Bodies in glass

This book is dedicated with gratitude and great respect to my friend Debbie Epstein

BODIES
in GLASS

Genetics, eugenics, embryo ethics

Deborah Lynn Steinberg

Manchester University Press

MANCHESTER and NEW YORK

distributed exclusively in the USA by ST. MARTIN'S PRESS

Copyright © Deborah Lynn Steinberg 1997

Published by Manchester University Press
Oxford Road, Manchester M13 9NR, UK
and Room 400, 175 Fifth Avenue, New York, NY 10010, USA

Distributed exclusively in the USA
by St. Martin's Press, Inc., 175 Fifth Avenue, New York, NY 10010, USA

British Library Cataloguing-in-Publication Data
A catalogue record is available from the British Library

Library of Congress Cataloging-in-Publication Data
Steinberg, Deborah Lynn.
  Bodies in glass: genetics, eugenics, embryo ethics / Deborah
Lynn Steinberg.
    p.   cm.
  Includes bibliographical references and index.
  ISBN 0–7190–4667–X.—ISBN 0–7190–4668–8
  1. Human reproductive technology—Moral and ethical aspects.
  2. Medical genetics—Moral and ethical aspects.   3. Eugenics—Moral
and ethical aspects.   I. Title.
  RG133.5.S74   1997
  176—dc20   96–8351

ISBN 0 7190 4667 X *hardback*
     0 7190 4668 8 *paperback*

First published 1997
00 99 98 97 96   10 9 8 7 6 5 4 3 2 1

Typeset in Walbaum
by Northern Phototypesetting Co. Ltd, Bolton
Printed in Great Britain
by Biddles Limited, Guildford and King's Lynn

Contents

Acknowledgements

I would like to thank the following people who have provided considerable support to me at various stages in the process of researching and writing this book. To students and staff in the Departments of Cultural Studies, Birmingham, Politics and Sociology, Birkbeck College, and Sociology, Warwick University; to Manchester University Press; and to: David Abdi, Penny Bainbridge, Kitty Bednar, Avtar Brah, Helene Brown, Joyce Canaan, Marilyn Crawshaw, Kate Corr, Christine Crowe, Louise Curry, Paul Darke, Debbie Epstein, Christine Ewing, Sarah Franklin, Cyndy Fujikawa, Wendy Fyfe, Ann Grey, Marion Hamm, Richard Johnson, members of the JUNE collective, Adrian Kear, Mary Kehily, Liz Kelly, Libby Kerr, Renate Klein, Beau L'Amour, Les Levidow, Christine Lewis, Mairtin Mac An Ghail, Wendy Maples, Maureen McNeil, Noe Mendele, Maxine Molyneux, Eleni Prodromou, Darini Rajasingham, Tess Randles, Peter Redman, Birgit Reinel, Cathy Sandrich, Iram Siraj-Blatchford, Jeff Smith, Patricia Spallone, Jackie Stacey, David, Jacki, Irwin, Maxine and Taryn Steinberg, Ian Varcoe, Matthew Weait and Stephen Yearly, for the many ways in which they have contributed to this project, I would like to convey my profound gratitude.

A portion of the Introduction of this book appears as 'Power, Positionality and Epistemology: Towards an Anti-oppressive Feminist Standpoint Approach to Science, Medicine and Technology' in *Women: a cultural review*. Earlier versions of Chapters 1 and 2 appear as 'The Depersonalisation of Women through the Administration of In Vitro Fertilisation' in McNeil *et al.* (eds), *The New Reproductive Technologies*, London, Macmillan, 1990. Versions of Chapter 3 appear as 'Technologies of Heterosexuality: Eugenic Reproductions and the Professional Discourses of In Vitro Fertilisation' in Steinberg *et al.* (eds), *Border Patrols: Policing Sexual Boundaries*, London, Cassell, forthcoming; and 'A Most Selective Practice: The Eugenic Logics of IVF', *Women's Studies International Forum*, 1996.

Abbreviations

AID	artificial insemination by donor
AIDS	acquired immune deficiency syndrome
BMA	British Medical Association
BPAS	British Pregnancy Advisory Service
CCETSW	Central Council for the Education and Training of Social Workers (UK)
COD	*Concise Oxford dictionary*
DES	diethylstilbestrol
DHSS	Department of Health and Social Security (UK)
DI	donor insemination
DNA	deoxyribonucleic acid
ESHRE	European Society of Human Reproduction and Embryology
FINNRET	Feminist International Network on the New Reproductive Technologies
FINRRAGE	Feminist International Network of Resistance to Reproductive and Genetic Engineering
GIFT	gamete intra-fallopian transfer
Gn RH	gonadotrophin-releasing hormone
GP	general practitioner
HCG	human chorionic gonadotrophin
HFE Act	*Human Fertilisation and Embryology Act* (1990)
HFE Bill	Human Fertilisation and Embryology Bill
HFEA	Human Fertilisation and Embryology Authority
HMG	human menopausal gonadotrophin
HMSO	Her Majesty's Stationery Office
IBA	Independent Broadcasting Authority
IVF	*in vitro* fertilisation
MRC	Medical Research Council
NHS	National Health Service (UK)
PID	pelvic inflammatory disease
RCOG	Royal College of Obstetricians and Gynaecologists

SPUC	Society for the Protection of Unborn Children
UNOS	United Network of Organ Sharing
VLA	Voluntary (also 'Interim') Licensing Authority (for IVF clinics)
WHO	World Health Organisation
WRRC	Women's Reproductive Rights Campaign
WRRIC	Women's Reproductive Rights Information Centre

Introduction

Black Couples Beg Me to Give Them White Babies: Desperate Dilemma of Doc Who Has to Play God
'I Am Not Being Racist, But Mixed Race Children Can Suffer in Life And If There's a Benefit They Can Receive Then Why Not?' (*The Sun*, 1.1.94)

Made to Measure: Can we Deny a Mother's Right to Shop in the Genetic Supermarket for Healthier Babies? (*The Guardian*, 3.1.94)

France Plans Ban on 'Aged' Mothers (*The Guardian*, 4.1.94)

Dead-Donor Babies 'Soon' (*Daily Mirror*, 8.1.94)

Baby Drug Kills Test-Tube Mum (*Daily Mirror*, 24.2.94)

These headlines, along with recent contestations over 'Virgin Births' (in 1991), parental 'rights' over frozen embryos (in 1992) and 'gay genes' (in 1993–4) are characteristic of nearly two decades of popular controversies generated in the wake of *in vitro* fertilisation (IVF), recombinant genetics and related reproductive technologies. Since 1978, with the birth of Louise Brown, the first so-called 'test-tube baby', there have been ongoing professional, legal and popular struggles over the meaning, 'morals' and futures of these technological innovations. These contestations have revolved around a number of fierce debates about professional and state power, 'rights' over women's reproductive processes, the issue of selective breeding on grounds of race, sexuality, age and genetic 'risk', and the question of embryo/fetal 'personhood'.

Throughout the period of controversy over IVF futures, feminists have been amongst the most critical, yet most marginalised, voices in the struggle over the parameters of debate and the definition of key issues. At the same time, there have been significant differences within feminism over the terms through which a feminist political agenda around the new reproductive technologies should be constituted. Contested perspectives of the 'science question in feminism'[1] as well as that of women's reproductive rights, both of which come to the fore in feminist analyses of reproductive technologies, emerge from competing understandings of relations of power and knowledge, of ontology (experience) and perspective. In this context, questions of authorship and authorial power, of discourse and the processes of meaning, of readership and of the ways these have been formulated through feminist analyses of science, medicine and technology, constitute the key political and discursive matrices underpinning the interrogative framework of this book.

It is precisely these, the growing cultural currency of IVF and genetic discourses and the social relations that delimit their authorship and readership, that constitute the central concerns of this book. Taking IVF and IVF-based genetic screening capabilities as case studies, this work investigates the key themes suggested in the headlines above. Firstly, it explores the constitution of expertise through an examination of *authorial* (that is, professional and legal) cultures of IVF. Secondly, it examines the *selective rationalities* (eugenic sensibilities) underpinning professional and legal discourses of IVF and related practices. In this context there are four aspects of dominant IVF discourse that are of particular concern: the reproduction of dominant relations of expertise and the *authorial* power of science; the *genea/logic* preoccupation with tracing of familial pedigrees and the reproduction of conventional definitions of family; the *embryo/logic* preoccupation with definitions of embryo 'personhood' and 'rights'; and the *recombinant logic* or discursive processes of the erasure and recombination of women's bodies and reproductive processes central to IVF language, theory and practice. Finally, the book considers the ways in which IVF discourses re/produce and interpellate popular common senses of kinship, identity, and 'nature' and reinscribe ableist, (hetero)sexist and racist (among other) social divisions. This book is therefore intended as an intervention both within the dominant discursive field in which IVF and genetic innovations have been constituted and within the arena of feminist critique.

The book begins, then, with an exploration of the agency of the medical scientific inventors of IVF language, practice and theory. Chapter 1 examines the linguistic frame through which the practices and professional common senses of IVF are constituted. Here there is particular concern with the way in which women's bodies and reproductive processes are conceptualised in *recombinant* terms congruent with the dominant ethos and methodology of IVF. Chapter 2 considers the formation of the Voluntary Licensing Authority (the medical scientific pre-statutory regulatory body overseeing IVF and related practices). Central to this chapter are questions of medical scientific power, agency and accountability and the ways in which IVF discourse constitutes the reproduction of dominant relations of expertise as well as a *recombinant* and *embryo/logically orientated* management of women's reproductive processes.

Part II of this book is concerned with the complex *genea/logic* (eugenic) ethos underpinning screening practices within the IVF context. Chapter 3 focuses on the indices of patient screening in IVF clinics, with particular consideration of the ways in which such practices reconstitute conventional classed, heterosexist, and racialised notions of 'fit' families. Chapter 4 examines the development of IVF-based capabilities for the genetic screening of embryos (*preimplantation diagnosis*) and the technological and biological determinist arguments offered by practitioners to rationalise the genetification of notions of reproductive 'fitness'. Here there is particular focus on genetic discourses of disability in the IVF literature and the classist, (hetero)sexist and racist logics underpinning them both textually and historically.

The final section of this book examines the contestations

between the state and medical scientific professionals for *authorial* control over IVF futures. Here I examine significant aspects of the popular debates over the formation of IVF legislation and the terms of the *Human Fertilisation and Embryology Act* 1990. Chapter 5 focuses on questions of competing jurisdictional claims over IVF practice and, particularly, over IVF embryos. Chapter 6 examines the legal reconstitution of the *authorial, embryo-centred and recombinant logics* of professional IVF discourse, particularly in relation to women's bodies, reproductive processes and civil status.

IVF can be seen, in a number of respects, as emblematic of the gamut of new reproductive technologies and of a new era of reproductive politics. Firstly, the professional culture of IVF has become an increasingly prominent enterprise. For example, in Britain alone, over 42,000 women underwent IVF[2] in a five-year period (1985–90), with only just over 5,000 births resulting – 25 per cent of which were multiple births. IVF, moreover, has been pivotal to the development of genetic research on embryos, new techniques for pre-natal and preimplantation diagnosis (i.e. genetic diagnosis of embryos) and the general study of human genetics (e.g. the Human Genome Project). IVF also involves a range of other reproductive technologies (e.g. donor insemination, forms of 'surrogacy' including egg and embryo 'donation', and hormonal and surgical interventions associated with 'conventional' infertility diagnoses and treatments). It has also been a key area of expansion in the human tissue transplant 'market' (i.e. traffic in eggs and embryos). The advent of IVF, moreover, has been unprecedented in generating an enormous body of reproductive legislation internationally. In Britain, such legislation has been consolidated in the *Human Fertilisation and Embryology Act* 1990.[3] As pointed out above, IVF has caused considerable popular controversy that has tapped into wider debates about 'fit' families, sexual morality and the status of women. Finally, the invention of IVF has raised serious questions within feminism about 'old' orthodoxies relating to reproductive rights, consent and women's control over their own bodies.

Feminist approaches to science, medicine and technology

In her article, 'How the Women's Movement Benefits Science: Two Views', Sandra Harding identifies what she defines as 'two main feminist approaches to [a critique] of science' (Harding 1992, p. 59). These, I would suggest, are useful distinctions for considering feminist approaches to related issues about medicine and technology, including feminist debates about reproductive technologies such as IVF. These two approaches Harding describes as 'feminist empiricism' – or critiques of 'bad' science, and 'feminist standpoint' – or critiques of 'science-as-usual'.[4] It must be noted, however, that of feminist analyses of science, medicine and technology, few works fall easily into one epistemological position or another. In this sense, Harding's distinctions are more useful in relation to an assessment of particular arguments, approaches or assumptions within any one work, than as a conclusive classification system describing the (unified) positions of their authors.[5]

Central to 'feminist empiricism', Harding argues, is a critique of the failure of scientists to follow the normative principles of the scientific method – including those of objectivity or value neutrality, of legitimate laboratory methodology and of interpretation of data within any given field. Within 'feminist empiricist' analyses, what is problematised is 'bad' scientists – either as incompetent or prejudiced – rather than the norms and organisational structure within which scientists work. Scientific 'artefacts' are assumed to have no inherent political value or meaning – instead, these are taken to accrue from the use to which they are put. Moreover, there is a separation made between the social context of science and science itself. Science can be constructed as a privileged sphere, separate from and not fundamentally shaped by (or shaping of) the social relations of inequality (and non-'neutrality') that characterise every other social activity or institution. Thus, to summarise, 'feminist empiricism', as Harding defines it, consists centrally of a use/abuse analysis. The political meaning of 'science-as-usual' is assumed to accrue from the manner (and con-

text) in which its 'artefacts' are used, or the loyalties and dis-
loyalties of individual scientists to the basic principles of scientific method.

A 'feminist standpoint' position, by contrast, problematises
'science-as-usual'.[6] The central premiss of a 'feminist standpoint' position is that science is a site of power/social relations
that is shaped by and that shapes the power/social relations of
its historical and cultural context. That is, social relations are
understood as embedded in the knowledges (and 'artefacts')
produced by scientists; they are integrated in the basic episte-
mologies and practices of 'science-as-usual'. The activities and
priorities of particular scientists, therefore, are not understood
individualistically, but rather in the context of a particular
social location.[7]

Feminist approaches to IVF

Both feminist empiricist and feminist standpoint approaches
can be identified in the specific literature relating to reproductive technologies, particularly IVF. Elsewhere (Steinberg
1993), I have considered in detail two of the major feminist
texts (Stanworth 1987 and Klein 1989) about IVF published in
Britain during the late 1980s. Here I shall summarise my main
critiques of these collections, the problems they illustrate in
relation to feminist empiricist and feminist standpoint frameworks, and the bases they provide for the development of a
more complex, 'anti-oppressive', feminist approach to science,
technology and medicine.

Reproductive Technologies: Gender, Motherhood and Medicine (Stanworth 1987)

The Stanworth collection could generally be characterised as
one that takes a 'feminist empiricist' approach to science, technology and medicine, and I would add, to women's experiences
in relation to them.[8] The collection as a whole, and particularly Stanworth's introductory chapters, which frame it, focuses
on the *uses* of IVF (and other) technologies. To this end, the
social conditions of their use are targeted for critical analysis.
Most of the authors in this collection maintain that IVF (and

other technologies), under the right conditions, offer a potential for the expansion of women's reproductive 'choices'. However, they do not explain for which women this may be the case, and what kind of choice this involves.

Related to the 'empiricist' orientation towards science, medicine and technology, and IVF in particular, of most of the book, is the identification of infertile women's experiences and priorities (as opposed, for example, to practitioners' experiences, priorities, and their ideas about women) as *the* starting-point for a feminist analysis of reproductive technologies. Stanworth suggests that 'the authors [in this book] hope to provide pointers to the development of new strategies around reproductive technologies – strategies that are alert to the differences between women as well as to what they have in common' (1987, p. 9). However, the book does not, in fact, explore the social relations associated with, for example, race, class, heterosexuality or ability/disability around IVF, nor does it examine the varied experiences of different groups of women in relation to IVF, medicine, motherhood and other dimensions of the social context that Stanworth and others suggest are crucial to the use of IVF.

To take infertile women as the starting-point in such studies has many ramifications. Firstly, it may suggest that the experiences and needs of infertile women are representative of all women's experiences and needs. It may suggest, furthermore, that the experiences of infertile women are more important than those of other women, and indeed, in the context of IVF, that theirs are the only experiences that must be considered. In other words, it seems to posit that the women who have the primary (or only) stake in (or will be affected by) IVF, are those who might or do undergo it.

This stance ignores the wider implications of the medical scientific relationship to women's reproduction for all women, and the ways these vary for different groups of women. Suggesting that women other than those undergoing IVF treatment might be affected by it does not deny the importance of taking the experiences of 'infertile' women seriously. Just as all women are implicated in the development of medical scientific practices that are directed towards women, so too are all women implicated in the specific innovations relating to IVF.[9]

It has been noted that white, middle-class and heterosexual women have been predominant in IVF treatment[10]. The class (in terms of relative income) profile of IVF patients can be largely deduced from the high cost of the procedure (see, for example, Corea 1985; Scutt 1990; and Steinberg 1993).[11] Moreover, the vast majority of IVF clinics will provide 'treatment' only to women whom they perceive as living in 'stable' heterosexual relationships (Arditti *et al.* 1984 p. 4; Spallone 1987 pp. 166–83; Steinberg 1993). Therefore, to focus only on the experiences of infertile women obscures the different stakes of different women in relation to IVF and the politics of its production and deployment.

Moreover, the articles in Stanworth's book do not consider differences (of power and position) among infertile women themselves (the politics of how they came to be infertile and the divergent social meanings accruing to the infertility of different groups of women). Rather these articles focus on those for whom IVF is most likely to provide a 'choice' of motherhood. Thus, it is the experiences and needs of this group of women that predominate and are often taken as universal. If, as these authors suggest, IVF is desirable as a reproductive 'choice', they do not consider whether this is a choice, given the power of racist, classist and heterosexist discourses of motherhood and family, that makes most sense from a white, middle-class and heterosexual position.[12]

To summarise, the key features of the 'feminist empiricism' of the Stanworth collection are, firstly, the assumption that IVF derives its positive or negative implications for women solely from the social conditions of its use, as opposed to its nature and form. Implicitly, in this collection, both IVF and the conditions and context of its production are taken as being value-neutral. Following from this premiss, it was possible for the authors to argue that IVF is potentially beneficial for (all) women, constituting a 'choice' that could, in principle, enable (all) women to control our own reproduction. Secondly, there is a common assumption that the meaning of IVF for particular women, (mainly white, middle-class, heterosexual infertile women) is representative of its meaning for all women.

Infertility: Women Speak Out about their Experiences of Reproductive Medicine (Klein 1989)

In contrast to the Stanworth collection, that edited by Renate D. Klein articulates a 'feminist standpoint' approach to IVF, although both share a focus on infertile women. Most of the contributions to the Klein collection are written by women who had undergone either conventional infertility treatment or IVF and who had left the treatment programmes feeling angry and critical of their treatment. In an introduction and concluding essay, Klein frames the testimonies of the contributors to her collection with several starting assumptions about both the nature of IVF (and conventional infertility) technologies and about women's relationship to them. Firstly, her central premiss is that IVF is a product of patriarchal 'science (and medicine) as usual'. She rejects a use/abuse analysis, arguing instead that the patriarchal character of the professional context of IVF development and practice is fundamentally antithetical to women's interests and needs, and that IVF is, itself, fundamentally patriarchal in character. Klein argues that one key feature of the profession generally, and of the development of IVF more specifically, is the withholding of information (for example about 'side' effects and high failure rates) from potential patients as well as from the public at large.

Klein's main arguments are that IVF professionals misinform women about the potential negative effects of treatment and about the likelihood that it will fail in assisting them to have a baby. This, in the context of general social (patriarchal) pressures on women to become mothers and of the stigmatisation of infertility, accounts, Klein suggests, for why women choose to undergo the procedure. Women who come to understand the dangers of the procedure and to demystify the misinformation provided by practitioners (possibly, as with the authors in this collection, through the experience of undergoing IVF or infertility treatments) will be empowered to (and desire to) leave the treatment regime (Klein 1989 p. 6).

Although making a significantly different analysis of the meaning of IVF, Klein's framework shares several features of the Stanworth book. Like Stanworth's, Klein's volume focuses on the experience and needs of infertile women, although in this case mostly infertile women who have left and indeed who now oppose IVF (and conventional infertility treatments). As with the Stanworth book, neither Klein nor her authors deeply investigate the appeal and availability of IVF and infertility treatments in relation to particular groups of women (mainly white, middle-class and heterosexual women). Again, the experiences (this time negative) of these infertile women are implicitly taken as generic of all women's potential experiences.[13]

A second tension in Klein's framework is the way it shifts from a 'standpoint' approach to science, medicine and technology to an exploration and explanation of women's relationship to them that extrapolates chiefly from consideration of the meaning of science, medicine and technology to professionals. One of the dangers of a 'feminist standpoint' position approach can emerge when feminists attempt to extrapolate from assessments about the medical scientific framework, that is the way professionals construct women, to draw conclusions about women's view of themselves and their experiences of technology or medical scientific treatment. This can implicitly construct women as passive victims of medical scientists, even where the feminist author does not intend to do so. This results from the failure to recognise differences among women's experiences of science, medicine and technology – differences of social position among women *per se*; and differences in the kind of agency women may exercise, from different positions of inequality.

One of the strengths of Klein's book is the attempt to retain a sense of women's agency with respect to IVF and conventional infertility treatments. In creating a forum for individual women to speak about their experiences of reproductive medicine (although she problematically construes their individual voices as universal), she avoids the most overt form of extrapolating women's motives and consciousness from an assessment of the voices of the professionals who treat them. However, as I suggest above, in explaining women's decisions to undergo IVF centrally in terms of being effectively lied to or 'duped' by professionals, and of their opposition to the procedure in terms of unmasking those lies, Klein implicitly posits a move from 'false consciousness' to revelation. This, in my view, profoundly underestimates the complexity of women's agency (both in undertaking and in opposing IVF). It also underestimates the power relations (and inequalities) that result in some women's perceiving IVF as their only option (and having the option of choosing to undergo it), while others are not in this position.

Even beginning, as Klein does, with the notion that IVF as well as the social conditions under which it has been developed are fundamentally patriarchal, it is nevertheless possible to argue that women might undergo IVF being fully aware of the risks they are taking to their health and well-being. Indeed, I would argue that it is dangerously reductive to suggest that all women who undergo these procedures misapprehend the meaning and risks of IVF. What seems more important, as I have indicated in my critique of the Stanworth collection above, is an understanding of the complex social relations of inequality that make IVF seem an appropriate or even desirable choice for some women and not for others.

Feminist empiricism and feminist standpoint: epistemological questions

The strength of the standpoint approach lies in its potential in dealing with complexity. Whereas the empiricist framework is, as I have argued above, limited in its acceptance of 'science-as-usual', the standpoint approach is critical of 'science-as-usual'. This establishes a basis for problematising universalisation (i.e. inductive reasoning) as a process both within and outside the medical scientific context and in relation to women's experiences. It is therefore possible and, I would argue, necessary to use a standpoint framework to develop forms of critique that take into account a number of different social relations of inequality as analytical indices. In other words, I am arguing for the development of an integrated model of power relations that allows for complex analyses of (and related political struggles about) both medical scientific practice and women's differential experiences of it. That is, I am proposing a move from a 'feminist standpoint' position, as discussed above, to what I would term an 'anti-oppressive feminist standpoint' position.[14]

Challenges to essentialist standpoint: feminist post-modernism

Feminist post-modernism has made a fundamental critique of all forms of essentialism (see, for example, Butler 1990; Nicholson 1990; Modleski 1991). In particular, some feminist post-modernists have problematised the use of the category 'woman' in so far as it has been used to obscure differences amongst women:

> For the most part, feminist theory has taken the category of women to be foundational to any further political claims without realising that the category effects a political closure on the kinds of experiences articulable as part of a feminist discourse. When the category is understood as representing a set of values or dispositions, it becomes normative in character and, hence, exclusionary in principle. This move has created a problem both theoretical and political, namely, that a variety of women from various cultural positions have refused to recognise themselves as 'women' in the terms articulated by feminist theory with the result that these women fall outside the category and are left to conclude that (1) either they are not women as they have perhaps previously assumed or (2) the category reflects the restricted location of its theoreticians and, hence, fails to recognise the intersection of gender with race, class, ethnicity, sexuality and other currents which contribute to the formation of cultural (non)identity (Butler 1990, p. 325).

This is an important critique, but all too often post-modernism involves a discussion of difference without a discussion of power relations. The endeavour of feminist post-modernism is to take the insights of post-modernism regarding positionality and fragmented subjectivities and reinvest them with a feminist political agenda.[15] However, as Modleski (1991 p. 18) points out, post-modern critiques of various forms of essentialism do not, in and of themselves, necessarily lead to analyses that take account of the differences they consider so important:

> Ironically ... anti-essentialists may be no more prepared to deal with such issues as race or ethnicity than the 'essentialists' whom they criticise for neglecting these issues. (We may note, for example, that the anthology *Feminism/Post-modernism*, which frequently claims for post-modern feminism a superior ability to deal with issues of race, contains no substantial discussion of these issues.).

Related to feminist post-modernist critiques of essentialism is the problematisation of the Enlightenment notion that people are constituted as unified, rational individuals and the consequent investment in the search for (and possibility of defining) 'truth'[16] (see for example, Henriques *et al.* 1984; Barrett 1991). Haraway (1989), for example, challenges notions of scientific truth and rationality by suggesting that theories produced by scientists can best be understood as 'science fictions'. As Harding (1991) points out, some feminist post-modernist critics have suggested that the notion of a 'feminist standpoint' position is subject to a similar critique to that made of science in general. That is, both are engaged in a search for absolute 'truth', albeit, in the case of a 'feminist standpoint' position, a feminist 'truth'. The Klein collection, as I suggest above, could be seen precisely as positing the possibility of a feminist 'truth' and thereby reproducing the very logic of 'science-as-usual' that she otherwise critiques. However, Harding argues:

> [T]he logic of the standpoint approaches contains within it both an essentialising tendency and also resources to combat such a tendency. Feminist standpoint theory is not in itself either essentialist or nonessentialist, racist or anti-racist, ethnocentric or not. It contains tendencies in each direction; it contains contradictions (p. 180).

Similarly, feminist standpoint positions contain the possibilities both of accepting Enlightenment frameworks and of critiquing them.

Clearly, in its critique of essentialism and scientific rationalism, feminist post-modernism has important insights to bring to a feminist analysis of science as well as to critical reflection on feminism itself. However, as Modleski (quoted above) suggests, there are problems with the post-modernist tendency, including its feminist variant, which involve the neglect of relations of power and inequality.

Challenges to the essentialist standpoint: black feminisms

Unlike much post-modern feminism, black feminisms have focused specifically on issues of oppression and power relations.[17] Indeed, black feminists have demanded a complex and multi-layered approach to oppression, a demand that, in part, derives from their critiques of white feminism. One particular critique that has been frequently made is that white feminists have largely disregarded issues of racism in their analysis of gender relations (see, for example, Carby 1981; Lorde 1984; hooks 1982, 1989, 1991). Amos and Parmar (1984) argue that:

> [W]hite mainstream feminist theory ... does not speak to the experiences of Black women and where it attempts to do so it is often from a racist perspective and reasoning.
>
> ... The limitations of the [feminist] movement are expressed in the issues which are identified as priorities: they are issues which in the main have contributed to an improvement in the material situation of a small number of white middle-class women often at the expense of their black and working class 'sisters' (p. 4).

Although, in 1984, Amos and Parmar did not use the term 'essentialism', this critique of 'imperial feminism'[18] is antiessentialist in its rejection of the universalisation of white, and, often, middle-class women's priorities and experiences.

This critique of white feminist agendas can be usefully employed in understanding some of the problems with the Stanworth and Klein collections, which, as I have argued above, take as primary the experiences and priorities of a 'small number of [mainly] white middle-class women'. What black feminists like Amos and Parmar are suggesting, therefore, is a reframing of the starting-point(s) for feminist analysis. As Patricia Hill Collins (1990) succinctly puts it: 'Black feminist thought consists of specialised knowledge created by African-American women [and, of course, other Black women] which clarifies a standpoint of and for Black women. In other words, Black feminist thought encompasses theoretical interpretations of Black women's reality by those who live it' (p. 22). A similar set of arguments can be made in relation to the formation of a variety of standpoints. Among these, Harding (1991) discusses those of some Third World women and lesbians. What these have in common are both an acknowledgement and centralisation of the specificity of positionality in relation to (different forms of) oppression and the development of an agenda for social change based on lived experience.

In reframing the agenda, black feminists have characteristically explored intersections of racism, class oppression and sexism, thus opening a way to consider other social inequalities.[19] As Amos and Parmar (1984) conclude: 'We cannot simply prioritise one aspect of our oppression to the exclusion of others, as the realities of our day to day lives make it imperative for us to consider the simultaneous nature of our oppression and exploitation. Only a synthesis of class, race, gender and sexuality can lead us forward ...' (p. 18). It is important to note that Amos and Parmar do not provide an exhaustive list of aspects of oppression that need to be understood as interrelated. For example, they do not mention disability/ableism. However, they have provided a model for an integrated analysis of oppression that addresses not only issues of positionality (of both researcher and researched), but also of indices of analysis and priorities for activism.

Towards an 'anti-oppressive feminist standpoint' position

In the light of the critiques that I have made of both Stanworth's and Klein's books, it is clearly important to move away from universalising the experiences of any particular group of women. For, as Harding says: 'We should redirect our analyses of women's situations and our agendas so that they are significantly closer to the more comprehensive ones advocated by women who suffer from more than what some women frequently see as simply "gender oppression"' (Harding 1991 p. 193).

This redirection will, I would suggest, involve an understanding of what is meant by 'standpoint' at three levels – that of positionality; that of the indices of analysis; and that of feminist politics. In terms of positionality, 'standpoint' can refer specifically to one's experiences (of oppression and/or privilege) as the point or location from which one develops an analysis of social relations. This is one of the respects in which Klein's analysis can be seen as a 'standpoint'. However, as I have argued, this can lead to a form of essentialism which posits that: (1) women have an inherent ability to 'know' patriarchy; (2) feminism can be located within the 'true consciousness' of womanhood; and (3) it is sufficient to consider only one index of social relations (i.e. gender) for an analysis to be feminist. Because of these problems, positionality alone is not a sufficient basis for understanding social relations. However, it is important to acknowledge that lived experience does make a difference to how one interprets the world.[20] It is, of course, not only the complex positionality of research subjects that is important but also that of the researcher.

A second component of a feminist standpoint position revolves around the selection of indices for the analysis of social relations. This selection process can be limited, as I have argued above, to only one index, or it can be more complex and multi-layered. This relates both to positionality and to political priorities. As Harding points out, the selection of gender as the only index has been characteristic of many 'white, Western, economically advantaged and/or straight women' (1991). What one privileges for the purpose of critical analysis is a political decision. To privilege gender inequality can have the effect of marginalising related struggles against other forms of oppression. In so doing, it can also have the effect of erasing the experiences of many women, which is precisely, as I have discussed, the central issue of contention within black feminist critiques of white feminism (for example, Carby 1981; Lorde 1984; hooks 1989).

There are a number of key social relations that are commonly neglected in an exclusive feminist focus on gender. These include relations around ability/disability, class inequality, heterosexism and racism, among others. My review of the Stanworth and Klein collections has highlighted some of the dangers of disregarding these forms of social relations. However, while it is important to consider forms of social relations in complex ways, it is not necessary that any one piece of work using an 'anti-oppressive feminist standpoint' approach explores each and every form of oppression.[21] I would suggest, instead, that the process of developing a complex, integrated analysis of some forms of power relations opens up the possibility of exploring others in a similarly integrated way. So, it is the model of considering power relations as complexly interrelated, rather than attempting exhaustively to track all forms of these relations, that is most important.

Finally, implicit in the term 'feminist' in the phrase 'feminist standpoint position' is an agenda for political activism towards social justice for women.[22] It can be distinguished, for example, from a primarily positional (and, it could be argued, dangerously essentialist) notion of 'women's standpoint', since solely positional standpoints do not necessarily imply struggle for social change. A *feminist* standpoint, by contrast, must, by definition, involve a will to social change, that is, a praxis in which there is 'a continuing shared feminist commitment to a political position in which "knowledge" is not simply defined as "knowledge *what*", but also as "knowledge *for*". Succinctly the point is to change the world, not only to study it' (Stanley 1990, p. 15, emphasis hers).

The additional term 'anti-oppressive', then, is intended specifically to locate this version of a 'feminist standpoint' approach within a complex political agenda of change aimed at social justice. The language of 'anti-oppressive practice' is not current in analyses of or in political movements challenging 'science-as-usual'. It is to be found more often, for instance, within social work[23] (see, for example, Langan 1992a) and education (see, for example, Epstein 1991 and 1993). An 'anti-oppressive' political orientation involves: (1) a recognition that 'difference' is often, if not always, attended by unequal relations of power; (2) an understanding that unequal power relations are produced in and through the discursive practices[24] of powerful institutions; (3) the perspective that no one form of power relations can be understood in isolation; rather, they are intertwined and mutually reinforcing; and (4) a commitment to developing analyses and practices that challenge the institutionalisation of oppression.

Taken together, these elements of an 'anti-oppressive feminist standpoint' approach radically shift an analysis of science, medicine and technology. With respect to an analysis of IVF, for example, women's experiences of and relationships to IVF and women's agency in this context can be seen neither as singular (universal), nor as divorced from the complex power relations of social institutions *including* science, medicine and technology. To utilise 'anti-oppressive' analytical indices, I would argue, contributes to the development of a feminist praxis that centralises the considerable differences of power among women as well as the considerably different ways that powerful institutions affect different groups of women. Such an approach elaborates and contributes to a feminist framework that challenges the privileging of particular female experiences. It also provides a model for the analysis of power that neither constructs women as passive victims nor denies female agency, but contextualises that agency within complex relations of social inequality.

(Re)Reading reproductive technologies: (re)writing feminist reproductive politics

With respect to the analysis of dominant discourses of IVF, an anti-oppressive interrogative framework brings to the fore a number of questions. Firstly, what, in their own terms, are the priorities of IVF inventors and practitioners and how are women and women's bodies, reproduction, agency and status differentially constructed and constrained within and through professional discourses? For example, innovation of new reproductive technologies has given a new twist to long-standing debates about women's reproductive rights and the ideology of embryo 'rights'. The advent of IVF has been particularly key to the reconstitution of anti-abortion and, indeed, pro-choice politics. Because IVF has made it possible to create embryos outside and (re)place them in women's bodies, it has significantly altered the terms of debate around pregnancy, abortion and childbirth and the role of medicine and the state in relation to all three. In addition, the creation of extra-corporeal embryos has reconstituted questions of male reproductive rights. This was the central issue at the heart of the 1992 controversy in the USA courts (noted in the headline above) over who has custody of frozen embryos. Moreover, debates about abortion and women's right to choose have now become inextricably entangled with questions about IVF embryo research. This was exemplified in early debates about the Powell Bill (1984), which proposed to ban embryo research on the basis of the purported 'personhood' of embryos, a standard argument of anti-abortionists. Indeed, it can be argued that IVF has made material the ideological separation between woman and embryo that underpins anti-abortion ideology. The reconstitution of embryo-'rights' discourses in the light of the recombinant capabilities and ethos of IVF, and the recombinant embryo/logic terms through which professional and state agencies differentially delimit the agency of (women) patients, are clearly central questions for the delineation of feminist reproductive politics in the IVF context.

A second set of questions, relevant to an anti-oppressive analytical agenda, revolve around the ways in which notions of reproductive 'fitness' are articulated through IVF discourses. A significant absence in many evaluations of new reproductive technologies is an investigation of the eugenic politics underpinning professional practices and cultures. Few works have considered, for example, the centrality of patient and genetic screening in IVF practice, including both policies for selecting or rejecting potential parents (for example, on the grounds of whether or not they are married) and genetic and other forms of screening embryos for 'abnormalities'. Issues relating to screening in this context are important for the ways in which they draw on and (re)construct widely held common-sense definitions of 'normal' and 'abnormal' families, 'proper' and 'improper' parents and 'desirable' and 'undesirable' offspring. The absence of attention to the issue of eugenic screening and the broader agenda to reproduce 'proper' families can be said to reflect a broader cultural disowning of the history of eugenic and 'racial hygiene' movements in Britain, the USA and Europe (in particular under National Socialism in Germany). It is also reflective of a denial of the primacy of medical science in the development of eugenics movements generally. An analysis of the ways in which practices and policies surrounding new reproductive technologies might draw upon and reproduce eugenic thinking, particularly in the wake of emergent ideologies of 'ethnic cleansing', would therefore seem to be of urgent necessity.

Finally, to propose an 'anti-oppressive' feminist analysis of science, medicine and technology suggests the possibility of an 'anti-oppressive' feminist science. At one level this raises the question of whether developments such as IVF can be justified on anti-oppressive grounds, or can be seen as or transformed into an 'anti-oppressive' feminist science. But, perhaps more importantly, it suggests a radical shift in the terms with which we understand the politics of science, medicine and technology-as-usual in relation to feminism and the terms with which we constitute a politics of women's reproductive rights.

Notes

1 I borrow here the title of Harding's (1986) book.

2 Most underwent IVF in the private sector.

3 British IVF constitutes a particularly good focus of study for several reasons. IVF on women was invented in Britain, which consequently set the agenda for the shape of developments elsewhere. This pattern, begun with the invention of IVF, has continued with later developments. For example, the first clinical use of genetic screening of IVF embryos (preimplantation diagnosis) occurred in a British IVF clinic. The Warnock Report 1984 was the first significant governmental document on new reproductive technologies produced in the world. It not only set the agenda for the British model of legislation, but also significantly influenced the shape of legislation in other countries.

4 Elsewhere Harding has also considered 'feminist post-modernist' approaches, in particular as critical responses to critiques of 'feminist standpoint' positions (Harding 1986, 1987, 1990 (a), and 1991). This is a point to which I will return below in the context of my own consideration of the first two approaches.

5 More commonly, feminist approaches have been classified as 'radical', 'socialist' and 'liberal' (and more recently 'post-modernist'), what I would term 'position' categories. These categories are often invoked in a rather monolithic manner, often underestimating: (1) the considerable differences of analysis and perspective among feminists classified within any one position; (2) the possible combination of approaches and priorities within any one work; (3) the commonalities across categories; or (4) the changing ideas of any one writer/activist over time. Used as labels, these categories can suggest that feminism is composed of separate and mono- lithic positions, and that these positions are somehow equivalent to or bespeak particular feminist identities. What is particularly useful about Harding's work, in my view, is that her consideration of feminist episte- mology – that is, of the questions feminists ask (what they problematise) and the assumptions underlying these questions – allows for the possibil- ity of a complex (and even contradictory) agenda in the way that posi- tional categories seem to obstruct. Moreover, Harding's categories are free of the pejorative or dismissive connotations often attendant upon the invo- cations of positions/categories when feminists critique the work of other feminists.

6 Harding associates this approach with Marxist epistemology where 'knowl- edge is [seen as] grounded in experiences made possible by specific social relations' (1991 p. 60). Within this perspective, Harding points out, 'there is no possibility of [a] perspective that is disinterested, impartial, value- free or detached from the particular, historical social relations in which everyone participates' (ibid.).

7 Margaret Lowe Benston, for example, argues that technology is a male- dominated (androcentric) 'language' of social action – providing a range of options for acting in the world' (Benston 1992 p. 35). The technologi- cal world-view revolves around the 'science-as-usual' principles of objec- tivity, rationality, control over nature and distance from human emotions – a schooled orientation for males (i.e. components of the definition of 'normal masculinity') (1992 p. 38). The principles of 'science-as-usual' form conditions for male dominance within and outside science, and in turn male dominance within and outside science reinforces the androcen- tric epistemology of science. Particular technologies, Benston argues, are consequently encoded with the fundamental values and social relations that underpin their production, and in turn (re)produce male dominance in our society.

8 One exception is Ann Oakley's article which makes a critique of obstet- rics-as-usual, focusing on the technologies 'for viewing the interior of

[women's] wombs' (Stanworth 1987 p. 5) and on the medical attitudes characterising the development and practice of these technological capabilities (Oakley 1987). Ros Petchesky's article combines both 'standpoint' and 'empiricist' orientations to questions surrounding (fetal) ultrasound monitoring of pregnant and birthing women. She begins with what could be described as a 'standpoint' critique of the objectification of women's experience characterising the practice and underpinning the philosophy of practitioners who use it. The second part of her article examines the mixed (often positive) experiences women have with the technology. In this part, there is a shift in her analytic premiss – arguing against a 'standpoint' critique of the technology that characterises the beginning of the article and concluding with a much more ambivalent use/abuse perspective.

9 For example, practices and policies relating to abortion are important for all women, not only for women who undergo them. There is an extensive feminist literature discussing how all women's social position and rights are shaped by the legal and medical status of abortion (see, for example, Oakley 1981; Fried 1990; Science and Technology Subgroup 1991). Black feminists have also pointed out that abortion policy and women's stake in it will be different for different groups of women. Moreover, pro-choice campaigns do not include only those women who will want or need abortions.

10 See, for example, Arditti *et al.* 1984 p. 5; Corea 1985 pp. 144–5, 276–7. Moreover, in media coverage of IVF birthday parties or announcements of new IVF births (since 1978, with the birth of Louise Brown), images of white patients, children and doctors/scientists have predominated.

11 This does not mean, of course, that working-class women do not undergo IVF. However, the financial burden for women undergoing IVF will obviously bear more heavily and therefore be a more significant deterrent for poorer women.

12 For example, it is possible that the pressures of compulsory motherhood and the stigmatisation of infertility are not likely to be experienced in the same way by lesbians. It is also possible that women who feel that they cannot afford 'treatment', or feel that they would be discriminated against by clinics, might be less likely to experience IVF as a 'choice'.

13 It must be stated that there is an important tension, in this regard, between the self-representations of the contributors to this collection and Klein's framing and interpretation of them. The contributors write as individuals, none claiming to speak a universal voice of 'female experience'. The tension arises in the way that Klein frames and interprets these individual voices as universally representative of women's relationship to reproductive medicine. I do not suggest that there is an inherent problem with examining the experience of women on IVF programmes. Indeed, the authors in the Klein collection provide disquieting and important testimony about their experiences of reproductive medicine. The problem, instead, is both with generalising from their experiences and motives as

characteristic (or even potentially characteristic) of all women and with neglecting to specify and examine the particular political dimensions of their social positions and context.

14 I recognise that feminists across a range of positions have expressed concern for and have struggled against many forms of oppression. I would not like to disparage or underestimate this. My use of the term 'anti-oppressive' is, in this sense, a gesture towards a conceptual opening up of the field rather than a dismissal of other feminists' positions and interventions.

15 See, for example, Linda J. Nicholson's edited collection *Feminism/Postmodernism* (1990).

16 Thus, for example, Martin Hammersley (1992) in criticising feminism and defending positivism argues that a finding should be accepted as 'truth' when there is consensus amongst a scientific community of rational individuals that it *is* the 'truth'.

17 I am not suggesting that this is related to some essential characteristic of 'blackness'. However, the self-conscious adoption of the label 'black feminist' indicates a deliberate critique of [white] feminist neglect of issues around racism. A similar point could be made about lesbians adopting the term 'lesbian feminist'. Indeed, to challenge Catharine MacKinnon's (1987) formulation, feminism *modified* implies a critique of feminism as identified by the modifier.

18 The title of their article is 'Challenging Imperial Feminism' (pp. 3–20).

19 It is notable, in this context, that many black feminists have been concerned to integrate, into their analyses of racism and sexism a consideration of issues of homophobia and heterosexism (for example, Lorde 1984; Jordan 1989; hooks 1989, 1991).

20 This represents what, I would suggest, is most significant about the notion that 'the personal is political'. It is not just that experience is central, but rather the question is *how* to centralise it in a political way, that is, in a way that accounts for the complexities of the social relations of oppression and privilege.

21 Indeed, this would be impossible, both because of limitations of space (we cannot write infinitely long books or essays) and because it is not possible to know all forms in which oppression can and does exist. In other words, we cannot presume to state categorically all of the variables that play out in any one moment or situation.

22 See, for example, the Bowles and Klein (1983) collection in which feminist research is defined in several articles as research for, not simply about, women.

23 Training in anti-discriminatory and anti-oppressive practice is a requirement of social work training as laid down by CCETSW [Central Council for the Education and Training of Social Workers (CCETSW 1991).

24 Discourse can be defined as ways of speaking and seeing that construct what counts as meaningful knowledge. A discursive field consists of competing ways of giving meaning to the world and organising social institutions and processes – which can be defined as discursive practices.

Part I

The agency of invention

The discursive inscription of female (and male) bodies and female (and male) 'nature' through medical scientific languages, texts and practices has been a major preoccupation of contemporary feminist critical theorists. Both medical sciences and female bodies/'nature' have been constituted in this context as contested territories and as bodies of knowledge through which professional agency is writ large as both authorial voice and voice of authority. The history of modern medical science has produced a progressive delimitation of what is socially accepted as legitimate expertise and a procession of specialists with specialised techniques, technologies and texts of which, this book will argue, *in vitro* fertilisation (IVF) can be seen as emblematic. In this context, it can be argued that women have been constructed simultaneously as docile[1] but also dangerous bodies[2] and, with particular reference to pregnant women, as divided bodies. Much feminist critique of contemporary reproductive technologies (including IVF) has revolved around the extent to which they can be read as reproducing the increasingly recombinant, embryo-centred logics that have historically underpinned medical scientific discourses.

Languages of risk

The advent of IVF and related capabilities reflects and reproduces trajectories of inventive thought and the power relations and logics of inventive agency located within the history of reproductive medicine and science. Ann Oakley (1984), among others, has examined the rise of professional medicine, for example, as a simultaneous professionalisation and masculinisation of healing that reconstructed women as both dangerous carers and dangerous bearers. Indeed, many commentators have identified the nineteenth century not only as an era that established science and medicine as dominant professional discourses, but as a period in which medicine and science became invested with moral regulatory power. As Lupton (1994) has noted, the incorporation of medical scientific expertise has, at least in part, revolved around the ways in which professional discourses have imbued biological reproduction, specifically female reproductive processes, with racialised, class-specific and (hetero)sexist notions of physical, social and moral risk.[3]

Dangerous/docile bodies

These professional languages of risk have, in turn, underpinned professional investments in decoding the mysteries of female bodies and managing the dangers or dysfunctional potentials that are seen to inhere in female reproductive processes and female agency. An increasingly *recombinant* logic can be traced in this project. The investiture of medicine as a profession was founded, for example, on a developing male, middle-class monopoly of surgical tools and techniques, a development grounded methodologically in a discourse, characteristic of Western allopathic medicine, of bodies as composites of component, rearrangeable parts. As noted by Usher (1991) and Witz (1992), the surgical management of female bodies was central to the economic viability and closure of professional specialisms, including Obstetrics and Gynaecology and Psychiatry. Usher has noted that if medicalisation underpinned the stigmatisation of women as dangerous bearers, carers and carriers (of physical and moral disease), Psychiatry singled out the organs and properties of the female body as harbingers of madness. Both Usher and Witz noted the central role of surgery on female reproductive/sexual organs[4] as the central avenue through which the gendered, class-specific closure of professional expertise and the construction of female bodies/women as dangerous breeders of individual and social chaos were consolidated.[5] Both Obstetrics and Gynaecology and Psychiatry were constituted, in this sense, as disciplinary regimes through which the female body was discursively constituted as (fragmented) object of hierarchical observation, normalising judgement and examination.[6]

Divided bodies

The languages of risk and recombinant logics that underpin dominant Obstetric and Gynaecological constructions of women and female bodies have also underscored the medico/legal construction of pregnant women as divided, adversarial bodies. The construction of a pregnant woman as not only two people (*sic*), but two patients, with separate, indeed hostile, interests, which has had powerful currency within anti-abortion discourse, has its roots, in part, in medical scientific discourses, of (female) reproduction. A plethora of feminist commentators have noted, for example, the increasing embryo/logic orientation of Obstetric technologies and medical treatment of birthing women, with the consequence that women's self-determination over the management of their pregnancies and the conditions of their birthing have been seriously eroded.[7] Franklin (1990), moreover, traces the underpinning construction of women as dangerous docile bodies housing 'fetal martyr/victim/hero' (p. 205) in the 'fetal fascinations'[8] of the medical sciences of embryology and fetology – specialisations that have emerged out of the specialisms of Obstetrics and Gynaecology. This construction of maternal danger constitutes a significant dimension of the conceptual trajectories through which have emerged the perceived 'need' for embryo protectors (who by definition cannot be (pregnant) women); an ongoing medico/legal/religious struggle for 'protective' custody of the fetal territory of pregnant women; and the invention/use of technologies aimed to image, manage and, more recently with IVF, create embryos as separate, if not extracorporeal, entities.

Textual bodies: technological texts

> To write is to assume a position of authority. To write as a scientist doubles the authority, because an authoritative account of reality is being established. Scientists and medical practitioners who put pen to paper are claiming to 'tell it as it really is' (Jordanova 1986 pp. 20–1).

The examination of medical scientific texts and of medical scientists as authors, both of practices and of texts about those practices, is central to an analysis of professional culture, agency and ethos. As Jordanova argues, professional writings reproduce professional authority and both reveal and constitute professional common senses through the ways in which they position readers and the modes, contexts and character of the writings.[9] They are also key sites through which popular common senses around medical scientific power, entitlement and agency and medical scientific discourses of health and illness, of kinship and other social/power relations are mediated: '[T]he social status of science, and, to a lesser extent, medicine depend[s] on the power of the written word to reach audiences, to change their ways of thinking, to persuade people of the value of science and to legitimize the position of the practitioners' (Jordanova 1986 p. 23).

If the writings (and by extension technical vocabularies) of medical scientific professionals can be read for the ways in which they (re)inscribe professional power and common senses, so too can the techniques and technologies which constitute medical scientific practice be 'read' as text. Medical Scientists are authors in both senses – inventing and 'owning' terminology, text and technique.[10] In both contexts, the delimitations on the speakable/doable constitute textual closures integral to the 'defensive élitism' of professional cultures. Medical scientific technique, terminology and text consolidate the specialised knowledges, monopoly of practice, autonomy in organising, self-policing and social status Friedson (1970) identified as characteristic of professional exclusivity. Technical processes mediate the reading as well as writing of bodies of knowledge. In decoding the technical, terminological and literary 'texts' of IVF, then, I am interested in examining the authoria/logics underpinning IVF as a professional praxis (theory and practice) and the ways in which IVF discourse (re)produces (female) reproduction.

Notes

1 I refer here to Foucault's discussion of the discursive production of 'docile bodies' through élite, disciplinary discourses, which themselves are characterised by hierarchical observation, normalising judgement and examination (Foucault 1975, Vintage Books edition).

2 Women are discursively constituted as 'dangerous bodies' in two senses: in the sense of a danger immanent in the literal bodies of women and in the sense of female will as dangerous. Within this discourse, the female body is inscribed at once as 'docile' and as a 'body of resistance'.

3 See also Walkowitz (1980); Oakley (1984); Mort (1987); Davis (1990) and Weeks (1991) for extended discussion of this point.

4 These included surgical management of birthing in the context of Obstetric medicine and treatments involving the amputation of sexual/reproductive organs (clitoridectomy, ovariectomy, hysterectomy) in the context of Psychiatry (see Oakley 1984, Witz 1990 and Usher 1991).

5 Walkowitz (1980) has noted that the Contagious Diseases Acts of the late nineteenth century reproduced this disciplinary ethos through the legal/medical regulation of working-class women working as prostitutes. Here the working-class prostitute was constructed as the transmission vector of sexually transmitted disease, class corruption and social disorder.

6 See Foucault (1975) for a discussion of the processes through which disciplinary power is constituted.

7 This is perhaps epitomised in both the imagery and the reality of the pregnant woman strapped down and connected externally and internally to 'fetal monitors' and in the increasing number of cases where hospitals have sought and won legal rights to suspend women's rights to refuse treatment, as in court-ordered Caesarean sections, in favour of the 'welfare' of the fetus. The appellation 'fetal surgery' encapsulates this logic in its linguistic erasure of the fact that 'fetal surgery' is performed on pregnant women.

8 The title of the article is 'Fetal Fascinations: New Dimensions to the Medical–Scientific Construction of Fetal Personhood' (see Franklin 1990 pp. 190–205)

9 Specifically, Jordanova argues that the treatment of professional writings as literary texts:

    involves asking questions about genre, about the relationship between reader and writer, about the use of linguistic devices such as metaphor, simile, and personification, about what is *not* being said, or cannot be said, and hence about the nature of conscious and unconscious constraints on writing, about the models and sources a writer employs, and about the relationship between the form and content of arguments. The end result of such investigations should be a much larger sense of how science is located in its social and cultural context (Jordanova 1986 p. 20).

10 Marion Lowe Benston has argued, for example, that technology should be understood as a language that reflects and reproduces male domination both of expertise and as a social condition more generally.

1

Writing recombinant bodies: the professional genea/logics of IVF

> *The idea behind test-tube babies is very simple. It involves removing an egg from the woman's ovary, collecting and cleaning her partner's sperm, mixing the sperm and egg in the laboratory and, if fertilization occurs, inserting the developing egg or embryo into the woman's uterus* (Professor Robert Winston 1987, p. 153).[1]

Professor Winston's statement encapsulates much that is of interest in this book. First is the question of expertise and the positionality of practitioners both as authors of technologies and texts and *vis à vis* patients. For whom is IVF a 'simple' idea? Who is in a position to invent, manage and offer authoritative representations of the procedures involved? Second are questions pertaining to the character of the 'text', the ethos or professional common senses encoded in both IVF procedures and professional accounts of such procedures. What does IVF 'involve'? What are the ideas underpinning what IVF involves? How are the central constituents – women, partners, their body parts, the laboratory, the techniques, the practitioners – constituted through technological and linguistic 'texts'? What do these encoded meanings suggest about the power relations of IVF treatment? about the professional culture? about the 'authorship' and 'readership' of these texts? Finally are the questions of selection and selectivity. What is included or omitted in the textual representation of IVF? Who may be included as patient or partner or practitioner? How do these *selective rationalities* constitute a discursive field in and through which the corporealities of reproduction and their social relations are constituted and contested?

In this first chapter, I am interested in exploring the sexual politics of the professional ethos of IVF through an examination of IVF procedures (professional practices), the professional lexicon of IVF (terminology) and a selection of textual representations of IVF authored by practitioners during the 1980s, the first, crucial decade of practice. Because I am neither an IVF patient nor practitioner, my analysis and understanding of the first two subjects are, of necessity, mediated through the last. My concern is not so much the 'truth' or accuracy of correspondence between IVF practices and representations of the practice. Rather, I am interested in the technological/procedural *as* text and both technique and writings as sites through which meanings are produced, power relations are mediated and subjects, objects and logics are constituted.

Sexual textual politics[2]: languages of IVF

'In vitro fertilisation'

As Professor Winston's description both reveals and conceals, *in vitro* fertilisation is a series of procedures that, while they may be simplistically represented, are in fact complicated and, unpredictable, and involve serious risks to the health of patients who undergo them. References to the involvement of 'partners' notwithstanding, IVF is a regime and regimen of treatments undergone by women alone, under the supervision and management of a team of specialised practitioners and involving considerable self-discipline to accommodate the technical and administrative requirements of the technique, practices and practitioners involved. IVF has emerged as a multi-disciplinary medical scientific enterprise and a capital-intensive economic venture. The process involves not only a range of practitioners and fields of expertise, but a complicated array of biochemical products, technical instruments and difficult and exacting protocols, most of which carry as yet unmeasured (and perhaps immeasurable) risks to women's health.

The technical lexicon – the professional vocabulary of IVF – is, like Professor Winston's description, interesting both for what it identifies and what it conceals. For example, '*in vitro* fertilisation', the term, means literally fertilisation in glass. As such, it identifies only one part of the extensive array of procedures that constitute IVF, indeed the one part in which women are physically absent.

The more popular term 'test-tube babies' not only replicates this erasure of women and the procedures women undergo, but compounds it in several ways. It misnames even the site of fertilisation, which does not in fact occur in a test-tube, but in a Petri dish. Moreover, the term 'baby' modified by 'test-tube' suggests that the act of fertilisation, and even the entire process of conception and 'pregnancy', is not only unrelated to women, but entirely extracorporeal, outside a woman's or any body. Furthermore, this term names only the (desired, but usually not achieved) product of the (misnamed) process – the 'baby', instead of the persons (women) who undergo the process.

Both of these terms, '*in vitro* fertilisation' and 'test-tube babies', with the Latin (technical jargon) words of the former and the reference to laboratory paraphernalia in the latter, implicitly recognise medical science as the central (if not the only) domain of this reproductive practice. By extension, these terms implicitly privilege medical and scientific practitioners – the IVF team, the 'test-tube baby' doctors. They are not only implicitly identified as present, as constituents, but as agents of IVF, and most importantly as agents of (women's) reproduction; the ones who make it happen. Women who undergo IVF, on the other hand, are not only not identified as agents of their reproduction, but they are not identified in any capacity; neither as participants nor, more specifically, as patients.

The procedures that constitute the IVF process and that are obscured by the term '*in vitro* fertilisation' comprise an ever-growing, extensive array of physiological interventions on women.[3] These include: (1) continuous and varied chemical alteration and reconstitution of women's reproductive functions: 'superovulation' (and other hormone drug treatments) ; (2) surgical removal and transfer of women's body tissues to medical scientific custody and treatment: 'egg recovery'; and (3) replacement of women's altered and fertilised tissue into their bodies: 'embryo transfer'.

'Superovulation'

'Superovulation' entails the administration of large doses of various synthetic hormones. These include, but are not limited to: clomiphene citrate (Clomid), human pituitary gonadotrophins HCG and HMG 2 (Pergonal)[4] and progesterone (Walters and Singer 1984 pp. 5–6). The designated function of these drugs is to induce women to ovulate more than one egg, in fact as many eggs as possible. The greater the number of women's eggs ovulated, the more likely it is that practitioners will extract one or more 'viable' (sufficiently mature) egg(s) for fertilisation, and the greater is the potential number of women's eggs that can be fertilised in glass. Equally important, hormonal induction of women's ovulation makes it possible for IVF practitioners to time the next phase of the procedure – the removal of women's eggs. According to practitioners Carl Wood and Ann Westmore,

> the use of fertility drugs also makes organisation of the procedure considerably easier. Operating theaters can be pre-booked for egg pick-ups at times compatible with the staffing situation and other requirements of the hospital (Wood and Westmore 1987 p. 60).[5]

The overall effects of these hormones on women's health have not been extensively documented, nor explored in any depth by that sector of the scientific community particularly concerned with the development of IVF, although some exploration of adverse effects of these drugs does appear in other treatment contexts.[6]

Most research and documentation on the long-term effects of Clomid (like those of more notorious drugs such as diethylstilbestrol [DES][7] and thalidomide[8]) are limited to its effects on fetuses and offspring rather than on the women who take it. These include teratogenic (producing congenital abnormalities) malformations,[9] anencephaly (absence of brain), ovarian dysplasia (abnormal ovarian cell growth) in female fetuses, congenital retinopathy, and bilateral breast cancer (in two daughters of women who took these drugs) (Crook 1986; Cunha *et al.* 1987). Detrimental effects of Clomid on *women* noted briefly by Dr Mary Anderson[10] include 'hot flushes, palpitations, visual blurring and abdominal discomfort'. Anderson reports moreover that one risk of gonadotrophin therapy is excessive stimulation of the ovaries, with cyst formation and, in the worst cases, '"blowing up" of the ovaries producing acute abdominal pain' (Anderson 1987 p. 68).[11] However, while other authors give limited acknowledgement to the possibility of adverse effects (many gave significantly less information than Anderson and none considered what the combined effects of the 'hormone cocktails' might be for women or their offspring), none questioned the ethics or desirability of their use on women or whether the risks entailed (and the lack of research and understanding of them) should preclude their use.[12] It is clear, despite the scarcity of research and documentation on the subject, that 'superovulation' entails barely estimated and perhaps even immeasurable risks to women's health and that of their offspring (Crook 1986).

Finally, the 'superovulation' phase of IVF treatment necessitates that women are monitored throughout the period of the administration of fertility drugs, with procedures that include blood tests and ultrasound scans. This continuous scrutiny is requisite as practitioners attempt to time the actual moment when women are ready, through hormonal induction, to 'release' their eggs (their point of ovulation). This point, where women are (made) ready to ovulate, is the point of transition to the next phase of IVF – 'egg recovery'.

'Egg recovery'

'Egg recovery' is the most common of the names given by IVF practitioner/authors in this collection of readings for the second phase of the IVF process. The *Concise Oxford Dictionary* defines the term 'recover' as 'to regain possession of or use or control of'. The term 'egg recovery' thus implies that

IVF practitioners are regaining possession of something that is theirs, when in fact they are dispossessing women of what is ours. Other terms for this procedure, including 'egg pick-up', used by Carl Wood and Ann Westmore, share with 'egg recovery' a focus on the tissue removed and the medical/scientific process of removal without reference to the person (a woman) from whom it is removed (Wood and Westmore 1984 p. 66). Mary Anderson uses the agricultural metaphor egg 'harvest' (Anderson 1987 p. 71), evoking vistas of 'crops' or fields of disembodied 'eggs'. Indeed, the conceptual separation of eggs and women implied in these terms, to a degree – as with the term 'harvesting' – that would make it seem as if eggs were never *of* women in the first place, is significant both for its recombinant and embryo-centred logics. Women's bodies are conceptualised in parts and taken apart and reconstructed; eggs become textually and materially disembodied from their original referents, are reconstructed as signifiers of the fertility of medical science, and reproduced as the metaphorical, technological and material seeds of extracorporeal embryos and 'test-tube babies'. The extracorporeal egg/embryo is a seductively 'simple' mythology that erases the very corporeal, protracted, invasive, often painful chemical and surgical treatment (excision, removal) of (parts of) a woman's body that produce it and through which it could not otherwise *be* produced as an 'it' separate from her. The conceptual separation of eggs and women that is made literal through 'egg recovery' techniques presages the conceptually separate/literally severed embryo to be (re)produced and subsequently 'transferred' (though not, it would seem, 'returned') to women.

In the 'egg recovery/pick-up/harvesting' phase of IVF, women undergo one of two surgical procedures, laparoscopic egg retrieval or one of at least three methods of ultrasound-directed 'egg recovery' that enable practitioners to extract women's eggs from women's ovaries.

Laparoscopic egg retrieval, the original procedure for 'egg pick-up', is a surgical procedure women undergo under general anaesthetic. Three incisions are made through a woman's abdomen so that practitioners can insert a laparoscope (a fibre-optic viewing tube), forceps and a teflon-coated needle. Practitioners hold her ovaries with forceps while inserting the needle into each of her stimulated follicles and, using a vacuum pressure device, extract her eggs. This procedure can damage women's ovaries and poses additional risks that are attendant upon general anaesthetics (Wood and Westmore 1984 pp. 66-8).

Ultrasound-directed 'oocyte recovery' is the more recently developed procedure for 'egg pick-up'. In this type of procedure, women are awake. Practitioners may first 'overfill' women's bladders with a saline solution. They then distend women's abdominal cavities with a carbon dioxide gas mixture. Under continuous ultrasound monitoring, they guide a hand-held instrument with a needle at one end through women's bladders and into each of their mature (stimulated) follicles to suck out their eggs. According to Bruel and Kjaer, who manufacture ultrasound 'oocyte pick-up' equipment: 'The puncture procedure can be performed by three different routes for needle insertion: A) Transvesical (through the bladder) with an abdominal transducer; B) Perurethral (through the urethra) with an abdominal transducer; C) Transvaginal with an abdominal transducer or a vaginal transducer' (Bruel and Kjaer (UK) Ltd pp. 4–5). As documented on film, this method of 'egg recovery' is painful for the women and poses the risk of infection from the incision through their bladders (*Panorama* 1988).[13]

As a sales pitch in another of their brochures, Bruel and Kjaer report their 'high recovery [of women's eggs] rate':

> On average five eggs are obtained per patient; the largest number of eggs retrieved from one patient so far is twenty-two (Bruel and Kjaer (UK) Ltd 1986 p. 2).

They do not mention or assess how this 'high recovery rate' affects women's health.

Assuming that women's eggs have been 'successfully' removed from their bodies, alive and sufficiently mature, the phase for which the process is named IVF – fertilisation in glass – follows. Women's extracted eggs are placed in a Petri dish with (usually their husbands') sperm with the objective that some or all will fertilise. Any resultant embryos are maintained *in vitro* for at least twenty-four hours. During this time a woman is continuously administered hormones to prepare her for the final phase of the IVF process, 'embryo transfer/replacement'.

'Embryo transfer/replacement'

This procedure, as described by Mary Anderson, entails the

> transfer [of] the now growing egg and implant[ation of] it into *the* uterus previously primed with hormones so that *its* lining endometrium is in a receptive state (Anderson 1987 p. 71, my emphasis)

Dr Anderson's reference to a singular fertilised egg is somewhat misleading as there is rarely only one fertilised egg reimplanted in women. The whole point of 'superovulation' is to induce women to produce more than one. To write of one egg is to obscure the character of 'superovulation' procedures and to erase the risk to women of multiple pregnancy that is necessarily posed by a routine reimplantation of more than one of their fertilised eggs. In Britain, since 1986 (VLA 1986 p. 16) the recommended and most common number of women's extracted, fertilised and then reimplanted eggs is three or four. In some countries, such as Ireland, all women's extracted and fertilised eggs must by law be reimplanted in them.

Despite claims by some IVF clinics of success rates upwards of 20 per cent, Gena Corea and Susan Ince found, in a survey they conducted on clinics in the United States, that success rates for IVF treatment are routinely manipulated by clinicians in various ways. These methods of 'success enhancement' include: (1) careful selection of IVF patients; counting so-called 'clinical pregnancies' (a label which refers to a rise in a woman's HCG hormone level; 'clinical pregnancies' are not ongoing pregnancies and cannot lead to a live birth) and ectopic (tubal) pregnancies (which are also not ongoing pregnancies and usually lead to irreparable damage to or loss of a woman's fallopian tube); and (2) removing certain (unsuccessful) patients from their accounting. Actual success rates of IVF, measured in terms of likelihood of a woman ending up with a live birth, are extremely low. Corea and Ince found in the United States no rates of live birth higher than 10 per cent, and even those occurred only at the best clinics. (This figure does not reflect the total number of IVF attempts these women underwent.) By and large the success rates at most clinics they surveyed approached or were zero per cent (Corea and Ince 1987 pp. 133–9).

In Britain, medical scientists reported a 1986 pregnancy rate of 9.9 per cent, 24 per cent of which were multiple pregnancies. They reported a live birth success rate of only 8.6 per cent. They did not, however, specify the percentage of these which were the result of multiple pregnancy. Thus the 8.6 per cent do not represent the number of women who gave birth after IVF treatment, but rather the number of babies born. Nor, again, do the figures represent the number of live births per cycle of IVF. The success rate of live birth per woman per cycle would therefore be much lower than 8.6 per cent (VLA 1988 pp. 21–2).

Any or all of the IVF procedures can fail. These so-called 'drop cycles' 'most commonly occur because hormonal therapy has not induced an adequate number of follicles to mature, rang[ing] from less than 10 percent to around a third of all cycles at some clinics' (Corea and Ince 1987 p. 136). Cycles can also be 'dropped' at the 'egg recovery' stage because no women's eggs, or eggs too immature for fertilisation are 'recovered'; at the fertilisation stage, where no fertilisation takes place, or fertilised eggs are too damaged to be viable; or, most commonly, at the 'embryo transfer' stage, where none of the woman's fertilised eggs implant in her uterus. Renate Klein and Robyn Rowland report an 80 to 95 per cent failure rate for embryo transfer (Klein and Rowland 1988a p. 3; 1988b p. 10). Even when an ongoing pregnancy occurs, women frequently miscarry. As one clinician reported in the Corea and Ince study, miscarriage (so-called 'preclinical abortion') rates were 25 per cent at his clinic and up to 50 per cent at others (Corea and Ince 1987 p. 138).

Thus, owing to the high likelihood of 'dropped cycles' at every stage of treatment, women may undergo any or all IVF procedures more than once, and probably several times. This repetition of IVF procedures compounds the considerable risks to women's health already posed by a single cycle of IVF treatment, a point that the modes in which 'success rates' are typically recorded obscure.

'IVF couples'

Your Search for Fertility [offers] ... a detailed index to offer childless couples the help they need (blurb of Barker 1981).

This book was written to help those couples contemplating In Vitro Fertilisation, for medical or counselling professionals in a position to offer advice about the method and for all those interested in the ethical, legal or social consequences of using this method to by-pass infertility (blurb of Wood and Westmore 1984)

Designed to meet the needs of every couple confronting possible infertility (blurb of Winston 1987).

If women are on the one hand rendered invisible through IVF terminology and in characteristic practitioner accounts of the process, they are also discursively (re)constructed both bodily through the recombination of their body parts and reproductive processes and textually through constructions of 'ideal' patient/reader. The simultaneous erasure and construction of women in the context of IVF is perhaps epitomised in ubiquitous references to IVF patients as 'IVF (infertile or childless) couples', by which, as all of the texts I read make clear, is meant heterosexual couples. Indeed, in her study of popular representations of infertility, Sarah Franklin (1990) notes that the discursive construction of IVF patients as conventional heterosexual couples thwarted from the natural progression of marriage to children and 'desperate' to fulfil conventional (white, middle-class) definitions of family infuses both popular media representations of IVF and practitioner-authored texts. As I discuss in depth in Part II of this book, underpinning this positioning of patients/readers is an implicit construction of an 'ideal' IVF woman who fits the discourses of acceptable, 'normal' heterosexuality, of 'ideal' family.

If the terminology of 'IVF couples' constitutes an exclusionary, heterosexist construction of the idealised woman patient, it also erases the woman *as* IVF patient. The notion of an 'IVF couple' equates women's and men's positions in relation to IVF treatment, implying that both receive it, and that they do so equally. However it is women, not their putative male partners, who undergo IVF, and women who bear the risks to health, life and livelihood IVF entails.

Infertile imaginings: 'infertility' as a suspect classification

IVF treatment is classified medically, legally and popularly as an 'infertility treatment', and more recently as a method for diagnosing 'infertility'. Not only does IVF have bearing on the meaning and 'management' of 'infertility', but, conversely, the meaning of 'infertility' itself has a necessary relationship to the the complex genea/logics underpinning IVF treatment that I have examined in this chapter. In what follows, I shall argue that 'infertility' is a fundamentally contradictory classification, displaying the principle that Simone de Beauvoir identified as 'an embarassing flexibility on a basis of rigid concepts' (de Beauvoir 1974 p. 42).

Rigid concepts

'Infertility' is constituted as a pathological medical category. As a conceptual framework, it is intrinsically a 'disease' model for understanding 'childlessness'. As a medical concept 'infertility' problematises 'childlessness' individualistically and as a matter of 'dysfunction' or 'what can go wrong' strictly within the body of the 'infertile person' (Anderson 1987 pp. 27–41). Likewise, the phrase 'infertile woman/man' establishes a pathological identity, orienting an individual's personhood around 'dysfunction' or 'disease'. As a diagnostic category, the classification 'infertility' rationalises, justifies and calls for medical intervention, interpellating not only the state of 'childlessness', but

---

those individuals who are childless (defined as 'infertile') and their feelings[14] about it as appropriately, even necessarily medical territory – problems that require medical solutions.

'Infertility' carries gendered cultural resonances with earlier notions of 'barrenness', a concept (of failure) firmly associated with women. These resonances infiltrate the literature on infertility and IVF even where author/practitioners provide carefully worded explanations of 'infertility' as physiologically originating in either or both men and women. For example, qualifying her acknowledgement that 'infertility' can be located in men as well as women, Dr Mary Anderson writes:

> some men cannot accept the possibility that they may have a problem and so refuse [infertility] investigation. There are ways of overcoming this as we shall see and the writer feels that no criticism should be levelled at the man by the doctor, especially to the woman. This can only increase tension, which is hardly the background for successful conception (Anderson 1987 pp. 2–3).

Anderson does not include a similar proviso for protecting the sensibilities of women. Nor does she question men's sensitivity on the subject, but simply assumes it as given. She also expects that women will feel similarly distressed at the idea that their male partners are 'infertile' (but will apparently be able to accept the idea that they themselves are).

The gender bias of the category 'infertility' is further revealed in the structure of 'infertility' investigations. Women bear the brunt of these diagnostic investigations, experiencing a level of intervention that is in no way comparable with the markedly less invasive investigations of male 'infertility':

> In outline, investigations for the male partner will be on his semen, and for the female partner on her ovaries and whether they are producing eggs satisfactorily, on her tubes and whether they are functioning normally, on her uterus and cervix and their capabilities and of course on the ability of her partner's sperm to enter her genital tract and reach an egg successfully (Anderson 1987 p. 3).

Routine 'infertility' investigations of women are primarily internal, entailing at the least post-coital internal examinations (to check the 'ability of her partner's sperm to enter her genital tract and reach an egg successfully'), and, at much greater risk to her health, laparoscopic (surgical, and under general anaesthetic) examination of her reproductive organs. Investigations of men on the other hand are usually (though there has been some growth of more invasive assays more recently) external (analysis of sperm and semen), posing minimal (if any) risk to their health.

Finally, the gender bias of the category 'infertility' is compounded linguistically by the designation of patients undergoing 'infertility' investigations as 'infertile couples', with similar implications to those discussed above in relation to 'IVF couple'. The 'gender neutrality' of the phrase 'infertile couple' may appear to avoid apportioning 'blame', allocating each partner equal weight and significance in the process of reproduction, regardless of who is 'unable' to contribute to that process. But in fact this terminology does not equalise the position of women in relation to men. Rather, it subsumes the unequal burdens of intervention and risk involved for women in undergoing 'infertility' investigation.

That women bear the primary burden and risk of 'infertility' investigations in the first instance reflects, I would suggest, an assumption that 'infertility' itself is both a 'woman's problem' and a problem with women (whether or not the 'problem' eventually diagnosed is theirs).

Embarrassing flexibility

While the category 'infertility' is conceptually rigid on the one hand, the specific conditions that are classified under this heading betray on the other hand a disquieting lack of consistency and clarity. The categorical 'flexibility' of the meaning of 'infertility' is particularly apparent in the variable ways it articulates with IVF treatment. This 'embarrassing flexibility' in the meaning of 'infertility' can be seen in a number of contexts, including: in definitions of the aetiology (origin of disease) of 'infertility'; in clinical indications used for offering IVF; in the conflation within IVF literature of 'infertility' and 'childlessness'; in the definition of IVF as an 'infertility treatment'; and finally, in the use of IVF as a tool for the diagnosis of 'infertility'.

Suspect aetiologies

The aetiologies (origins of disease) of 'infertility', even at a strictly physiological level, are poorly understood. Hence, accounts of such 'origins' of the condition are deeply problematic. These suspect aetiologies include:

1. Idiopathic or 'unexplained infertility', which is a common indication for a variety of 'infertility' treatments (primarily on women) despite the fact that no physiological reason for 'failure to conceive' can be found;

2. Environmentally induced 'infertility', which may result from exposure to pathogenic (producing illness), teratogenic (producing malformation in pregnancy), or mutagenic (producing mutations – for instance, cancer) substances including chemicals and radiation, either in the workplace or the general environment; and

3. Iatrogenic (medically induced) 'infertility', which is particularly common for women. It can result from direct surgical damage; post-surgical infections, as in septic (botched, usually illegal) abortions; pelvic inflammatory disease (PID), the most common source of physiological infertility in women, which if not treated in time can cause irreparable damage to women's fallopian tubes; misdiagnosed or undiagnosed sexually transmitted diseases such as chlamydia, which, if untreated, can cause secondary PID; tubal sterilisation; oral and particularly injectable contraceptive drugs such as the pill or Depo Provera; and, hormone treatments – including those used in the IVF regimen, which may damage women's ovaries or facilitate ectopic (tubal) pregnancy (Anderson 1987 pp. 27–41).[15]

'Infertility' can involve either one or both partners, although both cases are commonly conflated into the category 'infertile couples' and in most cases 'infertility' investigations and treatment, as noted earlier, are carried out disproportionately on women. Significantly, 'infertility' can, particularly in the case of 'idiopathic infertility', sometimes disappear without medical intervention.

However, within the rigid, medicalised conceptual frame-

---

work of 'infertility', all of these 'suspect aetiologies' will constitute individualised diagnoses which rationalise similarly individualistic medical intervention and treatment. This is despite the fact that environmentally induced and iatrogenic 'infertility' clearly constitute (often preventable) problems which do not originate in the individual affected. However when infertility is strictly a diagnostic/treatment question, the power relations surrounding the relationship between infertility, environmental polution and adverse effects of medical treatment become begged.

Suspect indications: clinical criteria for IVF treatment

Any and all of the aetiologically 'suspect' diagnoses, plus a wide variety of other conditions called 'infertility', can be designated by practitioners as indications for IVF treatment on women. 'Suspect aetiologies' in particular contribute directly to the expansion of indications for IVF, thereby co-opting a greater number of women into the IVF treatment programme. According to Françoise Laborie:

> The indications for IVF have expanded enormously ... [to include]: tubal damage (61%), male infertility (11%), both tubal and male infertility (11%), idiopathic [unexplained] infertility (12%), immunological infertility [for instance women producing antibodies against their partner's sperm] (1%) and multiple causes (2%) (Laborie 1987 p. 51).

With regard to the use of IVF on women with tubal damage, the cause of which is not infrequently iatrogenic, Robert Edwards writes:

> The majority of patients presented with tubal disorders (81%), Pelvic Inflammatory Disease caused irreparable damage and blockage of the oviducts in many of them, tubal surgery having failed to restore function (Edwards *et al.* 1984 p. 3).

In cases of idiopathic (unexplained) 'infertility', William Walters and Peter Singer suggest that:

> Another group of women with infertility which may be considered suitable for IVF is that comprising women who, although having

---

no problems after routine infertility tests, fail to conceive after more than one year with AID treatment (Walters and Singer 1984 p. 3).

However, Carl Wood and Ann Westmore add that:

such couples [*sic*] may become pregnant without any treatment; 40% after two years infertility (Wood and Westmore 1984 p. 28).

Walters and Singer also suggest male infertility as a diagnostic indicator for IVF on women:

IVF and ET [embryo transfer] are being explored in the treatment of male infertility where the number, movement and structure of sperm are considered to be abnormal (Walters and Singer 1984 p. 3).

Thus not only are women treated with IVF on the basis of possible prior medical malpractice (as involved in many cases of damage to women's tubes from misdiagnosed or untreated pelvic inflammatory disease), but, according to Laborie's statistics, at least 12 per cent undergo IVF despite the lack of diagnostic pathology (their own and their partner's), and at least 11 per cent of these women in the clinics she surveyed undergo extensive medical intervention for their male partner's condition. It would seem an unprecedented move in medical circles to subject a person to such an invasive and risky treatment regimen for the purpose of treating someone else's condition when that condition is non-fatal (and that person is himself not undergoing treatment).[16] Neither Walters and Singer, nor any other author/practitioner in the sample I read, raise questions about the ethics of treating women with IVF for the 'infertility' of their male partners.

As noted earlier in this chapter, the misleading 'gender neutrality' of the patient signifiers 'infertile couples' and 'IVF couples' (and 'pregnant couples') masks the fact that diagnosis of 'infertility' may not refer at all to women, and that IVF treatment may not in fact be treating a woman's fertility 'problem'.

Suspect elisions: 'infertility' and 'childlessness'
The terms 'infertility' and 'childlessness' are used interchange-

ably by practitioners (a situation that is reproduced in popular and legal discourses around IVF and infertility). Thus IVF treatment has come to be known as a way of 'achieving pregnancy for childless couples' (G. H. Barker 1981).[17] However, 'IVF couples' are not necessarily childless. According to IVF practitioners Carl Wood and Ann Westmore:

> It makes no difference to the priority given to couples if they already have children – either adopted, conceived before the infertility problem occurred, or achieved through artificial insemination or a previously successful In Vitro Fertilization attempt (Wood and Westmore 1984 p. 56).

William Walters and Peter Singer write, moreover, that:

> Previous childbearing suggests that factors contributing to infertility, with the exception of tubal disease, are unlikely to be present. Women who have already had a child also have a significantly better chance of an easy ET [embryo transfer] because the neck of the womb, having been stretched during delivery of a baby, is wider (Walters and Singer 1984 p. 4).

Thus, as these practitioners explain, IVF is more likely to be successful when women have had a previous pregnancy.

This interchangeable use of the terms 'childlessness' and 'infertility' obscures the fact that 'IVF couples' may indeed already have children, albeit they may be biologically related only to one (or, in the case of adoption, neither) of their parents. It is also a misrepresentation that fosters a categorical expansion of the use of 'infertility' treatments as IVF on a growing number of women (who may not have 'fertility' problems and/or who may already be parents).

Suspect definitions: IVF as an 'infertility' treatment

IVF is typically represented by practitioners (as well as in popular and legal discourses) as an 'infertility' treatment. This representation misleadingly implies that IVF treats or cures the causes or source of 'infertility'. This is not the case. IVF only bypasses 'infertility' – a point which is noted quite carefully by Wood and Westmore, who then however go on to discuss IVF as a method of 'overcoming' infertility. IVF, then, may be a tool for medical scientists to attempt to engineer a woman's pregnancy; but it does not treat any physiological fertility 'problems' she may have, and it most certainly is not a cure. If a woman undergoes IVF treatment because her tubes are damaged, her tubes will remain just as damaged during and after IVF treatment. Moreover, as I have discussed above, IVF not only does not enhance women's health, but jeopardises it in ways that are so far barely estimated or explored. Thus, a woman undergoing IVF treatment may emerge in worse condition, or with more fertility 'problems' than she had before treatment (or with fertility problems she never had before).

Suspect diagnostics: IVF as a tool for diagnosing male 'infertility'

Complicating the already questionable use of IVF to treat women who are not diagnosed as 'infertile' but whose male partners are, IVF has also been posited as a tool for diagnosing 'infertility'; particularly male infertility. William Walters and Peter Singer suggest IVF for diagnostic use, particularly for women with unexplained infertility (such as women who may not have any physiological fertility 'problem', but whose male partner may or may not):

> IVF is a new technique which may be used for diagnostic as well as therapeutic purposes. In women with unexplained infertility, IVF can be used to diagnose the level of fertility defect, that is in sperm, eggs, fertilization or tubal transport (Walters and Singer 1984 p. 8).

Previously, this type of test for sperm motility (ability to fertilise eggs) has involved the use of hamster ova, which were removed and then placed in a Petri dish with human sperm. The use of IVF for diagnosing male 'infertility' means that women and women's eggs, in effect, replace hamsters and hamsters' eggs.[18]

Recombinant bodies

As I have argued throughout this chapter, an examination of the terminology and procedures of '*in vitro* fertilisation' reveals a complex interplay of textual/procedural *genea/logics* which foreground: the reconstruction of women's reproductive processes, while erasing women as autonomous persons and primary patients (*recombinant logics*); technique, expertise and expert (*authorial-logics*); the production of embryos/children (*embryo/logics*); and the making of conventional families.

That the extraction, management and recombination of women's reproductive processes involve and are predicated upon a *deprivatisation* of women's bodies seems taken for granted within professional accounts of the process and is implicit in the terminology. Physiologically, women's bodies must be opened, monitored, and made increasingly visible, with parts extracted and then reintroduced. Thus even as women are *invisiblised* as autonomous persons and primary patients, their bodies are increasingly *visiblised*, conceptually and literally transferred from the 'private'[19] domain of the woman's body to the public gaze of (mostly private) medicine. Crowe (1987) has argued, furthermore, that the premium placed on women's physical visibility is matched by professional interest in and interrogation of women's personal lives and lifestyles. As part of the diagnostic and treatment regimen of IVF, women are routinely required to reveal the details of their sexual and reproductive histories and practices; their domestic arrangements; their attitudes towards mothering; and their willingness to co-operate with practice protocols and practitioners.

IVF treatment entails extensive surveillance of women's hormone levels, the (induced) maturation of their follicles, the 'accessibility' of their ovaries. Women are expected to make themselves continuously available to the schedules, scrutiny and management of practitioners and to hospital and clinical routines. Sometimes this requires an exhausting amount of travel for women who do not live near the clinic, or that they take temporary accommodation (at their own expense) near the clinic. As is acknowledged by Professor Winston:

> Test-tube baby treatment requires a great deal of commitment from the couple and from the staff carrying it out. You may be

asked to attend the clinic at very unsociable hours and at repeated intervals. There is no doubt that you will be required to make some sacrifices to have the best chance of success. For example, it is very difficult to carry on working during a treatment cycle. So it is important that you are certain you want to try everything to get a child of your own, otherwise it really is not worth the effort (Winston 1987 p. 153).

Professor Winston's statement encapsulates well the implicit assumption that a 'couple's' commitment is carried by women, whose willingness to subject themselves to the requirements of treatment protocols, hospital routines and practitioners' expectations, Winston links directly with 'chances of success'. Clearly it is not male partners who are expected to 'sacrifice' their paid work (particularly given the exorbitant costs of treatment even when offered on the NHS).

If the professional *recombinant* logic of IVF assumes a disproportionate burden of commitment for women, it also involves the assumption that women should bear the entire burden of physical risk.[20] Moreover, as IVF has developed over the years, the tendency has been to increase and complexify the level of medical intervention and surveillance on women. Thus the *recombinant* logic of IVF technique is both pervasive and progressive. In other words, IVF constitutes an approach to the management of women's reproduction that is intrinsically orientated to the progressive dis-integration and reconstitution of women's bodies. The professional texts and terminology emphasise the recombinant, scientific character of the treatment, while redirecting attention away from the involvement and position of women in this process. The IVF author/authority writes him/herself through the inscription of women as recombinant bodies. In the authoritative narrative, the professional culture would appear to be the primary culture medium of IVF – that through which reproduction, women's bodies and Petri dish media are (re)constituted and eggs, embryos, children and 'fit' families are (re)produced.

The meaning of 'infertility' is clearly central to the administration of IVF treatment on women. Not only is 'infertility' the categorical context of IVF treatment, but as such, it is the chief means of facilitating the use of IVF on a growing number of women. The contradictory meanings of the category 'infertility' constitute an *a priori* framework through which the recombinant logics underpinning IVF techniques and terms are reproduced and the recombinant bodies of women are 'written'. Moreover, both the rigid conceptual parameters and the 'embarrassing flexibility' of the classification 'infertility' bespeak the authorial power of medical practitioners. If IVF and 'infertility' investigations reflect an impetus to demystify, manage, 'fix', reconstruct women's bodily processes, the reductiveness and contradictions of practitioner accounts of these practices mystify and maintain the hegemonic mystique of their expertise and agency in 'authoring' the texts and techniques of IVF. Finally, as with IVF, the ubiquitous references to couples, marriage, 'husband's sperm', etc. permeating this literature suggest that while 'infertility' is rigidly construed as a medical condition, only some people's 'infertility' is a medical problem.

Notes

1 Robert M. L. Winston is a Professor of Fertility Studies at the University of London Institute of Obstetrics and Gynaecology, Hammersmith Hospital, London, whose public profile as an IVF practitioner and researcher and public spokesperson on behalf of developments in reproductive technologies has been considerable. His clinic is the first in Britain to have undertaken preimplantation diagnosis (genetic screening of IVF embryos) as a clinical practice.

2 I have 'borrowed' the suggestive title of Toril Moi's (1985) *Sexual/Textual Politics*, though my use of the term 'text' is expanded to include technique and technology (Benston 1992) and my analysis is not, as is Moi's, drawing on the (inter)disciplinary tools or field of feminist literary criticism/theory.

3 The components of the misleadingly termed '*in vitro* fertilisation' process can vary widely, although they all depend on similarly extensive intervention into women. The basic or routine 'IVF' protocol includes four stages of treatment: 'superovulation', 'egg recovery', fertilisation and 'embryo replacement/transfer'.

4 Human chorionic gonadotropin (HCG) is a hormone produced by pregnant women and can be extracted from their urine. Human menopausal gonadotropin (HMG) is a term used to describe a form of follicle-stimu-

lating hormone extracted from the urine of post-menopausal women (Barker 1980 p. 172). The gonadotropin drugs are extremely powerful, and risks include hyperstimulation and enlargement or rupture of women's ovaries; used in 'conventional' (chemotherapeutic only) infertility treatments they pose significant risks of multiple pregnancy.

5 Mary Anderson reports that women may additionally have administered 'gonadotrophin releasing hormone (GnRH): '[p]ulsed doses are given at 90-minute intervals and the equipment for injecting subcutaneously can be worn by the patient in the form of a small box not much bigger that a cigarette packet'. She adds that a prolactin-suppressant drug called 'bromocriptine' may also be administered to women who 'fail' to ovulate owing to 'high levels of the hormone prolactin'. She notes that bromocriptine causes 'side effects' such as dizziness and nausea (Anderson 1987 p. 68).

6 Indications of some adverse effects of hormone drugs used in the IVF context appear in drug manuals such as the *Physician's Desk Reference* (PDR) in the USA or MIMS in the UK, in texts concerning 'conventional' infertility treatments (i.e. treatments taking only a chemotherapeutic approach) and in some feminist and other critical examinations of drug treatments and allopathic medicine.

7 See Note 4 above.

8 Thalidomide is a drug that was administered to pregnant women in the 1960s to prevent morning sickness and subsequently was found to cause serious teratogenic effects in their children, notably the 'mal-' or non-formation of limbs.

9 One teratogenic effect identified by Crook (1986) is the production of hydatidiform moles, or 'molar pregnancy' – terms used to describe a cystic mole that 'looks like a bunch of grapes' that grows in a woman's uterus and gives the appearance of a normal pregnancy (p. 5).

10 Although Anderson's book *Infertility: a Guide for the Anxious Couple* mentions IVF as one of many possible clinical treatments for infertility, her book mainly provides clinical information.

11 According to Mary Anderson, as regards fertility treatments that are limited to hormone therapy: 'with Clomid, multiple pregnancy, especially twins is a possibility (15–25%); with gonadotrophin therapy it is a real risk (over 50 percent...)' (p. 68). Thus women who conceive before completing the rest of the IVF procedure that follows superovulation can run the risk of a multiple pregnancy, particularly in the case of women diagnosed as having *idiopathic* (unexplained) infertility and treated with IVF. IVF practitioners Wood and Westmore (1984) state: 'such couples (*sic*) may become pregnant without treatment ...' (p. 28). Moreover, as discussed later in this chapter, many or all of women's superovulated eggs may be reimplanted – reinscribing the risk of multiple pregnancy.

12 The identification of the action of drugs in terms of effects (meaning

desired effects) and 'side-effects' is a cliché of both medical and pharmaceutical professional cultures. It is worth noting that practitioner/authors in this sample characteristically name and describe the administration of 'IVF' hormones to women strictly in terms of their desired effects: hormone administration is called 'superovulation', and is described only in terms of stimulation to 'the' ovaries. This misleadingly suggests that these hormones affect only the organ or tissue to which they are directed and act on women only in the way practitioners purposefully administer them. Hormones, however, are administered in tablets (orally) or by injection (intravenously), and therefore circulate through a woman's whole body systemically, affecting not only the balance of her entire endocrine (hormone) system, but all the organs and tissues that constitute her body.

13 Similar footage of this procedure appeared in the (UK) Channel 4 television documentary 'Soft Cell' (11 January 1988).

14 In this context, men's as well as women's feelings and experiences of 'childlessness' take on a diagnostic significance – they are interpellated as part of the general pathology of 'infertility'. This is not to suggest, however, that men's feelings and experiences of 'childlessness', nor their experiences of 'infertility' investigations and treatments (most of which are undergone by women) are equivalent to women's. My argument here is that the medical approach encapsulated in the medical classification of 'infertility' eclipses social, political and psychological analyses of and approaches to experiences and feelings about childlessness.

15 Dr Mary Anderson explains two sources of iatrogenic infertility:
    Infection [pelvic inflammatory disease] can distort the tube, pin it down to surrounding structures, damage its fimbria, block its canal and destroy the specialised lining cells and their hair-like projections. Such infection is, unfortunately, not infrequently seen nowadays. Bacterial infection associated with abortion, the use of the coil or from surrounding structures such as appendicitis may result in damaged tubes. Gonococcal infection [gonorrhoea] may be the cause and there are several other implicated organisms (Anderson 1987 p. 36).
    Dr Anderson also points out that hormone therapy used in the treatment of 'infertility' can also cause infertility in women, as for example from hyperstimulation of women's ovaries (p. 68).

16 It is, on the other hand increasingly common for pregnant women to (be required or at least pressured to) undergo invasive treatments including surgery for the purpose of treating her fetus. In this context, the fetus is commonly regarded (both within and outside the professional medical context) as both a separate person and the primary patient who has 'rights' and 'needs' that supersede those of the pregnant woman. (See Daniels 1993 for an extended discussion of the politics of fetal rights and medical treatment of pregnant women.)

17 The title of Dr Graham Barker's book (1980): *Your Search for Fertility: a Sympathetic Guide to Achieving Pregnancy for Childless Couples* is char-

acteristic of the conflation of 'infertility' and 'childlessness' permeating the sample of literature I investigated.

18 Walters and Singer go on to write:

> Because normal IVF and embryo growth rates are less than 50 per cent, a control system is needed when testing the sperm–egg interaction in unexplained infertility. This control is applied by placing one egg with fertile matched donor sperm as well as another similar egg with the husband's sperm (Walters and Singer 1984 p. 8)

Thus women (for whom, along with their partners, practitioners have been unable to diagnose a physiological cause for their biological childlessness) undergo IVF in order that practitioners can test 'sperm–egg interaction'. Practitioners place one of her eggs in a Petri dish with donor sperm and one in a dish with her husband's (*sic*) sperm. The test requires that practitioners extract at least 2 eggs from a woman; if not, the cycle of hormone stimulation and 'egg recovery' procedures must be repeated.

Walters and Singer go on to posit several rather odd interpretations of the results of this diagnostic test:

> Successful fertilisation with the husband's sperm followed by pregnancy after ET [embryo transfer] would indicate that some immunological, chemical or physical barrier is preventing pregnancy.

Yet a far less risky (though not unproblematic) test for 'immunological [or] chemical … barrier' already exists: the 'cervical mucus hostility' (*sic*) test involves a 'post-coital' examination of the mixture of a woman's cervical mucus and the sperm of her partner. Walters and Singer do not explain why the risky and unpredictable process of IVF should be considered a suitable replacement for the old test.

Walters and Singer go on to suggest that 'in cases where eggs cannot be fertilised by either the husband's or donor's sperm, abnormalities of the egg may be responsible'. However this could equally indicate 'abnormalities' in both men's sperm, or, a possibility Walters and Singer do not consider, problems with IVF as a diagnostic test (for instance adverse effects of superovulation and 'egg recovery' or of a problem in the Petri dish culture medium).

19 I am aware that the notions of 'private' and 'private bodies' have essentialist connotations, suggesting a division between ontology and epistemology, between individuals and their social context, between subject and discourse, that is problematic to say the least. I therefore use the term with a certain ambivalence to acknowledge that bodies are not, on the other hand, without boundaries (however contested). To deny the existence of boundaries between bodies would render concepts of violence, violation, invasion, invasiveness, commodification, or objectification all but meaningless.

20 As my friend Debbie Epstein said to me in conversation about this point: 'No man ever died of wanking.'

2

Defensive élites and definitive practices: modelling medical scientific (self-)regulation

In Chapter 1, I explored several dimensions of the professional common senses around IVF. I suggested that the protocols and character of IVF technique as well as IVF terminology and practitioner-authored texts constitute part of a discursive field through which a particular set of genea/logical relations are constituted. In this chapter I am interested in extending my discussion to consider the ways in which a professional common sense was consolidated through the formation and Reports (particularly the *First Report*) of the Voluntary Licensing Authority (VLA) – a body created by medical scientific practitioners to articulate and 'enforce' a code of practice for IVF and related processes.

Both the literature I examined in Chapter 1 and that published by the VLA were produced during a period of escalating public debate about the ethics and legitimacy of IVF and related practices – debates to which both literatures refer explicitly. This took place in a context in which statutory regulation was clearly imminent and potentially constricting both of the unfettered 'progress' of developments in reproductive technologies and the traditional autonomy and self-regulation characteristic of professions in general and of medical scientific professions in particular. Both literatures, moveover, can be read as having similar aims: to 'sell' IVF and related practices *to* potential patients; to sell them *as* ethical and legitimate practices; and to reproduce the authorial voice and power of

medical scientific practitioners against the threats of public disapprobation and statutory co-option. In this context, the establishment of a code of practice and a voluntary licensing
authority emerge as, at least in part, defensive as well as discursively productive gestures. What is particularly interesting
here is the way in which the production of a code of practice
coalesces and produces a professional common sense. Whether
or not it 'really' reflects professional consensus, a code of practice discursively produces one. What the emergence of the
VLA represents, then, is a moment when hegemonic struggles
over defining practice appear to be resolved and the authorial
voice reproduces its own authority.

The Voluntary Licensing Authority: a model of medical science self-regulation

The VLA was set up in Britain in 1985 by a coalition of the
Medical Research Council (MRC) and the Royal College of
Obstetricians and Gynaecologists (RCOG) in response to a
Government Committee (The Warnock Committee) recommendation 'that a new statutory licensing authority should be
established to regulate both research and certain types of infertility services. One such service [is] IVF' (VLA 1986 p. 6). In
the absence of specificity on the part of the Warnock Committee as to who exactly should constitute this regulatory
authority, 'the VLA was proposed by the sponsoring bodies as
an interim arrangement pending the setting up of a statutory
licensing authority for human IVF and research on pre-
embryos' (p. 20).

The medical scientific community therefore established
the VLA as a non-statutory (not legally empowered or binding) interim medical scientific model for the regulation of
what it distinguished as the separate practices of IVF 'treatment' and 'pre-embryo research'. It not only provided a model
regulatory framework for eventual legislation, but a potentially incumbent or heir-presumptive body for statutory self-
regulation (in which intentions, as I discuss in Chapters 6 and

7, success in the former, if not the latter, was eventually achieved).

Despite their claim that the VLA had been established to allay public concerns and anxieties about IVF and, indeed, to involve the public in guiding the direction of 'this new but fast growing area of medical and scientific knowledge' (p. 1), an examination of both the membership and the remit of the VLA reveal a much more self-interested agenda. As with the terminology and other professional literatures of IVF, the central proccupations underpinning the VLA Reports concern professional licence, scientific 'progress' and embryos – and the absence of women is writ large.

The authorial voice: who's who in the VLA

The VLA was composed of fifteen members. Four were nominated by the Medical Research Council (MRC), and included a professor of medicine, a director of medical research, a director of veterinary research and a hospice medical director. An additional four were nominated by the Royal College of Obstetricians and Gynaecologists (RCOG): these were all doctors specialising in obstetrics and gynaecology. The chair of the VLA, Dame Mary Donaldson, was also a medical scientist.

In her foreword to the VLA report, VLA 'chairman' [*sic*], Dame Mary Donaldson (GBE) wrote '[l]ay members now comprise half the membership of the Authority'. The term 'lay members' suggests persons with no professional or personal ties or obligations to the medical scientific community. However, the 'lay' members (7 of the 15 total members – less, in fact, than half) of the VLA were all nominated jointly by the MRC and the RCOG, and three of them had existing or prior ties with either the administration of health services, or research science or population 'planning'.[1] All had obvious status as professionals of one sort or another.

While several of the VLA members were women, including the 'chairman', none had any obvious affiliations with women's/feminist health and reproductive rights groups. Given the nature of the procedures in which the VLA were interested and the obvious, though marginalised, profile of feminist debates around reproductive technologies and their implications for women's health and women's reproductive rights at the time, the absence of members clearly designated to represent women's and feminist interests is significant. This is not to suggest that there is (or can be) a simple consensus about what constitutes 'women's' or 'feminist' interests. But if the membership was ostensibly intended (as is suggested by the considerable attention the question is given in the VLA reports) to reflect 'public debate' in microcosm, it is clear that women's/feminist interests, whatever these might be, did not figure in the equation. Nor, as we shall see, does the remit of the VLA centralise considerations of women's health, rights or interests. Indeed, women are rarely mentioned in the VLA report.

Modelling self-regulation

The *First Report of the VLA* (1986) outlines a hierarchy of medical scientific accountability both within the medical science community and between IVF practitioners and (women) patients. Here the VLA proposes to establish a system of internal accountability that is strictly within the confines of medical science, specifically the MRC and RCOG. To this end IVF practice, practitioners and local ethics committees are placed solely within medical scientific jurisdiction. The VLA defines itself as both the standard-setting body for IVF practice and the central referee to whom practitioners are directly accountable through a system of licensing. The report states that the remit of the VLA is:

1. To approve a Code of Practice on research related to human fertilisation and embryology.

2. To invite all centres, clinicians and scientists engaged in research on *in vitro* fertilisation to submit their work for approval and licensing.

3. To visit each centre prior to its being granted a licence.

4. To report to the Medical Research Council and Royal College of Obstetricians and Gynaecologists.

5. To make known publicly the details of both approved and unapproved work (VLA 1986 p. 3).

The VLA then delegates strictly implementory responsibility to local ethics committees, which are expected to enforce VLA standards on a day-to-day basis:

> The local ethical committee is, in terms of day-to-day supervision, better placed than the VLA to ensure that only work which has been approved is being done in its centre: the VLA's role is to give more general guidance on acceptable work (p. 9).

Thus the VLA establishes a restrictive system of internal, that is, medical scientific, self-regulation. Accountability to patients (women) and 'public' are mediated through mechanisms of self-regulation.

Indexing acceptable practice

The Code of [IVF] Practice set out in the VLA report establishes, by intention, minimal standards of 'quality' control of IVF:

> The intention was not to draw up restrictive and rigid guidelines which might have been unworkable in practice, *nor to constrain further progress in areas in which research was considered essential for medical advance.* The Guidelines are intended to set the minimum acceptable standards ... (VLA 1986 p. 8; emphasis mine).

The central index of acceptable practice, then, is not the safety of IVF for women, but rather the facilitation and prioritisation of 'medical advance' and medical research. IVF is defined centrally as a research project whose research status, interests and potential far outweigh its 'clinical application' in importance (p. 30). The putative distinction made between research and clinical IVF is, as we shall see, central to the agenda outlined in the VLA *Reports*[2] and a key means through which women are discursively *disappeared.* For example, the distinction obscures the fact that 'clinical' IVF is the source of material (embryos) for IVF research.[3]

The specific series of thirteen policy guidelines that constitute the VLA 'minimum standards' regulating IVF reflect two fundamental concerns that directly reflect the VLA's central objectives: (1) the preservation of exclusive medical scientific control over IVF; and (2) the facilitation of the research potential of IVF. In keeping with these priorities, the VLA standards simultaneously effect a linguistic erasure of women, even as they interpellate women (patients) into the research objectives/ethos of IVF.

Interwoven with proposals to regulate the standards of IVF clinical and laboratory facilities and equipment, a significant portion of the VLA guidelines are concerned with the maintenance of the professionalism (and the professional exclusivity) of IVF teams. Guidelines specify that IVF teams must consist of 'appropriately experienced medical, nursing and technical staff' (p. 32). In a section entitled '[i]nvolvement of non-medical staff on IVF programmes', the *First Report* notes that some clinics employ 'specially trained' counsellors so that 'patients who fail to achieve a pregnancy have the opportunity to discuss their problems and decide on future treatment' (VLA 1986 p. 16). This *Report* does not indicate whether this special training is medical or non-medical however, and does not discuss the conflicts of interest that accrue if counsellors are members of the IVF team. The subsequent *Third Report* (VLA 1988) did recognise the conflict of interest arising when IVF practitioners provide counselling, but only when the prescribing doctor acts as counsellor:

> Proper counselling is only possible if space and time are available to the couple in a neutral atmosphere with a fully-trained counsellor, *possibly a member of the team*, who is not the prescribing doctor (p. 15; emphasis mine).

Other members of the treatment team are, presumably, 'neutral'. Moreover, while the VLA applauds the *de facto* provision of counselling at some clinics, they do not mandate the provision of counselling services in their guidelines (VLA 1988 pp. 29–32). The construction of good practice posits a medical scientific professionalism which may also serve as a medium for the provision of 'non-medical' services that are seen as desirable but not necessary.

The two sections of the VLA guidelines proposing to regulate the professionalism of IVF practitioners and the quality of premises do not consider questions surrounding [the protection of] women or women's health as part of the indices of good practice. Although they are classified as 'Guidelines for both Clinical and Research Applications of Human [*sic*] In Vitro Fertilisation' (VLA 1988 p. 30), not one of the VLA guidelines establishes standards for the administration of hormones and surgeries to women that constitute the actual procedures of IVF. The VLA guidelines do not discuss either the so-called 'clinical administration' of IVF, nor by extension, any procedures women undergo, whether classified as 'clinical' or 'research'. Nor in fact do they ever mention the word 'woman'. The only clear exception to this regards the number of embryos reimplanted in women with respect to the risks of multiple pregnancy. The VLA Report recommends (though it does not mandate) a limit of three or, occasionally, four (VLA 1986 p. 16). This recommendation is not included in the Guidelines (code of practice), which appear as Annex 1 at the end of the Report. Aside from this consideration, nearly all the VLA guidelines are concerned exclusively with: (a) the status of IVF as a justified experiment; and (b) the status of 'the' embryo. Both concerns can be said to represent a frontal assault on the agency and social status of women.

'Scientifically sound research'

In the absence of standards around (or discussion about) the health of women patients[4], the Report makes it clear that scientificity rather than safety is the primary index of the legitimacy of IVF and related practices:

> Scientifically sound research involving experiments on the processes and products of in vitro fertilisation between gametes is ethically acceptable subject to certain provisions detailed in Sections 2–10 below (VLA 1986 p. 31).

The preoccupation with IVF as a research project has two significant effects. Firstly, as I discuss earlier in this chapter, it posits a false distinction between research and clinical IVF practice. The fact that 'research involving experiments on the processes and products of *in vitro* fertilisation' is predicated on the 'clinical' practice of IVF on women patients, that research on IVF 'products and processes' is, inescapably, research on women, is entirely obscured. The euphemistic language of the passage above illustrates this erasure perfectly. Secondly, the drawing up of a code of practice that only considers the research practices in which, like fertilisation in glass, women are physically absent, implies an *a priori* construction of clinical IVF (the IVF practices women undergo) as both 'scientifically' and ethically unproblematic. The position of women in IVF research (as IVF researched) is simultaneously taken for granted, denied and validated.

Within the rigid framework of scientificity, the VLA defines three wider-ranging or flexible aims that it considers appropriate, indeed necessary, to justify any IVF project:

> The aim of research must be clearly defined and relevant to clinical problems such as the diagnosis and treatment of infertility or of genetic disorders or for the development of safe and more effective contraceptive measures, (VLA 1986 clause 3 pp. 31 ff).

While appearing to construct boundaries that limit IVF research practices, these aims are so broad-based as to validate just about any study of the 'products and processes' of women's bodies – and for reasons, moreover, which may have nothing at all to do with her specific health 'problems' (or with the reasons for which she is undergoing IVF treatment).[5] For example, research 'relevant to clinical problems such as the diagnosis and treatment of infertility' would not exclude using IVF on women as a tool for researching male infertility. There is, furthermore, a disturbing irony in the use of a procedure which may cause damage to women's reproductive organs (as well as other adverse effects) to undertake research to 'improve' the diagnosis and treatment of women's infertility.

This problem is not limited to IVF research. It can be

argued that clinical treatment is the primary context for medical research, indeed is, in and of itself, research. However, IVF research can be distinguished by several features. The gender-specificity of IVF practices, for example, means that, as I note above, women are the research subjects for research interested in clinical 'problems' associated with men. Moreover, unlike other contexts where the clinical experiment is (represented as) orientated towards the improvement of the clinical treat-ment itself so as to improve the health (or save the life) of the research/clinical patient, with IVF most of the stated goals of research often have nothing directly to do with improving IVF treatment on women, and none seem geared to minimising its risks for women or towards improving women's reproductive health. Finally, there are many contexts where a medical research practice undertaken in a clinical context is identified as research involving patients. IVF research is represented as if both its clinical practice and its women patients do not exist (or as if their existence were entirely unrelated to it).

Ultimately, what is interesting here is that the language of limitation implied in the setting of these guidelines would appear to address the 'public' debates and anxieties around out-of-control scientists that were rife at the time, while not actually imposing substantive limits on IVF research possibilities. This is in part facilitated through the representation of IVF research as if it had no relationship to (the treatment of) women.

Embryo/logical agendas

The erasure of women in the VLA's preoccupation with research is brought into stark relief by its preoccupation with embryos. Most of the VLA guidelines for acceptable IVF prac-tice (8 of the 12 separate clauses) are concerned with the treat-ment of 'pre-embryos' in either a clinical or a research setting (VLA 1986 pp. 31–2). These include establishing conditions preventing the re-use (implantation in women) of research embryos in clinical treatment; the requirement of signed con-sent from women and their male partners for the clinical and research use of the gametes and embryos; the legitimate use of 'surplus' embryos from clinical treatment as research material; the limitation of research to embryos up to 14 days after fertilisation (termed 'pre-embryos'); conditions for the freezing and storage of embryos and subsequent use of frozen embryos; and legitimation of the cross-fertilisation of animal ova and human male sperm as long as development of the embryo does not proceed beyond 'early cleavage stage'.

The language of IVF embryos constructs a conceptual (made literal) division between women and embryos that parallels the division made between clinical and research IVF. In both, the position of women, the treatments women undergo and the implications for women's health and social status are eclipsed. It is embryos, not women, that would appear to be the subjects/objects of clinical treatment and research. An important consideration here is the way in which the construction of embryos as extracorporeal entities (both literally and linguistically) represents a reconstitution of anti-abortion discourses. Indeed, as I discuss later in this book, because IVF has made it possible to create embryos outside of and replace them in women's bodies, it has significantly altered the terms of debate around pregnancy, abortion, childbirth and the role of medicine and the state in relation to all three.

It can be argued that IVF has made material the ideological separation between woman and embryo that underpins anti-abortion ideology. The VLA *Report*'s discussion of clinical and research IVF solely in terms of its effects on (the status) of embryos participates in this discourse by implicitly laying out an agenda of embryo interests with no reference to women. At the same time, its renaming of the 0–14 day embryo as a 'pre-embryo' attempts to recuperate early embryos as legitimate materials (that have no personhood because they are not really embryos) for scientific research.[6]

The notion of separate embryo interests resonates with the adversarial construction of women and embryos in anti-abortion discourses. Where embryos have been seen as having separate interests, women's interests have been construed as in conflict with the putative interests of their embryos and embryos have been constructed as a kind of *endangered* species.[7] The growing currency of embryo/fetus as primary patient and first person is a direct consequence of this embryo-centred rationality. However, because the VLA never refers directly to women, the adversarial resonances of its embryo/logic remain implicit.

Most of the VLA guidelines not only discuss IVF in terms of embryos, but do so, most significantly, in terms of removing them from women's control and transferring them into the custody of IVF practitioners. In this sense, the VLA would appear to be establishing guidelines for protecting embryos in the context of IVF and designating IVF practitioners as both embryo custodians and embryo protectors. At the same time, although the VLA also establishes guidelines to protect the viability and integrity of embryos in their 'care', practitioners' research interests (their prerogative to determine how they 'dispose' of embryos) clearly supersede those of embryos. As we shall see, within the VLA guidelines embryo 'interests' effectively supersede women's interests and practitioners' interests (within the 14-day margin) explicitly supersede embryos'.

'Consent': contractual embryo/logics

The 1986 VLA *Report* provides their first model of what they term a 'Specimen Agreement for *In Vitro* Fertilisation', which is in effect a model contract of prior consent (pp. 41–2). The terms of this original model contract clearly illustrate the primary interests of the medical/scientific community in securing the materials (women and women's eggs and embryos) and licence to promote the research potential of IVF.

Prior consent contracts, sometimes also referred to as 'informed consent' forms, may appear to be an explicit vehicle for ensuring the protection of patients from medical malpractice and a moment at which the patient's agency is recognised and (re)inscribed into the doctor–patient relationship. The VLA, however, states that the importance of prior consent is:

> 1. that [the prior consent form] is a 'useful document to remind ['patients'] of the exact terms of their consent' ; and

2. that it provides 'additional security' for the doctor, giving evidence that he [*sic*] has explained 'what the treatment involves' (p. 13).

Both reasons suggest that the primary function of consent forms is to protect the practitioner from liability, not to protect the 'patient' from injury or abuse.

As I discuss below, the specific terms of the VLA 'Specimen Agreement for *In Vitro* Fertilisation' contractually bind 'IVF patients' to the research objectives of IVF treatment. More specifically, this form is a model for the contractual subordination of women.

Custodial bodies

The assumption of heterosexuality and the constitution of IVF as a means through which heterosexuality is maintained and reproduced are firmly established in the requirement that both partners of the 'IVF couple' agree to the procedure. The 'couple' are referred to as 'gamete donors', a term that (re)constructs the IVF 'couple' as altruistic and voluntary research participants rather than as patient (and male partner) involved in clinical treatment. Thus the terms of the contract interpellate clinical patients as voluntary research subjects (even where 'gamete donors' choose to refuse to release their gametes/embryos for research). 'Gamete donors', like 'IVF couple', constructs a misleading linguistic equivalence between the position of women and men in relation to IVF treatment. While both may 'donate' gametes, men's masturbation to provide sperm is not comparable to the chemotherapeutic and surgical interventions of 'egg recovery'. The notion of 'donation' is a particularly odd construction in relation to women IVF patients. Does one 'donate' parts of one's own body to one's self? Perhaps most important, despite the fact that it is women who undergo IVF, the specimen consent contract makes women's treatment with IVF conditional on the consent of their male partners. This contingent consent resonates with a sense of male 'right' over a woman's body, a conventional heterosexist construction that is clearly fostered by the embryo/

logic emphasis on gametes. It also makes a woman's reproductive agency a rather meaningless concept if her consent to treatment is not meaningful on its own.

Transferring custody: contractual 'ownership' of embryos by IVF clinics

Directly reflecting the VLA guidelines' primary objective of promoting the research potential of IVF, the IVF consent form, with the exception of the above clauses, is almost exclusively focused on the transfer of women's embryos to medical scientific control. Clause 4 is a detailed five-part provision for what is effectively a transfer of custody of embryos from 'donors' to the IVF clinic. Sections (a), (b), and (c) provide that embryos that are not 'replaced' in women should be preserved [cryogenically frozen] for 'not more than two years', within which time 'donors' may request subsequent embryo 'replacements' (only into the woman signing the contract). Ultimately, however, decisions both for the preservation of embryos and for subsequent 'replacements' remain the prerogative and at the discretion of the clinic. The 'donors' may request them, but as established elsewhere in the contract, the clinic is not obliged to provide them. Section 1 of Clause 4, for example, establishes that the couple agrees to the 'transfer of [practitioner-] selected "pre-embryos" to the woman'. This is corroborated in Clause 5, which states:

> We accept that the decisions as to the *suitability* and number of pre-embryos for replacement at any time and whether frozen or not will be at the *absolute sole discretion* of the medical and scientific staff of the [IVF] Centre (p. 42, my italics).

In addition to establishing that it is practitioners, not patients, who decide on embryo transfers, Clause 5 also invokes the power of screening as part of both practitioner prerogative and IVF method. While the term 'suitability' might be read as referring to the viability of embryos, it also leaves open the possible selective criteria used to screen embryos, a point that will be taken up in Chapter 4.

Section (d) of Clause 4 specifically establishes the custodial relationship between IVF practitioners and the embryo:

> We agree that no stored pre-embryo shall be removed from the custody of the medical and scientific staff of the Centre without the written consent of both of us (or the survivor), such consent to be given within 28 days before such replacement or removal.

Finally, section (e) states:

> We agree that after the period of two years (or such extension as may be agreed [at the discretion of the Centre]) has expired the Hospital or Centre (subject to the general terms of this agreement) may *dispose of* the stored pre-embryos at their discretion (my italics).

While the term 'dispose of' may strongly imply 'discard', other potentially relevant meanings include: 1a. 'deal with', 1c. 'finish', 1d. 'kill' and 2. 'sell' (COD), the first of which meanings is clearly more congruent with 'research' than with 'discard'. It could be argued that unless any of these treatments is specifically excluded elsewhere in the Guidelines, they can be construed to confer the right to do any of these things on the 'Hospital or Centre'. Effectively, then, and under the cloak of what appears merely to stipulate a right and obligation to discard embryos on the expiry of a fixed time-period, the entire *ownership* of the 'stored pre-embryos' (including any potential economic value and the right to sell) is effectively transferred to the 'Hospital' or 'Centre'.[8] The clause can therefore be read to establish that after two years the 'donors'' already limited claim on their embryos ends, and practitioners may, at their discretion, use them for research.

As I have already discussed earlier, IVF procedures are designed to produce the maximum number of embryos (more in practice than are 'replaced' in women). While the language of limitation may suggest otherwise, this contract expressly facilitates the stockpiling of embryos garnered from IVF treatment of women for research. Taken together, these provisions mean that women who consent to undergo 'clinical IVF' necessarily consent to research IVF. Agreement to one is, by definition and by contract, agreement to the other.

The original 1986 version of the VLA specimen consent form provided a deletable clause which states:

> We understand that pre-embryos not used for replacement or storage and any pre-embryos remaining after the agreed period of storage may be used for the advancement of medical and scientific knowledge and we welcome such use. We realise that the development of such pre-embryos cannot proceed for long outside of the [*sic*] body and the period of survival will be brief (VLA 1986 p. 42).

This interestingly prescriptive clause not only reflects an explicit acknowledgement of the intrinsic interlinkage between clinical and research IVF, a relationship that is otherwise obscured, but represents this relationship as the agenda of patients (and their male partners) rather than of practitioners. Moreover, if the term 'gamete donor' constructs IVF patients (and male partners) as 'altruistic', this clause would construct those who delete it as 'selfish' beneficiaries of the very 'advancement of medical and scientific knowledge' that they would withhold from others. Significantly, even if this clause is deleted, the transfer of custody of gametes and embryos to practitioners such that they eventually become available for research is already established by other clauses. Thus the deletion of this clause would not prevent gametes/embryos from eventually becoming research material. While the presence of this clause would suggest otherwise, 'gamete donors', in the terms of this consent form, cannot opt out of the clinical/research connection of IVF.[9]

In sum, the VLA model consent form, in keeping with the VLA minimum standards of acceptable IVF practice, betrays three fundamental goals: the establishment of IVF practitioners' discretionary authority over the practice of IVF and by extension over women's bodies; the transfer of custody of embryos from women ('donors') to IVF staff; and in so doing, the establishment of a necessary link between 'clinical' and 'research' IVF.

The agency of invention

The regulatory guidelines and specimen consent form proposed by the VLA explicitly codify the implicit values and priorities of the medical science community built into IVF procedures and language. As I have discussed throughout this chapter, both the apparatus and the medical scientific administrative framework of IVF consolidate and reproduce the recombinant, embryo-centred genea/logics explored in the preceding chapter.

The apparatus of IVF together with the medical scientific code of practice articulates a double standard of accountability that constitutes an oppressive power relationship between practitioners and women. The apparatus, practice and medical scientific administration of IVF at once minimise the accountability of practitioners to women (and the general public) and at the same time maximise the accountability of women to medical scientists and their priorities within the context of their IVF project.

The structural lack of accountability of practitioners to women is constituted and protected by means of several processes and initiatives that I have described throughout this chapter. Practitioners use misleading language to name and describe IVF tools and procedures such that IVF appears to be a practice unrelated, or, at best, inconsequentially related, to women. With IVF treatment, they actively dis-integrate women's bodies and limit women's agency. Thus, women's reproduction is increasingly controlled, monitored and organised by medical scientists. Women's agency is eroded, to be replaced by the increasing power of practitioners over women's reproductive processes, bodies and lives. Moreover, the medical scientific code of (IVF) practice explicitly structures a model of medical scientific self-regulation that is a system of internal professional accountability. Their model consent contract which, as they themselves admit, protects practitioners from accountability (and liability) to the women whom they treat with IVF, constructs a compromised model of women's reproductive agency.

This dual meaning of accountability is interlinked with a concomitant double standard in the meaning of choice for practitioners and women. Within the IVF context, the priorities and prerogatives of scientific research and 'progress' are defined and exercised as the relatively unrestricted practice of researchers. Hence the simultaneous concentration of IVF practitioners on the research potential of their IVF project and on a regulatory framework that structures minimum restrictions on the discretion and authority of practitioners *vis-à-vis* their patients. Thus, the structural lack of direct accountability of IVF practitioners to women is central to their (practitioners') increasing agency.

The agency of IVF innovators differs significantly in character from that exercised by women patients. The agency of practitioners is authorial. It is they who direct and initiate the developments, directions, methods, language and standards of their own practices. Within the context of treatment, it is IVF practitioners who establish criteria of eligibility for treatment. It is they who determine the particulars of treatment regimes.

By contrast, women (as patients) have had little or no directive or initiative impact on the development and practice of IVF. Choice for women in this context is *post facto* and mediated by and within the parameters of professional authority. Women may consent to pre-existing options that they have had no substantive role in determining. As I have pointed out above, women may desire to have IVF treatment, but only their doctors may determine, ultimately, whether they are accepted for treatment. As I discuss in Chapter 3, the extent to which women's ability to gain practitioner consent to their treatment with IVF depends on their 'fitting' with practitioner's ideas of 'fit' families is a significant question in this context. Moreover, women may attempt to exercise control over the course of their IVF treatment, but again, treatment regimens are ultimately not up to women. Indeed, if women attempt to intervene too strenuously, they may be judged by practitioners as unco-operative and jeopardise their access to treatment (be dropped from the programme, or not be permitted to try again in the [likely] event that treatment does not result in [their] pregnancy). Finally, women have the choice not to be treated with IVF. For many women, however, this may mean that they are 'choosing' in effect to remain biologically childless (or live with husbands who are) in a social context that stigmatises 'infertility'. The choice between IVF and social stigmatisation is not one that empowers women. Clearly the agency of consent does not substantively subvert either the authorial power of practitioners or the recombinant, embryo-centred genea/logics inscribed in both professional practice and model code.

Notes

1 These included the former Health Service Commissioner for England, Scotland and Wales, a research psychologist, an actress who was also on the Executive Committee of Population Concern, a magistrate, a theologian, an editorial director who was on the General Advisory Council to the IBA (Independent Broadcasting Authority) and, finally, a research consultant for the International Centre for Child Studies.

2 By the Third Report of the VLA (1988) the distinction between experimental and clinical IVF as separate projects is set in stone.

3 As was noted in Chapter 1, superovulation and 'egg recovery' processes generally 'produce' more eggs than are re-implanted in women's bodies. This 'surplus' is the source of IVF research embryos.

4 In this context the VLA 'agreed that soundly based clinical practice involving *in vitro* fertilisation should proceed and it should be regarded as a therapeutic procedure covered by the normal ethics of the doctor/patient relationship' (VLA 1996 p. 30). The guidelines do not state what constitutes 'soundly based' clinical practice but take it for granted that 'normal' channels of medical self-regulation will ensure 'sound' practice. The treatment of women with IVF, from the practitioner perspective, was, clearly, never an issue.

5 The VLA prefaced the guidelines with three specific limitations on research that would not be approved: 'modification of the genetic constitution of a pre-embryo; the placing of a human pre-embryo in the uterus of another species for gestation; cloning of pre-embryos by nuclear substitution' (VLA 1986 p. 31). These limitations corresponded to the three major issues raised in public debate about the ethics of IVF research: genetically engineering 'designer' people, cloning human beings, and creating human–animal hybrids (specifically, creating humans out of or incorporating animals).

6 See Crowe (1990) for an extended discussion of the construction of the 'pre-embryo' as a medical scientific category.

7 Elsewhere I have considered the adversarial construction of woman and embryo/fetus within anti-abortion discourse (Steinberg 1991).

8 I am grateful to David Phelps for this point.

9 Interestingly, this clause was dropped from versions of the contract provided in subsequent VLA *Reports*.

Part II

Genea/logical trajectories: the ethos of screening

Eugenic conceptions

The common-sense and traditional meaning of 'eugenics' as both a philosophy and a historical set of practices has been embedded in the rationality of twentieth-century science and medicine. Eugenic science has simultaneously emerged as a project of social engineering based on medical scientific theories of heredity, of natural inheritance, and a more general logic of selection and impetus to control the reproduction of desired and stigmatised social categories, groups and characteristics. Eugenic discourses have linked notions of natural (i.e. genetic) 'fitness' and judgements of social acceptability in a project of social engineering. In Foucauldian terms, the eugenic gaze is at once a praxis of hierarchical observation and normalising judgement, a scientific and socialising disciplinary regime of reproduction.

Conventionally, eugenics is primarily understood as a (discredited) genetically based science of racial and racist selection, though one whose tentacles of reproductive control have also incorporated class and ableist elements (Mort 1987; Morris 1991; Proctor 1988). Less commonly is eugenics directly associated with or seen as expressive, indeed productive, of a dominant discourse of family, that discourse of 'legitimate' kinship in which class, gendered and racialised inequalities are normalised and in which heterosexuality is assumed and (re)inscribed. In other words, in its widest sense, the project of eugenics is a project for the reproduction of the 'legitimate' family and the social relations of inequality that underpin it. The ethos of eugenic screening is, in this sense, a *genea/logic* tracing of the putatively biological markers of inheritance and heritage to produce both retrospective and prospective family trees. In this context, scientific notions of heredity and modes of medical control over reproduction can be understood as components of a much more complex logic of controlled reproduction that is, itself, embedded within what Adrienne Rich (1978) has termed 'compulsory heterosexuality' and Judith Butler (1990) 'the matrix of heterosexuality'. In other words, eugenic ideas and practices are about not only racialised and classed but also gendered and heterosexist notions of nature, and the heritability of normality and abnormality.

I am not the first to suggest that new reproductive technologies, including IVF, bespeak or are at least linked with a logic of social engineering.[1] However, it is significantly the case that most debates around IVF and related practices have not been concerned with the ways in which these practices may reflect, reproduce and, perhaps most importantly, (re)normalise eugenic sensibilities. Nor have critical studies either of the history of eugenics or of reproductive technologies considered the reproduction of heterosexuality as a specifically eugenic project in the terms I discuss above. I would suggest, however, that whether or not heterosexuality has been theorised specifically as hereditary, it is not only assumed to be so in and of itself, but is intrinsically bound up with those characteristics (desired or derided) that have been understood more conventionally as appropriate (or inappropriate) objects of eugenic practices.

Selective reproductions

Any evaluation of contemporary practices in reproductive medicine needs to be considered in the context of the historical relationship between medicine, women's reproductive autonomy and health; the role of medicine as an institution of social control and in the formation of dominant discourses of family and breeding. As I discussed in the previous section of this book, feminist and other commentators have given complex accounts of the heritage of compromised autonomy, bodily alienation and professional disenfranchisement for women, both as practitioners and patients through the medicalisation and masculinisation of health care, and particularly of sexuality and reproduction. In this context, the significant role of professional medicine in the (re)production of class, gendered and racialised social divisions,[2] and in the formation and policing of dominant discourses of family and (hetero)sexuality are widely documented (Butler 1990; Fried 1990; Mort 1987; Oakley 1976). Barker (1981) has argued, in the context of the contemporary character of racism in Britain, that class and racialised divisions have specifically been mediated through (medical and) scientific discourses of breeding and nation.[3] Mort (1987) and, more recently, Anthias and Yuval Davis (1993) have explored the ways in which discourses of breeding and nation interface with and intensify gender divisions more widely. The history of reproductive medicine, in other words, has been deeply invested in and formative of eugenic ideologies of kinship, family and reproductive heritage. Medicine as a profession, and reproductive medicine in particular, have played central roles in the mediation, (re)production and regulation of sexuality and of particular definitions of the 'legitimate' family. These, in turn, have had serious implications for the shaping of a range of social inequalities and specifically for the importance of medicine in that process.

This history raises important questions for an evaluation of contemporary innovations in reproductive medicine. As I have noted in the previous section, criteria by which IVF and related practices are given to or withheld from women patients are established centrally by medical professionals (though other institutions, including the law[4], are implicated). In this context, it is important to evaluate the social relations of diagnostic and treatment decisions made by practitioners – i.e. the criteria by which practitioners select or de-select potential patients, specifically with reference to questions about the regulation of family and sexuality. Similarly the historical centrality of genetic theory in and to eugenic discourses raise questions about developments in genetically based screening capabilities through and within the context of IVF. The ways in which practitioners conceptualise and normalise the *selective rationalities* and *genetic genea/logics* of IVF practice is, then, the focus of the following two chapters.

Notes

1 See, for example, Arditti *et al.* 1984; Spallone and Steinberg (eds) 1987; Spallone 1989. Erica Haimes (1990) has also discussed the impetus, from many quarters, to harness the disruptive potential of such practices for the reproduction of conventional forms of family.

2 Consider, for example, the complex power relations of expertise (McNeil 1987) underpinning the professionalisation of medicine; medical–scientific theories of class, race, gender and other categories of 'difference', particularly in the context of the history of racial hygiene and eugenics movements (Mort 1987; Proctor 1988).

3 While not specifically focusing on science or medicine, Cohen (1989) has extensively discussed the ways in which notions of breeding related to class became interpellated within the imperial context to notions of race.

4 See the *Human Fertilisation and Embryology Act* 1990.

THE ETHOS OF SCREENING

3

Selective rationalities and the politics of patient screening[1]

This chapter explores the eugenic genea/logical sensibilities underpinning IVF practice as they are revealed through patient selection policies. Drawing on examples from a survey I undertook of criteria for patient screening in British IVF clinics, I shall examine the ways in which IVF practice is permeated with notions of reproductive 'fitness' that are elaborated within and through the boundaries of conventional heterosexuality. Specifically, I shall argue: (a) that while the survey reveals a continuum of overt to covert forms of patient screening, there are significant contradictions regarding what practitioners regard as discriminatory or legitimate screening; and (b) that these contradictions reflect a commitment to the principle of screening within which it is possible to be engaged in the very forms of selection to which practitioners may state opposition. A central theme that emerges in this context is that practitioners seem to regard IVF practice as one of making/authoring families – a practice that they seem to feel involves an obligation to make 'fit' families against a range of criteria. I shall argue that patient selection both reflects and reproduces a eugenic sensibility organised through a matrix of dominant discourses of 'fit' heterosexuality, a matrix through which, in turn, a range of social divisions (classed, racialised and genetified) 'speak' and are 'spoken'. I shall also consider the implications of selection policies in relation to the social profiles of IVF patients; and, perhaps most importantly, the ways in which IVF selection practices can be seen to relate in direct and indirect ways to the reproduction of ableist, class oppressive, heterosexist and racist social divisions. Finally, I shall argue that together with emergent genetic screening capabilities (both of patients and of embryos – touched on here and discussed more fully in the next chapter), IVF emerges not simply as a technology *used* to reinscribe and reproduce conventional families, but one whose invention is embedded in such sensibilities.

Surveying selective rationalities

Between January and April 1990, I conducted a postal questionnaire-survey, with open-ended questions, of all registered clinics offering *in vitro* fertilisation (IVF) and gamete intra-fallopian transfer (GIFT)[2] in Britain.[3] The survey had several aims: (1) to gain some insight into the attitudes of IVF/GIFT professionals[4] regarding their practices; (2) to gain information beyond that provided in the Voluntary Licensing Authority (VLA) *Reports* about the types of practices conducted at the clinics; and (3) specifically to investigate screening policies, that is, criteria and rationales for accepting or rejecting potential patients and embryos. With respect to patient screening, questions were asked about physiological and non-physiological criteria (for example age, marital status, socio-economic status, race, etc.) for providing IVF/GIFT. Questions were also asked about policies around genetic screening criteria with respect to both patients and embryos. A total of 75 questionnaires were sent out, out of which 35 (47 per cent) were returned to me and 24 (32 per cent) were completed.[5]

As with the rest of the research for this book, the survey took place during the period leading up to the passage of the *Human Fertilisation and Embryology* (HFE) *Act* 1990. Thus, responses provided by practitioners to this survey emerge from that particularly sensitive and key historical moment of negotiation of 'legitimate' IVF and related practices. Although not raised as a major issue during the dominant debates over statutory regulation of IVF, responses to this survey suggest that the issue and practices of selection, both of patients and of embryos, have been central to the practice, ethos and future direction of IVF and GIFT. As we shall see, while there appear to be a number of differences amongst clinic screening policies, there are a wide range of similarities in practitioner responses, suggesting a shared professional common sense about 'appropriate' reproduction (i.e. who should and should not be parents) and about the 'appropriate' role of practitioners in managing it. The responses to this survey, while representing a small number in 'real' terms, nevertheless suggest fairly widespread assumptions by practitioners that IVF professionals are entitled (perhaps even obliged) to have and exercise power, through the medium of IVF/GIFT practices, over the reproductive decision-making of others. This chapter will concentrate on responses of practitioners about non-physiological criteria for screening patients and their evaluations of the importance of genetic screening of patients and embryos.

Finally, it must be noted that preceding studies (for example Arditti *et al.* 1984; Corea 1985)[6] of IVF patients have indicated the predominance of white, middle-class, able-bodied women living in heterosexual couples amongst those undergoing treatment. A similar social profile of IVF patients emerges from the media coverage of this field of medicine. For example pictorial representations of parties assembling large groups of IVF children (which also feature white, male IVF doctors) or announcements of the births of various IVF children, as well as descriptions in nearly all IVF literature of IVF 'couples' (see Steinberg 1993) suggest this profile. It is in this context that I am interested to consider what responses to this survey suggest about the relationship between patient screening practices and the dominant profile of IVF patients.

The survey results indicate a variety of selection criteria for IVF/GIFT treatment. These include intelligence, sexuality and lifestyle as well as age, financial status and attitudes to treatment. As I shall suggest, the use of such social criteria, which bear no necessary or straight-forward relationship to a woman's physiological condition, raise a number of questions about practitioners' positions with respect to women's reproductive decision-making.

'Fit' fertilisations: reproducing heterosexuality

An important question in the survey concerned categories of women accepted for or rejected from treatment.[7] With one exception, all clinics (23 out of 24) in this response pool refused to treat women who were not either married or in long-term (marriage-like) heterosexual partnerships. It is interesting that the one respondent who indicated that his/her clinic would treat all categories of women listed in the questionnaire (married, single, divorced and widowed women as well as single lesbians and lesbian couples) was from a private clinic. It is, of course, possible that this apparently liberal access policy may have been motivated by financial factors. Indeed, this same respondent, unlike all of the others, also indicated that all listed physiological conditions were used as indicators for IVF treatment. In other words, this respondent seemed willing to treat any woman without restriction.

There were two related arguments used to justify the restriction of treatment to married women or women in long-term heterosexual relationships. The first expressed an unwillingness in principle to assist any but heterosexual married (or akin to married) women to reproduce. The second, more subtle version of this position forwarded what I would term the 'scarcity' argument about IVF/GIFT provision.

'Ethically dubious' women

Many clinicians took the position expressed in the *Warnock Report* (1984) (and eventually in the HFE Act 1990[8]) that children should be raised by heterosexual couples and that women living in anything other than this kind of arrangement should not be assisted to reproduce:

> I would personally have reservations about doing for [lesbians] – I
> feel a child should much preferably have a father as well as a

mother in their formative years. [Divorced women], same effectively as [lesbians] (C17).[9]

We do not consider categories [single, divorced, widowed, lesbian women] as ideally suited to managing GIFT treatment and having a child (C22).

Like to think child born to stable relationship with a mother and father (B9).

ethical considerations (B28).

Respondents indicate two possible sources for such a policy. One, as suggested by (C17) above, comes as a result of clinicians' personal views about appropriate parenting, or as another respondent put it 'personal choice' (C18). Only one practitioner (see (B14) below) indicates any reservations about imposing personal views about who should be appropriate parents or potential patients. These responses are significant not only for the ways in which they seem to reproduce dominant common-sense definitions of 'legitimate' family, but also for what they suggest about the discretionary character of professional power and accountability *vis-à-vis* patients. Clearly these respondents implicitly define the imposition of value judgements on their patients' social profiles as a legitimate component of their medical responsibilities. In this respect the reproduction of 'acceptable' heterosexualities is congruent with the reproduction of professional power and domain. Also interesting in these responses is the way in which they designate only particular forms of heterosexuality as ethically acceptable. Thus heterosexuality is policed not only against the prospect of lesbian parenting, but indeed what are quite explicitly constructed as deviant familial heterosexualities (families without fathers). The resonances of this construction of acceptable and unacceptable heterosexualities was later reproduced in the 'Virgin Birth' controversy,[10] which hit the media in the Spring of 1990 (before the passage of the HFE Act). There too, the spectre of illegitimate medically assisted reproduction was linked explicitly to single (in that case celibate heterosexual) mothers, and only implicitly to lesbian mothers.

Other respondents attribute the source of heterosexist selection policies to ethical committees:

> At present we are planning for group a, b [married, married-like] to avoid confrontation with ethical committee and other [indecipherable] (C23).

> ethical committee advice (B3).

One response suggested that selection of heterosexual patients reflected NHS policy:

> Policy aimed at meeting NHS commitment of service primarily (C35).

Still others referred to fears of adverse media attention:

> You must be joking. I have conscientious objections to treating women in these ethically dubious groups. I certainly do not wish to end up in the National Press! (CAA).

> Exclusion predominantly because of fear of public reaction and reservations from some team members. Acknowledge little evidence suggesting excluded groups could not make satisfactory parents/family units (B14).

The last comment suggests that even where a practitioner does seem to have reservations about exclusionary policies, the ideology of the traditional nuclear family and heterosexist pressures seem too great to allow for resistance.

A second type of justification for heterosexist selection policies were arguments about the 'scarcity' of provision:

> More than enough work for 'straight couples'. No sperm freezing facilities easily available (C16).

> Lack of time and facilities. At present we are limited to the above [married, cohabiting (heterosexual) couple] (C10).

> Pressure of numbers in totally NHS clinic (C19).

> Service developing and enough work by providing a and b (C29).

> Totally NHS funded clinic with a long waiting list of heterosexual couples, therefore some criteria for inclusion had to be applied and the decisions were taken after discussion with colleagues (B24).

The 'scarcity' argument, however, only explains the perceived need to restrict services. It does not explain the categorical exclusion of all women not living in heterosexual couples. Indeed, the policy could just as easily have been run on a first-come, first-served basis, or, indeed, based on physiological health considerations.[11]

A final reason suggested for heterosexist exclusions implied self-selection:

We have no requests from the groups bracketed above (B19).

In the context of a complex system of professional referral, it is important to ask what 'no requests from the groups' means. There are several possible interpretations. It is possible that GPs make no requests for IVF or GIFT on behalf of patients who are not heterosexual (as this is the regular avenue for specialist consultation). If this is the case, this would indicate that a heterosexist selection ethos (and practices) not only operate at specialised gynaecological and obstetric levels, but at all relevant levels of the medical hierarchy. However, this practitioner might also be suggesting that only heterosexuals are presenting themselves to GPs (with infertility problems and/or requesting IVF or similar treatment). If this is the case, this raises questions about a possible pattern of self-selection. Indeed, self-selection on this basis would be in keeping with a range of pointedly heterosexist elements of contemporary British society. These include financial constraints on many single and lesbian mothers, for example, who tend to experience greater poverty than white, middle-class, heterosexual, partnered women; legal constraints, such as the instability of custody for lesbians (Rights of Women 1986); and the broader social disapprobation of lesbian parenting and lesbian life. More subtly, it may well be that the heterosexist representations and marketing of IVF and GIFT services, which reproduce the language and narrative of 'couples' (Franklin 1990) are likely to reinforce the perception that the obstetric community would be unlikely to be sympathetic to lesbians' and single women's desires for children, or to their experiences of 'infertility' (a perception that would be born out by some of the disapproving comments of this sample of practitioners).[12]

Picking 'proper' parents

There were two other selection criteria that could be seen to contribute to the heterosexist screening practices around IVF/GIFT. These are reflected in responses to my questions about whether or not practitioners gave consideration to patients' (and partners') mental and psychiatric states[15] and the emotional dynamics (of the couple's relationship) in making treatment decisions.

Screening for 'stability'

Nearly all respondents (22 of 24) claimed that the mental and psychiatric state of patients and their partners was used as a criterion for IVF and GIFT treatment. Half also indicated that this was a 'very important' consideration. There were two reasons given for this selection criterion: ability to cope with the strain of treatment and, significantly, ability to care for children:

> Depends on ability to cope with stress of treatment and failure and ability to cope with baby/babies (C16).
>
> Ability to bring up child (C19).
>
> Only relevant where this would affect ability to deal emotionally with treatment/failure/pregnancy or with ability to care for child (C22).
>
> Pressure to avoid at all costs adverse parenting situations (B14).
>
> If psychiatric opinion indicates that pregnancy would be detrimental or that there would be disadvantage to the child (B19).
>
> Wish to bring children up in stable [healthy?] family (B3).

These practitioners clearly saw themselves as responsible for the creation of families and both obligated and entitled to judge parenting abilities to this end. The reference to 'pressure to avoid ... adverse parenting situations' distinctly suggests a worry about being held accountable for and implicated in 'bad parenting' practices. However, what, in Britain today, constitutes 'bad parenting' is constituted not only within medical but also through legal and popular discourses. In addition to a long history of medical opinion on and regulation of familial relations (from psychiatry to paediatrics to obstetrics and gynae-cology) has been a similar range of governmental policies around child protection and definitions of a proper family. Recent legislative policies such as the *Children Act* (1989), for example, effectively define proper families as heterosexual nuclear units (Langan 1992 p. 78). Section 28 of the *Local Government Act* (1988) defines lesbian and gay households as 'pretended family relationships' (see Stacey 1991); and les-bians, as I note above, are particularly vulnerable to losing cus-tody of their children and being defined as unfit mothers (Rights of Women 1986). As I also point out above, the *Warnock Report* (Warnock 1984) and eventually the HFE Act (1990) define the 'best interests of the children' in heterosex-ist terms. Furthermore, in practice, many commentators have noted that the authority of social workers to intervene in and regulate 'adverse parenting situations' is directed primarily to poor and black families, particularly those headed by single women (Bryan *et al.* 1985 pp. 112–20; Mama 1992; Dominelli 1992). It is notable in this context that two additional respon-dents indicated that the advice of social workers (as well as GPs and psychiatrists) regarding the suitability of prospective patients to parent was sought (A10; B16A).

Thus concerns about the mental and psychiatric state of prospective patients and partners and screening on this basis can be seen to reflect and (re)produce two related domin-ant common senses: a long-standing regulatory discourse of parental 'fitness' and specifically a professional discourse that constructs medical professionals as primary arbiters of 'good' and 'bad' parenting and, in turn, constructs judgements about parenting as medical matters. In this context, the dominant white, middle-class, heterosexual profile of IVF/GIFT patients 'fits' the dominant discourse of 'parental fitness' and is clearly consistent with judgements about 'ethically dubious women' discussed above.

It must be said that not all practitioners indicated that IVF and GIFT treatment would be ruled out entirely for those judged to be mentally and psychiatrically 'unstable'. One respondent commented that 'if at that time, [the prospective patient/partner were] psychiatrically unstable, I would delay until improved as it is a stressful procedure' (C29). Another stated that patients (and partners) 'must be normal to "endure" IVF cycle. Would treat mental state prior to IVF' (B9). The juxtaposition of 'normal', in this last response, with ability to cope with IVF is interesting. Indeed, all the responses discussed so far suggest that notions of personal and parental 'normality' are framed within an understanding of IVF/GIFT treatment as a project for the reproduction of 'traditional' family units. In so doing, IVF and GIFT practitioners join the ranks of other professionals (for example psychiatrists and social workers) whose job descriptions more obviously revolve around defining and regulating what is and is not considered 'normal' with respect to parenthood. Here this agenda is extended to the literal, hands-on, process of (re)generating familial relationships.

Regulating relationships: evaluating emotional dynamics

Most respondents (17 of 24) indicated that the 'emotional dynamics of the family/couple', that is, evaluation of the quality of marital (or marriage-like) relationships, were a criterion for treatment:

> Stable union required (C16).
>
> Vital that they should co-operate and work together to give support (C23).
>
> Would *obviously* depend upon stability of relationship (A10, italics mine).
>
> Would like to think they were stable (B9).
>
> Both must be wholeheartedly in favour of using this procedure (B14).
>
> Couple needs to be well motivated and in unison with the desire for a family and the desire for such treatment (B24).

Clearly, single women are excluded in this ethos of teamwork – a concept, like 'stability,' discursively tied to (heterosexual) couples. Here the emerging definition of an appropriate relationship is one in which two 'think and feel as one' and in which there is an unequivocal desire for children. This notion epitomises the conventional, romantic definition of marital union. Indeed, there is no consideration within these criteria of the possibility that few relationships lack ambivalence or are entirely stable and synchronous. Implicitly, these comments seem to indicate that prospective patients must at least act the stereotyped ideal of marital accord in order to be considered for treatment.[14] It is interesting that respondent A10 seemed to feel he/she was stating the 'obvious' in considering marriage assessment as part of IVF and GIFT protocols. This is a testament both to the ubiquity and power of conventional family discourse (despite the fact that most families do not conform to the ideal) and to practitioners' apparent sense of entitlement, even obligation, to make such assessments as part of their medical responsibilities.

Class(ed) conceptions

Two sections of the survey addressed the question of selection of patients on the basis of class[15]/economic factors: respondents were asked (a) about the costs of treatment in respect of NHS or private provision of services; and (b) as with the earlier questions, they were asked if financial status, ability to pay for treatment, educational qualifications, occupation and standard of accommodation were used as criteria for selecting or refusing prospective patients; here respondents were asked (a) if they selected on these bases and (b) (in a separate section) how important they considered these criteria.[16] The answers to these sets of questions were somewhat contradictory. One would, perhaps, expect that those respondents who identified their clinics as private (20 of 24 total responses) would have regarded the ability to pay as important and therefore as a criterion for selection (if they did not, then they could not survive as a commercial venture). However, 10 respondents (6 more than the number of NHS clinics in the sample) said ability to pay was not important and two more than that (12) indicated that this was not a criterion for selection. This discrepancy is significant because it suggests a breach between *processes* (for example costs), which may pre-emptively exclude poorer candidates from treatment, and the *perceptions* of those who implement or are responsible for those processes. Similar discrepancies were revealed by responses to all of my suggested categories.[17]

Nevertheless, whether or not respondents saw (or see) themselves/their clinics as operating a direct selection policy on the basis of these considerations, clearly the single greatest factor that accounts for the dominance of (white) middle-class patients in the IVF context is the direct cost of treatment cycles, together with the hidden costs of treatment.[18] Costs of treatment in 1990 ranged, in private clinics (over 50 per cent of my sample) at between £250–£1750 per cycle, with the price of drug treatments extra. It is important to note, in this context, that most patients will undergo several cycles in order to have at least a 10 per cent chance of having a live birth. At most NHS clinics from my response pool, costs of drugs are extra and borne by patients.

High-technology treatments like IVF and GIFT, moreover, require high levels of financial investment within the research and clinical context. Such investments, in an ever-shrinking NHS budget, can only divert attention and resources away from primary medical care, specifically in this context from primary infertility prevention (such as mass screening for sexually transmitted diseases). It can be argued that the hegemonic association of progressive medicine with developments of increasingly sophisticated technological processes and expertise marginalise alternative, less glamorous, and indeed, less medicalised approaches to health care. Indeed, characteristic of a medical model is a definition of ill health in terms of individual pathology, a definition that side-steps the complex social conditions/relations of adversity and class inequality (for example poor housing, poverty, environmental pollution and oppression) that are associated with ill health. Locker (1991) argues that: 'numerous studies have shown that social class measured by occupation, education, income or area of residence, is closely related to health ... As a consequence, social and political change may be necessary to modify the health experience of these groups' (pp. 20–1). Certainly treatments like IVF and GIFT do not represent strategies aimed at social and political change in the class conditions that might foster impaired fertility.

Thirdly, as a middle-class constituency, the medical profession has traditionally acted as an agency of social control that has been: (1) particularly directed toward controlling working-class people; and (2) aimed at reinforcing middle-class morality. As Frank Mort argues, the profession has laid 'claim to a middle-class monopoly over the issues of health and hygiene' (Mort 1987 p. 42). This general observation can be related directly to women's bodies and reproduction. Anne Witz (1992) has noted that the politics of expertise and professionalisation are class relations – relations that, I would suggest, are inevitably (re)produced in high-technology infertility treatments such as IVF and GIFT.

It can be argued that the policies delimiting access to IVF and GIFT on the bases discussed so far in this chapter reflect and reinforce what Mort (1987) terms 'medico-moral regulation', that is the growing hegemony of medicine as an apparatus of social control over sexuality and reproduction. Historically constituted, in class- and race-specific ways, ideas about who can legitimately reproduce and parent (and who should be medically assisted to or prevented from doing so)[19] have constituted the context in which IVF has been developed as a 'regulatory' approach (that is, a mode of managing women's reproductive processes), as well as elaborated in the subsequent (after the invention of IVF) policies of access revealed in this survey.

In this respect, like much traditional medicine, neither IVF nor GIFT can be said to address inequalities experienced by poor and working-class people (inequalities that foster ill health, including infertility). They are firmly entrenched in (and elaborate) the dominant paradigm of professional medicine as well as the notion of scientific 'progress', which is, itself, embedded in the promotion and production of 'high'-technology. This is a matter not just of access but of form, resources and priorities. Indeed, for this reason, it could be argued that a democratisation of access to IVF and GIFT, even if it were possible or likely in the context of increasingly privatised medical care, does not, in itself, alter the fundamental classist character of the high-technology approach to health care that they embody. Moreover, while it has been argued that medicine has been about class regulation and control, there have also been studies that have shown the class-specific appeal of medical models (see Reissman 1992 and Martin 1987). Reissman has noted, for example, that middle-class (white) women have historically had a disproportionate investment in the medicalisation of pregnancy and birthing. In this context, the disproportionate profile of middle-class IVF and GIFT patients may also reflect (intentionally and/or effectively selective) class relations that have characterised the process and reception of medical professionalisation more generally.

Racialised reproductions

Of all the questions asked in the survey, those regarding selection on religious or racial bases seemed to touch the nerve of an important tension that characterised all responses. All respondents either indicated 'no' (that race and religion were not criteria for treatment) and that they were 'unimportant' considerations, or declined to respond to the question at all. Significantly, while most respondents seemed pointedly untroubled at the idea of selecting patients on heterosexist criteria or on genetic bases (see below), the notion of selecting on racial or religious grounds was greeted as offensive by many.

Within a general expression of objection to the question, comments varied in significant ways. There were terse assertions that race and religion were 'not relevant' (C22) as selection criteria as well as the apparently liberal, democratically minded statements: 'Service for all' (C35), and 'if treatment is needed it should be given' (C10). These statements seem implicitly to claim both an anti-discriminatory and, in the latter case in particular, a narrowly physiological orientation in both the clinic policy and the medical context more generally.

While the tone remained consistent, it appeared that the prospect of selecting on racial grounds provoked more pointed objections than did the prospect of doing so on religious grounds. One respondent, for example, on the question of racial selection expressed what seemed a more pointed criticism of the question, asking 'Why should we?' S/he then provided a more ambivalent response to the question of religious exclusion:

> We do not wish to play god. Customer [*sic*] is usually right. We worry about group whose religion nominally precludes assisted conception because it divorces them from moral support if family remain unsympathetic (B14).

Another respondent with similar concerns wrote: '[religion] irrelevant if couples decide to continue after counselling'. I would suggest that, at least in part, the concerns expressed around religious beliefs in the context of IVF and GIFT reflect both the view of IVF/GIFT patients as 'couples' and 'family' members and the high visibility of objections to aspects of these treatments by right-wing Christian groups such as the Society for the Protection of Unborn Children (SPUC). It would be difficult to imagine reservations about giving medical treatment to a patient whose family or religious community were unsupportive in any other context. For example, would doctors feel reluctance or sensitivity of this kind in the case of Jehovah's Witnesses who, in their view, needed and, importantly, presented themselves for treatment that violated the religious beliefs of their families or community? Moreover, the question of embryo 'personhood', raised by powerful religious lobby groups, was, at the time of this survey, reflected in legislative debates about the possible banning of IVF-based (embryo) research. In this climate, I would suggest that religious sensitivities on the part of practitioners are likely to have been high.

The quotation above also raises the question of the perception by practitioners of their own role and position in the context of their patient's reproductive decision-making. Statements such as: 'we do not wish to play god' and 'customer [*sic*]

---

is usually right' deny that practitioners do make reproductive decisions for others. Another respondent, in a similar vein, commented: 'multiracial and multireligion country, therefore [screening on these bases] not appropriate' (B24). Yet, this is also a country where people have different sexual preferences and lifestyles. Nevertheless, all of these clinics discriminate on the grounds of sexuality and domestic arrangements, and as I discuss below, increasingly select patients and embryos on genetic grounds. Clearly there are circumstances in which discriminating or 'playing god' is considered more acceptable. Racial exclusion is seen here as discriminatory and illegitimate and an inappropriate exercise of practitioner power, while heterosexist exclusion, however, apparently is not.[20]

Why would practitioners feel concern about 'playing god' in the racial and religious context, but not in the context of sexuality (or genetic 'health')? I would suggest that the notion of racial exclusion raises the spectre of selection practices under National Socialism, and of what I would term the 'unacceptable face' of eugenics. As I discuss in more detail elsewhere (Steinberg 1993), one of the characteristic arguments put forward by IVF practitioners in their books and articles is the rejection of any relationship between 'Nazi eugenics' and IVF practices. To this end, concerns with reproducing heterosexual family units and genetically 'healthy' offspring (see below) do not seem to raise criticisms in the way that notions of racial selection do. In this context, sexual and genetic selection seem to be constructed as a non-discriminatory and entirely legitimate, precisely because they do not seem obviously to participate in the notorious discourse of racial hygiene. It would seem then, from the perspectives of my respondents, that heterosexist and genetic screening are understood as conceptually (and materially) separate from racism, indeed as having entirely different logics and ethos.

My respondents overwhelmingly claimed, then, that they and their clinics would find overt selection of patients on racial/religious grounds unacceptable (indeed, for many, repugnant). Taking it for granted that these responses are offered in good faith, nevertheless the overt and conscious rejection of racist selection criteria does not necessarily indicate the absence of racism in the overall selection process. Certainly the categories of selection respondents find acceptable are implicitly and historically racialised. The dominant discourse of family underpinning heterosexist selection policies is a case in point; dominant notions of legitimate family are not only about heterosexuality and child-rearing, but are also racialised (white) and classed (middle-class).[21] In this context, the coding of 'illegitimate' heterosexualities made explicit against the prospect of families without fathers is also implicitly a classed and racialised coding.

Secondly, the effective selection by economic status (discussed above) would disproportionately affect women of colour.[22] Thus mechanisms for effective selection based on class/economic factors might serve simultaneously to exclude or marginalise in racialised ways. Thirdly, these issues must, of course, be seen in the context of the history of professional medicine, which has been widely critiqued as an agency of social control[23] and for its institutional racism both generally and with particular reference to obstetric and gynaecological specialisations. Finally, as I noted earlier, media portrayals of IVF 'birthday parties' in Britain since the birth of Louise Brown have shown a striking predominance of white patients, children and practitioners. This stands as a notable contrast to the disproportionate representation of black women patients with respect to procedures such as sterilisation (Davis 1984; Fried 1990; White 1990). This both suggests at least some kind of selection process and reinforces a common sense of IVF as designated white.

Genetified selections

In addition to the validation of overt heterosexist screening criteria, genetic screening emerged as another acceptable face of selection in the IVF context. Responses to my questions about genetic screening and counselling[24] reveal some variation of opinion about their perceived importance and role in IVF/GIFT practice. However, they also provide a keen illustration of the shared commitment to the *principle* of screening, notwithstanding contestations about its appropriate form, context and targets:

> Question: How important is genetic screening/counselling in IVF/GIFT treatment?
>
>> Not very important except where age or family history of [?] indicate it (C19).
>>
>> Only important where there is a high risk or suspected risk of genetic abnormality (e.g. recurrent miscarriage) (C22).
>>
>> Very important (C35).
>>
>> For average couple it is irrelevant (B16A).
>>
>> Many of those over 35 years as would be the case for non-IVF pregnant women. 43% of our IVF cycles are to women 35 years and older (B16A).
>>
>> If genetic problem offered, otherwise I don't see the relevance. Not appropriate in terms of IVF, only in usual cases for anyone wanting a pregnancy spontaneously (B9).
>>
>> Not important unless history of problems (B3).
>>
>> Should be available if requested or patients in high risk group (B14).

With the exception of C35, these comments explicitly reveal that perceptions of legitimacy in relation to screening on genetic bases are negotiated through two key discourses: one of 'risk' and the other of voluntarism.

The designation of genetic screening for those who fall into the category of 'high risk' is an interesting construction of such screening as of limited importance. On the one hand, it appears that an 'average' couple is perceived of as having no genetic impairment. Genetic risk, therefore, seems to be perceived as a special case, rather than as a factor which would be routinely expected, at least as a potential problem, in the IVF/GIFT context. In this context, screening would, similarly, seem to be perceived as important only in exceptional cases. However, in order to designate prospective patients and/or their partners as 'high risk' in the first place, it would be necessary to undertake some form of genetic (family history) inquiry. Thus, this discourse of 'risk' depends on the wide-spread practice of precisely what it is perceived to limit.

Voluntary eugenics

That genetic counselling and screening should be voluntary rather than routinely imposed was explicitly indicated by most respondents:

> If couple accepted the risks I would proceed (C29).

> It is indicated in some but patients need to decide and choose (C23).

> Helpful in relation to couple's being more able to make an informed decision with respect to less 'crippling' anomalies and enables difficult decisions to be undertaken jointly and other more serious situations (B24).

One recurrent argument was that genetic counselling and screening are not routine for pregnant women (and their partners) outside the IVF/GIFT context, so routine screening within IVF/GIFT treatment would not be justified:

> We don't routine [sic] screen the normal fertile population. It is discriminatory to screen the infertile (B14).

> No evidence that there is increased risk of genetic disorder after GIFT treatment compared with spontaneous conception therefore why do counselling/screening? (C16).

One respondent suggested that routinised counselling and screening might undermine the morale of patients:

> Offered routinely it *may* upset some of the patients who are trying not to build up to [sic] much hope (C29).

It would, of course, make sense that in a context where patients have intensely invested in having children, the possibility of being screened before or after conception for genetic 'abnormalities' might well be extremely distressing, particularly in the latter situation, where they might be advised or feel compelled to terminate a 'high risk' pregnancy.

Indeed, the language of 'risk' is a loaded one. As a diagnostic discourse, it resolutely individualises the character of disability and thus side-steps an interrogation of the social attitudes, conditions and inequalities that shape the experiences of disabled people. It is both embedded in and reinscribes a pervasive common sense that disability is a natural and inevitable disaster. The call for voluntary screening places putative emphasis on patients' choice and on the perception that genetic counselling and screening enable patients to make difficult decisions.[25] Yet, it is questionable what 'choice' might mean in the context of the language of 'risk'. In this context, a practitioner's willingness to proceed 'if couples accepted the risks' underestimates the power of negative medical discourses of disability, and medical judgements expressed in the ableist language of 'risk'.[26] Considering the ableism endemic in our social institutions and dominant social (including medical) attitudes, how many patients would be willing to proceed with treatment if advised that there was 'risk' of producing disabled offspring?[27]

It is my feeling that most practitioners support genetic screening as a way to spare patients/offspring not only the perceived negative character of disability, but the negative social attitudes and conditions surrounding the lives of people with disabilities (and their primarily female carers). However, if the language of 'risk' assumes the natural negativity of disability, it also assumes the importance, even necessity, of preventing or terminating a pregnancy that 'risks' the reproduction of disability. The primary focus of concern in the context of genetic 'risk' assessment, whether performed on prospective parents or on embryos, is the genetic profile of offspring. At the heart of these practices is a concern to prevent the birth of disabled children. Ironically, this inescapably eugenic sensibility naturalises the very conditions and attitudes that practitioners may, through the practice of genetic screening, wish to spare prospective patients and their children. While practitioners may support genetic counselling/screening practices specifically out of a recognition of the harshly punitive realities of living as or caring for a person with disabilities in an ableist society, the underpinning ethos of genetic screening can also be seen to contribute to those very realities. If the emphasis on voluntary screening bespeaks a personal opposition to ableist discrimination, my respondents nevertheless clearly inhabit a discourse that normalises it.

Significantly, no respondents indicated that they thought these questions 'provocative' (including the respondent who made this comment about the section of the questionnaire addressing other possible screening criteria, including race). While there were differences in the relative importance given to the role of genetic screening and counselling in the IVF and GIFT context, none stated that they had reservations about the use of such screening *per se*. While most respondents explicitly rejected the notion of routine screening, genetic considerations were clearly perceived as an important and consistent component of IVF and GIFT treatment by all of them. It is important to point out here, moreover, that concerns about the genetic profile of offspring are consistent with the other patterns of practice emerging from my survey. Indeed, the concern with medicalised quality control of offspring, in this respect, fits with more emphatically supported concerns to diagnose the quality of marriages and the fitness of prospective patients (and male partners) to parent.

Authoring selective rationalities

Responses to my survey suggest, therefore, that IVF and GIFT projects are not simply about enabling the infertile to reproduce biologically, but constitute an extensive social reproduction package. I have argued from my survey findings that (familial) heterosexist norms have been central to IVF and GIFT practice in Britain. I have also indicated that racism, class and ableist inequalities form part of the matrix of this field. This survey provides direct evidence of selection overtly on heterosexist grounds and effectively on financial grounds. While it does not provide direct evidence of racialised selection, it does suggest that racialised selection may be more subtly mediated through ideas about what constitutes 'fit' parenting and through class relations at several levels. I have also argued that while respondents may differ on the importance they place on forms of screening, they nevertheless see screening in principle as an intrinsic (indeed necessary) genea/logic of their practices. What is clear is that practitioners in this field are positioning themselves, their patients and IVF/GIFT treatment within conventional, white, middle-class and heterosexist kinship discourses (which have, themselves, been historically constituted by the medical and scientific professions). In these ways, practitioners, even when opposed to particular forms of discrimination or eugenic practices, are nevertheless involved in the (re)production of key social divisions through the administration of IVF and GIFT and are positioned within a discourse in which eugenic sensibilities inhere.

Notes

1 The notion of 'selective rationalities' was prompted in discussions I had with Les Levidow.

2 Gamete intra-fallopian transfer, similar to *in vitro* fertilisation, implies that women undergo: (1) a regimen of superovulation treatment and (2) surgical extraction of their ova. However, where IVF involves fertilisation of ova and sperm in a Petri dish culture medium before fertilised ova are vaginally transferred into a woman, with GIFT ova and sperm are injected directly into women's fallopian tubes (Morgan and Lee 1991 p. 127).

3 All the clinics surveyed were registered and licensed by the Voluntary [Interim] Licensing Authority [VLA/ILA] and listed in the *Fourth Report of the Voluntary Licensing Authority for Human In Vitro Fertilisation and Embryology (1989)*.

4 Clinics were registered under the name of one clinician (usually the head of the team offering IVF/GIFT). Thus responses to the survey and representations of clinic policy were based on the perspective of an individual on the upper end of team hierarchies. This factor must be considered to be a significant limitation in the research. However, it can be argued that team leaders may be among the most likely members to reproduce dominant professional common senses and to shape disproportionately local and general professional cultures.

5 It should be noted that this is an average response rate to a postal questionnaire (Moser 1958; Moyser and Wagstaffe 1987). However, since the questionnaire was sent to *all* registered clinics, the percentage return rate is also a percentage of *all* clinics (rather than a sample) offering these services in Britain at the time. In the light of this, I would argue that it is possible, while taking into consideration the important limitations of postal surveys, to draw conclusions about IVF practice in the UK from the

returns which I have received. The remaining 11 returned questionnaires were accompanied with letters or comments declining to participate in the survey for reasons ranging from lack of time or length of questionnaire to lack of established service provision. Elsewhere (Steinberg 1993) I have discussed in detail the structure and format of the survey as well as a number of feminist methodological issues relating to researching professional groups and important advantages and limitations in undertaking a questionnaire survey approach.

6 An earlier study that I conducted suggested similar patterns with respect to patient profiles and access policies around donor insemination (see Steinberg 1986, 1987).

7 The question read as follows:
Does your clinic offer IVF/GIFT treatment to: (a) married women; (b) unmarried but living with male partner; (c) single women; (d) divorced women (with donor sperm); (e) divorced women (with ex-husband's sperm); (g) widowed women (with donor sperm); (h) widowed women (with husband's sperm); (i) lesbian couple; (j) lesbian (single). Please specify any reasons for including or excluding any of the above for/from treatment.

8 *The Human Fertilisation and Embryology* (HFE) *Act* 1990 stipulates that in making treatment decisions, practitioners must take into consideration 'the child's need for a father'. For extended discussion of the heterosexual politics of the HFE Act, see Steinberg (1993) and Chapter 6 below.

9 In order to protect the confidentiality of respondents, all responses were coded. For the purposes of discussion in this paper, responses quoted in this paper do not represent a sample. Rather, I have reproduced *all* responses provided to the questions analysed here.

10 The 'Virgin Birth' controversy, as I discuss in Chapter 6, concerned the provision of donor insemination to single women at British Pregnancy Advisory Service (BPAS) clinics. It was 'leaked' to the media coincidentally as an amendment to the Human Fertilisation and Embryology Bill was proposed to limit Donor Insemination and IVF-related treatments to heterosexual women in long-term partnerships with men. Following the 'controversy', the BPAS curtailed their Donor Insemination services.

11 This is not to suggest, however, that physiological criteria are unproblematic. The persuasiveness and ubiquity of the 'scarcity' argument was also indicated in Christine Crowe's study of IVF patients in Australia (Crowe 1987 p. 87).

12 Again a telling and related example of media hostility to the desire of women who are not married to have children was the 1991 'Virgin Birth' controversy. Here single women's access to donor insemination was brought under attack in tabloid and 'quality' press, as well as in television coverage of the allegedly selfish and deviant desires of some women to conceive without sexual intercourse and to mother without male partners.

This controversy was significant in the parliamentary decision to add a clause to the Human Fertilisation and Embryology Bill pressuring practitioners to treat only married women (or women with male partners) with IVF, DI and related procedures.

13 A related criterion, intelligence, was also indicated by most respondents.

14 Christine Crowe's early study of women undergoing IVF treatment in Australia suggested that outward appearances of conformity to such idealised definitions of coupledom and desire for children constituted a significant expectation and dynamic of the treatment experience (Crowe 1987).

15 I am not, in this context, using the word 'class' in a strict Marxist sense, i.e. to denote a relationship to the means of production. I am using it, rather, to indicate relative income and social status.

16 Here they were given a choice of 'very', 'somewhat' and 'not' important.

17 One respondent wrote 'as long as patient and husband can get to the clinic, it doesn't matter about occupation. [Twenty?] patients have taken 2 or 3 weeks holiday for the treatment' (C10). This statement again suggests a gap between practitioners' stated intent to be non-discriminatory and the ways in which they may be clearly implicated in such discrimination. Clearly, it is only patients/partners in particular occupations who can afford and arrange to have '2 or 3 weeks' holiday for the treatment' (and to do so repeatedly to accommodate the likelihood of repeated cycles of treatment).

18 Aside from the stated costs of treatment, and even for patients undertaking treatment on the NHS, there are a range of 'hidden' costs which may include: travel to the clinic and accomodation (if the clinic is not local); the costs of additional procedures (as I note, drugs costs are usually extra); the possible loss of the (woman) patient's income, as it may be difficult to continue treatment cycles while in paid employment; child-care costs if there are other children; etc.

19 See, for example, Davis (1990); Fried (1990) and White (1990).

20 One notable response raised questions about whether clinics do directly exclude potential patients on racial or religious grounds. In the margin of the questionnaire, next to the questions referring to screening patients on racial and religious grounds, this respondent wrote: 'Provocative questions. If I answered these questions I would be breaking the law' (CAA). This response hinted: (1) that selection practices on racial grounds might indeed be carried out at this and perhaps at other clinics; and (2) that admitting to that would create legal trouble for the clinic. Certainly in a pre-legislative context, where clinics would be pressured to present the most benign face of IVF and GIFT practice, if such selection practices were being carried out, it might seem politic to deny them, or to refuse to answer the question. In addition, this respondent was the only one to object to all of my questions on selection policies, except those on genetic bases, as 'provocative' and to refuse to answer any of them. However, as

with all the other respondents, the questions on racial and religious selection clearly provoked the most objection.

21 See for example: Carby 1981; Collins 1991; Anthias and Yuval-Davis 1993.

22 Government statistics and a wide range of commentators and monitoring groups have identified the disproportionate representation of black people, in particular women and their children, in poverty statistics.

23 See, for example: Illich 1985 [1976]; Mort 1987; Scambler (ed.) 1991.

24 Genetic counselling is an advice service offered by medical scientists (usually trained genetic counselling specialists) in which a medical history is taken of a woman and man who wish to reproduce together. The process is used to determine an 'inheritance pattern' of traits that are socially and/or medically defined as undesirable. Based on this pedigree, counsellors assess the statistical probability of producing 'genetically damaged' offspring; hence the terminology of 'risk' and 'risk groups'. Genetic screening involves the use of a variety of diagnostic tests to acquire genetic information about an individual. In the reproductive context it is used to identify carriers of heritable genetic conditions that may be transmitted to offspring.

25 Theresia Degener (1990) has argued that 'neo-eugenic population control policies no longer principally rely on compulsory state intervention but on *voluntary eugenics* from below' (p. 88). Voluntary eugenics presuppose a 'sovereign self-responsible individual with her/his own economic and social interests'. In this context, medical practitioners provide 'what appears to be neutral, objective information that is supposed to aid women in exercising their right to self-determination and facilitate decision-making'. Their power to do so is contingent on the cultural hegemony of, for example, negative discourses of disability.

26 In other words, the notion of 'risk' in itself constructs the condition in question as inherently and inevitably negative. I would argue that such constructions contribute to a social climate that is deeply intolerant of disability and that discriminates profoundly against people living with disabilities (see also Morris 1991).

27 It must be noted that while a hegemony of voluntarism seemed to emerge in the survey, some respondents indicated that genetic counselling and screening results *were* used directly as criteria for treatment, and some stated that IVF or GIFT were used specifically for genetic reasons.

4

Genetic genea/logics: the apologetics of preimplantation diagnosis

Scientists are almost ready to start testing human embryos for genetic defects (Veitch 1985).

[T]he genetic *in vitro* screening technique will shortly be put into practice ... at the Hammersmith [hospital] (Ballantyne 1988).

Scientists are preparing plans to remove embryos from mothers, screen them for genetic illnesses in the laboratory and then reimplant only healthy ones (McKie 1988).

Preimplantation diagnosis or embryo biopsy, catch-all terms for the examination of IVF embryo cells in order to diagnose gene or chromosomal 'abnormalities', is a specifically IVF-based development – an invention predicated on the creation, through IVF, of extra-corporeal embryos. As such, it constitutes an extension of the screening logic underpinning IVF patient selection and an important illustration of the ways in which screening is embedded, not only in IVF use, but in medical scientific conceptualisations of the properties of the technology. In this context, the language of selection gravitates around questions of genes, illness and disability, both mediating and mediated by the genea/logical politics identified in the previous chapter. Here, as I shall argue, the selective rationality of IVF clearly incorporates an ableist conceptualisation of illness and disability as a central dimension of the emerging IVF discourse of 'fit' reproductions.[1]

According to the Human Fertilisation and Embryology

Authority, the first baby born to an IVF patient following the use of preimplantation diagnosis was at the Hammersmith hospital, under the direction of Robert Winston, in 1990. Winston was also the first IVF practitioner in Britain to undertake research specifically on developing embryo-biopsy capabilities. The 'Annual Report' of the Human Fertilisation and Embryology Authority lists 14 of 22 current IVF-based research projects whose investigations either directly concern the development of preimplantation diagnosis, or clearly suggest a fundamental connection with such techniques (for example research concerned with genetic development and 'abnormalities') (HFEA 1992, Annexe 2). The development of preimplantation diagnosis techniques is clearly central to current and projected priorities in IVF practice.

The term preimplantation diagnosis, without directly involving the linguistic reference point of IVF, nevertheless places the procedure firmly within the IVF procedural sequence. 'Pre' precisely locates preimplantation diagnosis in the linear IVF ('treatment service') teleology, discussed in detail in Chapter 1. As I noted there, practitioners characteristically describe IVF as a linear progression from hormonal induction of women, to 'recovery' of their eggs, to fertilisation *in vitro*, to re-implantation of IVF embryos in women. In practice, of course, women's IVF experiences will very probably not follow this order (for example, early stages may be repeated many times before the reimplantation stage can ever be reached). Thus the description of IVF events as a linear progression represents not necessarily the empirical practice of IVF, but rather the neat, linear, medical scientific idealisation of what IVF is supposed to be. However, it remains the case that, while it may not proceed in orderly steps, preimplantation diagnosis is linguistically and empirically placed along this time-line, between the stages of fertilisation in glass and re- implantation. As with the term *in vitro* fertilisation, women and the IVF procedures they undergo are absent referents of the term 'preimplantation diagnosis'.

If 'pre' locates preimplantation diagnosis in time, 'diagnosis' locates it in orientation. In Chapter 1, I discussed the significance of the diagnostic framework in the context of the category 'infertility'. The diagnostic framework, I argued, is one that pathologises particular conditions or events, locating their sources in terms of individual biology, disease and disease-inducing agents rather than, for example, with respect to oppressive social, political and economic conditions and inequalities that dis-able. I argued, moreover, that the diagnostic framework operates as a kind of territorial claim for medical intervention. The term preimplantation diagnosis indicates that the techniques covered by the term are similarly orientated toward both the individualistic pathologisation of disease agents, and the establishment, in so doing, of a basis for further medical scientific interventions that characteristically involve the medical management, and in this case, prevention of the birth, of diagnosed/affected individuals.

As I have discussed earlier, the construction of reproduction in terms of danger and abnormality has historically been gendered. As Mary Douglas (1966) argues, reproductive processes, cross-culturally, are the sites of much ritual and mythic practice pertaining to notions of purity, pollution and danger, notions typically associated with women's ability to menstruate and procreate (or in the case of abortion, to decide not to reproduce). Douglas points out, moreover, that Western science has historically played a particular role in the construction of categories of danger, dirt and pollution, many of which similarly revolve around and elaborate notions about female sexuality and an insidious female nature. Thus it can be argued that this 'danger' attributed to the process of reproduction in Western medical scientific discourse, and here (re)invoked as 'abnormality' in the context of genetic 'biopsy' of IVF embryos, derives much of its power from deeply embedded notions in Western culture about women's dangerous sexuality. The absence of women as referents in descriptions of reproduction, and the pathologisation of female reproductive processes can be interpreted as linguistic and empirical strategies of containing, while (re)constructing, female reproductive 'danger'. From this perspective, it seems no accident that the linguistic erasure of women in preimplantation diagnostic terminology is paralleled by the empirical excision of 'key stages' of reproduction from women with IVF. Nor is it coincidental that the disproportionate burden of genetic diagnosis in both conceptual and, as I shall argue later in this chapter, material terms falls disproportionately on women.

Diagnostic relations: the apologetics of preimplantation diagnosis

In his study of the history of the scientific racial hygiene movement as a key predecessor of current practices and frameworks in genetic sciences, Robert Proctor (1988) argues that there are four interconnected priorities/functions of modern science; these are: enlightenment, production, social control and apology. This last function Proctor explains as the practices (by scientists) of convincing people 'that the social order is a natural order' (Proctor 1988 p. 2), or, to put it another way, scientific rationales for and about the inevitability of the social order, or indeed for the organisation and priorities of the scientific enterprise itself.

Mandates and justifications claimed by medical scientists for the development of preimplantation diagnosis capabilities characterise Proctor's notion of apology. They revolve around two interrelated modes of deterministic argumentation: one being technological, and the other, biological. The current existence of preimplantation diagnosis techniques is typically explained as the logical and inevitable outcome of both a linear trajectory of technological progress and the imperatives of biological nature in itself. Below, I shall examine each strand of the preimplantation diagnosis 'origin narrative' in turn, beginning with the posited technological trajectory, exploring the ways they, together, weave an apologia for genetic screening through which ableist and other oppressive social relations are both taken for granted and reproduced.

Machina ex machina: the technological trajectory

Dr Marilyn Monk, an IVF and genetics researcher in the veterinary context, has identified three technological developments that she argues were directly preconditional to preimplantation diagnosis practices (in both animals and humans). These include: IVF, recombinant DNA capabilities and the development of 'microassays to detect metabolic products and specific proteins in [embryo] cells' (Monk 1990 p. 56). Other writers have identified further technological sources that were key, both materially and conceptually, to the development of preimplantation diagnosis. These include: genetic counselling practices, already existing genetic screening (on prospective parents) tests, prenatal diagnostic techniques, veterinary IVF-based genetic research (particularly on mice) and embryo 'lavage' techniques.

What is significant here is not simply the identification of technological preconditions for the development of preimplantation diagnosis, but the particular deterministic way that the medical scientific writings I examined identify them as origins – that is, arguing that technology breeds technology.

The IVF Trajectory

One argument justifying the development of preimplantation diagnosis posits it as a logical outcome of the 'routine' technological nature of IVF:

> [I]t is conceivable that selected traits which can be easily detected and altered could be subject to systematic manipulation. This is particularly true of IVF programs where the gametes and embryos are maintained outside the body as a routine part of the procedure (Meek 1986 p. 43).

Implicit in this passage is a notion, which I would suggest is characteristic of the modern common sense of scientific 'progress', that technology does, shall and needs to breed new technology. Indeed the development of one technology is seen as only one step *en route* to the next. What is 'conceivable' is, as argued here, predicated on the nature of current technological capabilities. The use of the passive voice is significant, for instead of identifying a human agent (IVF practitioner) who conceptualises possibilities, the prognostication appears to be a product of the procedure in itself (which apparently performs itself). This erasure of scientific agency (by scientists) is characteristic of professional as well as popular representations of science and scientific 'progress'. It is the quintessential rhetorical formula of technological determinism.

While it is true that the use of IVF on women is a procedural precondition for the possibility of performing preimplantation diagnosis on women's embryos, another version of the IVF trajectory would seem to suggest that IVF emerged from interests in screening capabilities rather than the reverse:

> When the [IVF] programme started we were not certain that it would result in the achievement of pregnancies, but it seemed reasonable to believe that the basic information acquired from the work might help in the areas of sperm–egg interaction, contraceptive development and a greater understanding of foetal malformation (Wood and Westmore 1984 p. 103).

Thus Wood and Westmore state that the IVF project, rather than simply providing the basis and capabilities for preimplantation diagnosis, was itself the outcome, in part, of interest in 'foetal malformation'. Yet what both passages have in common is the implicit revelation that it is deterministic thinking on the part of practitioners (accompanied by a rhetorical erasure of that agency), as well as the social organisation of science and medicine (which offers resources that enable practitioners to mobilise and realise their ideas), rather than the nature of technology itself, that accounts for innovations. Clearly what is less important than what came first, is that IVF and an orientation to screening have been deeply inter-associated in the priorities of practitioners.

The recombinant DNA trajectory: when possibility is the father of necessity

That it can be a short step from identification of the possible to claims of necessity is exemplified by another author's account of the pivotal and preconditional role of recombinant DNA technology in developing preimplantation diagnosis:

> Because of the power of recombinant DNA techniques, it is now possible to study human inheritance and development by examining gene organization and expression in single cells or organisms. Since genetic disease either directly or as a paradigm accounts for a high proportion of serious handicap in children and young adults, such studies may represent the only way to understand and to prevent many abnormalities. The study of early embryos may also be necessary if we are to understand the normal development of the foetus during pregnancy ... (Williamson 1986, p. 105).

There is a deterministic subtext both in the claim that genes are 'paradigmatic' causes of 'serious handicap' and in the way in which the link made between genes and 'serious' disease implicitly constructs a moral imperative to follow the path that Williamson claims may represent the '*only* way to understand and to prevent ... abnormalities' (my emphasis). Indeed, it is precisely this imputation of a seemingly inevitable trajectory to a putative biological disaster that discursively transforms *a* possible technological trajectory (from DNA to preimplantation diagnosis) into the *only* possible one.

Technological determinist thinking is also exemplified in arguments justifying preimplantation diagnosis in the human IVF context with respect not only to the capabilities, but also to the limitations of pre-existing technologies. A particularly poignant example is the 'abortion–replacement' argument.

'New and improved': preimplantation diagnosis as abortion replacement

One of the most consistently asserted 'benefits' of preimplantation diagnosis is constituted as an 'abortion replacement' argument. This line of justification places preimplantation diagnosis in relation specifically to prenatal diagnostic screening. The claim is that while both perform the same type of function (diagnosis of genetic 'abnormality' in embryos), the benefit of preimplantation diagnosis is that it is performed before implantation and so the 'need' for (eugenic) abortion is thereby obviated:

David Weatherall asked what the benefit would be if these diagnoses could be made before implantation on *in vitro* material. Infertile couples who are at high risk from some genetic disease or chromosomal disorder would certainly benefit. We are not necessarily envisaging people [*sic*] having IVF in order to be diagnosed, but it must be a great anguish for an infertile couple [*sic*] of this kind to finally get pregnant and then to have the pregnancy terminated because the baby [*sic*] is affected (Mclaren 1986 p. 104, my emphasis).

Abortion 'for these reasons', then, is posited to be a trauma (for 'couples') that preimplantation diagnosis would purportedly eliminate. This assertion raises several important issues. First, it is abortion, rather than the oppressive social relations around disability, that is posited as the primary source of distress. In this formulation, abortion is taken as a *prima facie* necessity arising from the negative 'fact' of disability. Second is the extraordinary implication that preimplantation diagnosis, which necessitates that women undergo IVF, is not, itself, traumatic for women. The construction of preimplantation diagnosis as a neutral or beneficial procedure, in contrast to (eugenic) abortion, is strengthened by the use of terms such as 'couple' or 'people', which obscures the fact that it is women who bear the burden of both procedures.[2] It is not my intention here to suggest that eugenic abortion is not highly traumatic for women, most if not all of whom would probably go through such a procedure in the context of a wanted pregnancy. However, it is important to point out that, contrary to the implications of the abortion-replacement argument, it is not the case that preimplantation diagnosis obviates a termination of a pregnancy. It is debatable whether a termination of the wanted *prospect* of pregnancy after a woman has undergone the difficult process of IVF is less traumatic than the termination of an established and desired pregnancy. Certainly, it has been widely noted that 'failed' cycles of IVF have been experienced as traumatic by patients (Crowe 1987; Klein 1989a, b). Thus, my concern here is not to disclaim the ways in which terminations of wanted pregnancies might be traumatic, but rather to assess critically the terms in which trauma is discursively constituted in this context and, specifically, the ways in which it is disclaimed in relation to preimplantation diagnosis.

Implicitly, moreover, this comparative formulation links the technological nature of the abortion and preimplantation diagnosis procedures to the hegemonic 'moral' debate about embryo/fetal 'personhood', a dominant strand of both abortion and IVF professional/mainstream debates. As I note above, the 'benefits' posited are twofold: firstly, that preimplantation diagnosis is less procedurally traumatic; and secondly, that it obviates the 'need' to terminate a 'child':

> There are still many women particularly from the group who object to abortion, who would prefer antenatal diagnosis even earlier in pregnancy. There is a real demand for diagnosis of affected foetuses during the preimplantation stages of pregnancy, particularly after IVF (Williamson 1986 p. 12).

This formulation locates both demand for preimplantation diagnosis and 'object[ion] to abortion' with women. It resonates with the punitive social climate surrounding abortion more generally, and with anti-abortion initiatives of recent years. It is not surprising that the 'abortion replacement' argument was particularly popular with the mainstream media. For example:

> Embryo testing has obvious advantages over testing in pregnancy which is sometimes deferred until the 18th week. By this time the pregnant woman regards what is growing within her as her unborn child (Illman 1989).[3]

Anti-abortion rhetoric and legal initiatives (as well as embryo-centred thinking within the IVF context generally) have clearly had an impact on the argumentation about preimplantation diagnosis. To posit preimplantation diagnosis as the new and improved model of prenatal testing, a complex recourse to anti-abortion sentiment, assessment of technological capabilities and limitations and absolutist assertions of the essential negativity of disability were evidently considered politic. In other words, both anti-abortion and anti-disability sentiments provided powerful fuel for the techno/logical construction of preimplantation diagnosis as necessary, desirable and inevitable 'progress' over abortion-dependent forms of prenatal diagnosis.

'Inevitable' directions: gene therapy as the next trajectory

The final component of the preimplantation diagnosis trajectory story projects into the 'new and improved' future of genetic 'therapy', the alteration of the genetic structure of embryos with the aim of the superimposing of 'normal' functions on the 'abnormal', or of simply eradicating certain genetic expressions from the organism. 'The idea', explains Gail Vines, 'is that doctors could cure a person with a genetic disorder by introducing a gene to compensate for the faulty gene responsible for the disease' (Vines 1987 p. 3).

Interestingly, the projections with respect to genetic therapy differ from discussions about the other, related technological practices identified in this chapter. Unlike the formulations of the other practices in virtually uncritical, enthusiastic terms, those exploring the possibilities of genetic therapy are infused with a certain ambivalence. One author, for example, after suggesting that genetic therapy is the logical ('ultimate') result of DNA technology (Meek 1986 p. 42) (and implicitly of preimplantation diagnosis screening practices through which conditions 'needing' genetic therapy would be identified) nevertheless cautions:

> The possibility of curing genetic defects by inserting the correct gene or genes into the egg, sperm or developing embryo may appear to present a slightly *simpler* option than treating the mature individual. However, the resulting alteration would then be passed on to the next generation. The implications of interfering with the genetic make-up of our species, which has been selectively evolved over millions of years, must be *carefully considered* (my emphasis).

The ambiguity of this warning is disturbing. What is meant by 'simpler' is not explained. For whom and in what way is genetic therapy 'simpler'? Is it that it is 'simpler' for medical scientists to view 'disease' in reductionist genetic terms and treat the conditions accordingly than for 'disease' to be understood in complex, social terms that would necessitate equally complex, social intervention? Moreover, in the context of an argument that genetic therapy has the potential to 'alter the genetic make-up of our species', a call to 'careful consideration' seems extraordinarily understated for a consequence of such scale.

Apparent uneasiness about the safety of genetic therapy contributes a significant tension into the otherwise unproblematised trajectory formula used to explain the existence of this technological practice and its antecedents. However, even as medical scientific writers identify gene therapy's dangers, they none the less use several strategies to minimise the importance of those dangers.

One strategy has been to distinguish germ-line from somatic gene therapy. Weatherall *et al.*, writing in the CIBA text, argue:

> Here [germ-line genetic therapy] we would be moving into a completely different area of research because we would be manipulating genetic material which would be passed on to subsequent generations. This would be dangerous ground, and although we cannot imagine experiments of this type being done in the foreseeable future, it is a problem that we must keep in mind. Somatic cell gene therapy is only an extension of current medical practice; a transgenic man is another thing altogether (Weatherall *et al.* 1986 pp. 97–8).

The distinction being argued here is revealing about the narrowness of what is taken, in medical scientific circles, to constitute transformation of the genetic structure of an organism such that it affects future generations. 'Somatic' gene therapy certainly involves deliberate and direct manipulation of the genetic structures of an organism; yet any potential transgenerational 'side-effects' of this are sharply distinguished from 'germ-line' therapy, which is spoken of as if it were the only possible way in which 'manipulating genetic material' might have effects on 'subsequent generations'. There is, in this formulation, a reduction of the perceived potential effects of a genetic experiment into the specific purpose medical scientists have for using it. This kind of technological reductionism is reminiscent of the construction of 'superovulation' drugs as affecting only a woman's ovaries. The fact that non-genetically based therapies have been documented as having (undesired) 'transgenerational' effects[4] would call into question the easy assertion that somatic genetic therapy would not affect 'germ lines'. 'Germ-line therapy' might be the only genetic therapy explicitly aimed at transgenerational effects: but my argument here concerns the possibility that the constant insistence on the dichotomy between germ-line and somatic therapies may serve to conceal a deeper problem in the professional common sense about the relationship between intent and effect.

Weatherall *et al.* write, moreover, that 'we cannot imagine experiments of this type being done in the foreseeable future'; thus making the case that technological limitations, if not obviating the need for ethical consideration now, at least limit it to a 'problem' that should simply be 'kept in mind'. The projection that 'gene therapy is a long way from being a routine procedure' (Meek 1986 p. 42) is taken as a typical yardstick against which the necessity for ethical consideration is formulated. Williamson argues:

> Somatic gene therapy, where a gene is placed in cells of a relevant tissue but not in gametes, should not be confused with genetic therapy … Leaving aside any questions of public policy, gene-level therapy is not an issue today, because no one is even close to making it work for diseases such as thalassaemia or the haemophilias (Williamson 1986 p. 113).

The subtext of this argument is that until the procedure can be 'made to work', consideration of its meaning, which would include whether or not it should be done at all, 'is not an issue'.

The genetic therapy project, that is, the manipulation of the germ-line of human embryos, was declared off-limits within practitioner circles (i.e. in the VLA) and eventually unlicensable within the Human Fertilisation and Embryology legislation. Marilyn Monk offers a very clear summing up of this contradictory aspect of the politics around genetic therapy and its representation:

> The ILA [VLA] prohibits obviously undesirable research aims such as interfering with an embryo's genetic make up, attempts at cloning, and mixing human and animal cells in developing embryos (Monk 1990 p. 58).

Monk makes this statement in the context of a larger argument for the development of preimplantation diagnosis, in a self-evident attempt to allay perceived public fears about the prospect of transgenesis. Her own discussion captures the contradictory construction of genetic therapy pervading the literature I read: posited on the one hand as the 'ultimate' (and beneficial) outcome of preimplantation diagnosis (and thus of IVF) and on the other as an 'obviously undesirable research aim'. The spectre of restrictive legislation clearly underpinned tensions between the technologic (in which gene therapy is clearly constructed as the apogee of screening sensibilities) and political expediency (in which it is disclaimed). Ironically, one of the effects of this contradictory construction of gene therapy is the effective normalisation of preimplantation diagnosis (and genetic screening *per se*) and IVF by contrast as 'obviously desirable research aims'.

Machina ex corpore: the bio/logical trajectory

> The goal of 'preimplantation diagnosis' is to give couples known to be at risk of passing on a severe genetic disease the option of having their embryos screened in the laboratory. This procedure would enable the woman to begin a pregnancy knowing that the embryo would escape the disease (Vines 1989 pp. 49–50).

Embedded in the notion that preimplantation diagnosis is a techno/logically determined outcome of the properties of IVF (and other technical practices) is a parallel bio/logic that locates its origin in the putatively negative nature of disability (as 'inherited illness'). The language of genes – 'genetic abnormality', genetic defect', genetic disease' among many other such terms – permeates rationales for preimplantation diagnosis, forming the linguistic matrix and central theoretical framework explaining the 'nature' both of disability and of screening technology. The promise of 'escape' held out in Vines's claim bespeaks a reified conceptualisation of disability as a 'natural' disaster. It is precisely this posited trajectory from genes to disease-as-prison that is seen, literally, to incorporate the imperative for the technological trajectory of preventive genetic screening.

Genetic origins: sequences of cause and effect

If the biochemical basis for a genetic disease is known, it is usually possible to isolate the offending gene (Weatherall *et al.* 1986 p. 85).

This passage captures several features of the construction of disease and disability through the lens of diagnostic genetics. Firstly, genes, in such formulations, emerge as self-contained meaning units for which the capacity to be isolated is an inherent property.[5] As with the Vines quote above, there seems to be an inveterate optimism about the capabilities of scientists to 'know' the (seemingly singular) function of genes and to realise the 'goals' of genetic screening (an embryo that has 'escaped' the disease). The persuasive power of both statements owes much to the notions of 'risk' and 'offence' ascribed to the 'nature' of (bad) genes. Indeed, the notion of an 'offending gene', with its connotations of criminality, insult, affront, constructs genetic 'disease' as, at once, a natural fact and an unnatural, 'offensive' one. Secondly, genes seem to determine not only disease, but the negative social meaning of disease as an inevitable calamity. Moreover genetic disease is not only something terrible that someone *has*, but something someone *is*. More emphatically than the theory of germs as cause of disease,[6] with genes the 'foreign agent' of disease is incorporated in and of, indeed intrinsic to the very body of the person affected. In this context an 'offending gene' implicitly bespeaks an 'offensive' person, and is clearly implicated in the putatively imperative logic of genetic screening as a strategy to prevent the birth of persons with such 'diseases'.

The standardisation of gene function is paralleled by a standardisation of the conditions they purportedly cause:

At present more than 7,000 babies are born each year in Britain with some form of congenital disease, including many cases of inherited illnesses – such as cystic fibrosis, muscular dystrophy and sickle cell anaemia – that later lead to severe impairment or death in childhood (McKie 1988).[7]

McKie's construction of 'inherited illnesses' in such unrelievedly negative terms (and his elision of very different conditions) is characteristic of both the professional and the more popular literatures on preimplantation diagnosis. Implicit in such formulations is that all 'inherited illnesses' are not only equally tragic, indeed deadly, but essentially so. Clearly the investment of genetic disease with the spectre of an inevitably terrible life and early death fuels the sense that genetic screening is not only necessary but the only possible response. In this context, the fact that actual experiences of these and other 'inherited illnesses' vary considerably is eclipsed, as is the possibility that the problems of 'disability' are not biologically determined but produced through oppressive social responses to illness and disability.[8] This is not to deny the material realities of the body in these and other conditions, but to argue, rather, that one's quality of life is not determined, as is assumed in the bio/logic narrative of preimplantation diagnosis, by the state of one's body.[9] Rather, it is mediated through social processes that, for example, may foster or impair bodily and social mobility, and cultural regimes of meaning that inform broader common senses about illness and disability.

It is worth noting, for example, that the direction of cause and effect from genes to 'disease' eclipses the possibility that 'damaged genes' might be an effect of illness or other factors (for example, from radiation and toxic chemical exposures as well as iatrogenic effects of drugs). Such, however, is the narrative closure of the bio/logic origin story of preimplantation diagnosis that even where such effects may be noted, the overwhelming focus is on the (damaged) genes (the body of the damaged individual) and only in so far as they constitute bodies of risk for the next generation. Williamson (1986 p. 108), for example, argues that tracking the gene that purportedly controls 'normal' finger development can be compared to the action of 'viruses and teratogens [toxic exposures]' on abnormal finger development. 'In this way,' he argues, 'we

THE ETHOS OF SCREENING

should be able to stop these substances in the environment coming into contact with the pregnant woman at relevant times during embryogenesis.' It is rather curious to suggest that gene 'tracking' would stop exposures to toxic substances when already well-established knowledge about their adverse effects has not done so. What this argument does open up is the possibility of sanctions against pregnant women,[10] for example preventing them from working in certain jobs or during certain 'relevant times during embryogenesis'. Indeed, the term 'embryogenesis' for pregnancy captures exactly the ways in which the embryo-centred logic of IVF underpins and is underpinned by a genea/logical (eugenic) sensibility. Finally, it is also significant that while genes are posited, in all the literature I examined, as sites of 'risk' for 'disease', the recombinant processes of IVF and genetic science are not.

Natural(ised) disasters: normal(ised) selections

Knowing how precious the human baby is tends to lead us to take a similar attitude to the human preimplantation embryo. But facts of our biology and social life can give us another perspective. Because we have so much invested in the production and rearing of only a few offspring, it is even more important to invest that energy in offspring who will be free from serious disease. This is not to say that the life of those individuals afflicted with severe genetic or other disease is invalid. Nothing could be further from the truth. The appropriate question to ask an afflicted person is, if they were to have a child, and with the current technology available, would they want to be able to choose to have a baby free from the disease they themselves have suffered? (Monk 1990 p. 59, emphasis mine).

The inter-investments of popular and professional common senses of disability emerge with a particular edge in the more popularly orientated IVF/preimplantation diagnosis promotional literature.[11] Here, Monk's appeal clearly assumes a non-disabled audience in an 'us' that is inclusive of both practitioners and lay people and that, despite her disclaimer, clearly excludes disabled people (referred to as 'they'). Jenny Morris (1991) has argued that one of the dominant discursive constructions of disability is that of a life not worth living. The currency of this notion is conveyed both in Monk's invocation of a universal investment in 'non-afflicted' offspring and in her attribution of this attitude to disabled people themselves. Her assumption of family forms in which only 'a few' offspring will be reared also bespeaks a characteristically Western (white middle-class) eugenic discourse. Genes, moreover, would appear to determine not only disability, but ableism.[12] In this context, preimplantation diagnosis would seem to be a response to rather than a(nother) source of negative meanings of illness and disability.

The reification of disability as 'inherited illness' and both as natural disasters is intensified by the ways in which 'risk' is discursively linked with both 'choice' and 'demand'. As emerged in my survey, there is an emphasis in the preimplantation diagnosis literature on the voluntary participation of patients (and their presumed male partners) in genetic screening and on the technology as providing parents with the 'choice', as Monk puts it, 'to have a baby free from disease'. M. A. and M. E. Ferguson-Smith corroborate this view:[13]

> As with all genetic counselling, the advice given should be non-directive so that the couple [sic] has the opportunity to take the decision appropriate to their own particular circumstances. Once they embark on prenatal diagnosis, they should also have the freedom to change their minds at any stage ... *a couple's [sic] freedom of choice in this matter must be carefully guarded, although it may mean that a considerable burden, financial and other, may later be imposed on the family and social services* (Ferguson-Smith and Ferguson-Smith 1983 p. 188, emphasis mine).

Yet clearly the language of 'risks' (indeed of 'considerable burdens') that pervades genetic screening discourses would compromise (if not obviate) the possibilities of 'non-directive' advice and 'freedom of choice'.[14]

M. A. and M. E. Ferguson-Smith go on to state:

> A more usual and perhaps more ethical approach [in relation to genetic screening] is to discuss the findings carefully with both parents so that they may be helped to understand the likely prognosis and make an informed decision about continuing the pregnancy. *This is the approach favoured by this Department and our*

> *experience has been that most parents are not prepared to accept even a small risk of handicap [sic] in their future offspring* (1983 p. 196).

In a context where 'handicap'[15] is constituted in terms of 'risk', such a sentiment would not be surprising. Indeed such formulations interpellate the myriad oppressions (legal, economic, educational and through representation) experienced by disabled people into the properties of genes and the sphere of individual choice as if both were divorced from their social – in this case specifically their medical scientific – context. Thus it is posited that it is genes, not gene data, that, in Foucauldian terms, *produce* risk and constitute dangerous bodies of knowledge; it is individual couples [*sic*], not screening (and other eugenic) discourses that *produce* eugenic choices. As with the techno/logic trajectory, the agency of medical scientists as *authors* of screening technologies and of discourses of 'risk' is eclipsed. The screening ethos and impetus are located both within the properties of genes (which are understood to predetermine adverse social conditions for disabled people, locating the origins of oppression in the bodies of the oppressed) and the 'natural' demands of patients. Screening is normalised as a matter of common sense.

Diagnostic imperialism

The new genetics marks the birth of a new kind of medicine. It heralds the most comprehensive assault ever against disease and will have a profound impact on each and every one of us, influencing what we eat and drink, where we live, and even the jobs and hobbies we pursue. As children we will know if we will be at high risk in later life from diseases such as cancer and heart disease. As prospective parents we [*sic*] will no longer face the anguish of a pregnancy that may end in abortion if we are known carriers of defective genes (Illman 1989).

The advent of preimplantation diagnosis reflects and reproduces the growing currency of genetic perspectives of health and illness and of genetic screening as central to reproductive futures. As Illman notes, though presenting it as a welcome development, within the logic of genetic screening is also an

---

immanent potential to interpellate not only reproductive life, but, indeed, all aspects of our lives. His construction of genetics as an 'assault' on disease is significant not only for its recapitulation of a military metaphor typically associated with medicine,[16] but for the particular ways in which the genetic 'enemies' elide both 'defective' genes and 'carriers'. The power of such a discourse to intensify the stigmatisation of illness and people who are ill should not be underestimated. As Sue Meek has argued:

> Knowledge of the result of genetic screen tests may adversely affect marriage and employment prospects and health insurance status ... The development of increasing number [*sic*] of these texts is likely to exert a pressure for routine genetic screening of the foetus itself rather than just members of identified, at risk, family groups. Peer group denigration and potential prosecution by a child born with a genetic defect may await parents who decide not to have such screening performed, or who decide to continue with the pregnancy despite the outcome of the tests (Meek 1986 p. 41).

Barbara Katz Rothman (1986) has argued that while the creation of new technologies may herald new options, they may also foreclose others. As Meek suggests, such diagnostic imperialism is both embedded in and reproduced through the increasing currency of genetic screening as a genea/logical imperative.[17]

Selective burdens

Underlying the writings examined here are a number of assumptions about the position of women in the preimplantation diagnosis/genetic screening context, assumptions that are obscured in the gender-'neutral' language of 'couple', 'parent' and 'individual', as well as through a lack of exploration of the implications of such screening for women's health, well-being and social status. As with languages of IVF more generally, appeals for preimplantation diagnosis obscure social inequalities between practitioners and female patients and between patients and their male partners, while implicitly reinforcing and relying on these power imbalances. Indeed, preimplanta-

THE ETHOS OF SCREENING

tion diagnosis involves a heavy burden that disproportionately falls on women.

Firstly, preimplantation diagnosis is predicated on a procedural, diagnostic burden unevenly experienced by women and men. As I discussed in Chapter 1, women undergo the bulk of invasive diagnostic infertility testing and solely undergo IVF — the latter being an empirical precondition for preimplantation diagnosis. Thus, significant risks to women's health are essential features of preimplantation diagnosis. While women's bodies are in several senses *taken* as present, they are also discursively positioned as absent (yet docile/dangerous/divided) bodies and disclaimed (or disciplined) as bodies of resistance. This is reinforced through the construction of a discourse of 'risk' located entirely with 'inherited illness', while the procedural risks of IVF to women (and potentially their offspring) are discursively erased.

Rothman, examining the implications for women of prenatal diagnostic techniques, raises a number of issues concerning the nature of eugenic decision-making that are relevant to the preimplantation diagnosis context. First is the question of investing pregnancy with the question of genetic 'risk', which, as the women Rothman interviewed reveal, renders women's relationship with their own pregnancies 'tentative' and fragmented (the pregnancy cannot be part of them until 'abnormalities' are ruled out by the tests). This alienation is fostered through the embryo-centredness of concerns in the diagnostic context and the concomitant consideration of women as 'maternal environments ... increasingly seen as only one of the possible locations for the completion of fetal development' (Rothman 1986 p. 111). While preimplantation diagnosis takes place before pregnancy, it similarly involves an embryo-centred construction of pregnancy and injects a further 'tentativeness' into an already tentative potential pregnancy.

Rothman also argues that eugenic diagnosis involves the process of 'evaluat[ing] disabilities, deciding which disabilities make life not worth living for the disabled person, and also which disabilities demand too much or are beyond ... [parents'] competence' (p. 160). The procedure demands that women (with or without their partners) make ableist decisions, and then live with the consequences, a decision-making process that Rothman's interviewees describe as tragic, questioning whether this kind of choice is a desirable kind of choice (pp. 181–92). Moreover, the ableist notion of genetic 'risk' not only has consequences for women as bearers and carers, but also for women as 'carriers'. Preimplantation diagnosis (and other related diagnostic tests) are informed by a dominant discursive construction of women's bodies, reproductive processes and wills as, 'if not the enemy, then the battleground' (p. 111). The 'guilty' burden of 'risk' is, I would argue, disproportionately loaded on women, whose reproductive processes are already viewed with suspicion, if not opprobrium, within dominant medical scientific cultures. Thus, the notion of genetic 'risk' interfaces with already dominant notions of maternal 'risk' to women's embryos (and potential offspring).

Women, in the preimplantation diagnosis context, as evidenced by the texts examined here, are implicitly construed as bearers of 'nature's defects'. The pathogenic potential of their reproduction is construed simultaneously as intrinsic to their reproductive processes (increasingly their behaviour) and in their capacity as 'gene transmitters'. While men are also constructed as potentially pathogenic 'gene transmitters', they none the less do not bear an equivalent eugenic burden.

Finally, as with patient screening, infusing promotions of preimplantation diagnosis is a preoccupation with policing the reproduction of ab/normality and a conceptualisation of 'fitness' in genea/logical terms. Notions of normal and abnormal familial heritage implicit in heterosexist patient selection policies are, in this context, explicitly constituted as genetic mechanisms (which, as Williamson posits above, can be 'switched' on and off). In both contexts, prevention is the central diagnostic orientation and racialised, classed and heterosexist constructions of 'unfit' familial arrangements interresonate with those of 'offensive' disease. In this context, genes, like women, become the recombinant (docile,[18] dangerous and divided) bodies in the authorship of 'fit' genealogies through the linguistic and technological 'texts' of IVF. The disciplinary character, in Foucauldian terms, of the preimplantation diagnostic gaze is encapsulated in standardised representations of 'genetic disease' where the growth of extra fingers elides with cystic fibrosis, muscular dystrophy and sickle cell anaemia into equivalently intransigent tragedies in which the necessity of genetic prevention is seen as literally incorporated.

Notes

1 Most of the texts considered in this chapter have been authored by IVF practitioners (and geared to a range of readers, including: potential IVF patients, 'science buffs' and professionals, or those working in fields contributing to the wide variety of IVF practices. Several commentators are medical or science correspondents (predominantly having been trained in science) for broadsheet newspapers (no tabloids have been used). While these correspondents may not be practitioners in IVF or related fields and may not participate in policy decisions, their writings are none the less significant for the purposes of this chapter. Firstly, they help shape the social climate within which practitioners work and policies are decided. In a context of imminent legislative intervention into IVF practices, such a role would clearly have currency. Secondly, these commentators often derive their stories from culling professional journals. Thus they occupy an important mediatory role between practitioners and laypeople, and hold, as I argue in this chapter, significant power to contribute to popular *and* professional common senses of IVF genetic screening practices (and IVF itself) as socially necessary and legally acceptable.

2 It is also worth noting that Mclaren's implicit suggestion that IVF might be used, not as an infertility treatment, but rather 'in order to diagnose ... genetic disease' is not unusual. Marilyn Monk (1990 p. 57) also argues that 'success [with IVF] is perhaps more likely for th[o]se couples [*sic*] whose problem is not infertility but genetic risk in the offspring'.

3 A number of medical/science correspondents in my sample, including Andrew Veitch in the *Guardian* (1985, 1987) and Robbie McKie of the *Observer* (1988) advanced similar arguments.

4 As noted earlier, DES (diethylstilbestrol) has produced transgenerational adverse effects – notably vaginal cancer in daughters and granddaughters of women who took the drug.

5 Williamson (1986 p. 107) produces a similar formulation:

> We use the term 'candidate gene' to refer to any gene where there is a biochemical or biological or genetic reason to suppose that the sequence causes or contributes to an inherited phenotype. The advantage of this approach is that it allows definitive experiments to be done using such genes to track risks in families.

Thus, the assumption that genes are (singularly or contributory) causal factors in disease precedes 'definitive experiments' to definitively 'track' them. Genes define not only disease but families. It is significant that Williamson expresses his enthusiasm about 'this approach' in terms of how it facilitates scientific research. Clearly a social model of disease and social definitions of what constitutes family would create difficulties for such 'definitive' experimentation.

6 For an extended comparative discussion of germ theory and gene theory see Spallone (1992).

7 Robin McKie was writing as a science correspondent for the *Observer*, a (British) Sunday broadsheet newspaper.

8 In a recent letter to *Community Care*, Jenny Morris distinguished the essentialist and ableist construction of disability as 'impairment' with a perspective of disability as oppression: 'Disabled people ... are disabled by society's response to impairment' (Morris 1995 p. 13).

9 R. W. Connell (1995) has argued that the social meanings of bodily experiences are neither located/determined in the essence of the body nor in the unidirectional imposition of social meanings on the body. Rather, social meanings are produced through a 'body reflexive' circuit in which discourse (and the oppressive social relations they reflect and reproduce) constitutes a kind of matrix through which 'bodies of meaning' and 'meaning as embodied' are produced. In this context, negative social meanings of bodily experiences of illness and 'impairment' are produced in a 'body reflexive circuit' in which ableist discourses of (oppressive practices and perspectives around) illness and disability are central.

10 These implications are not limited to pregnant women, but may affect women and men more generally. For example, accumulating evidence as to the mutagenic effects of radiation and chemical exposures on reproductive organs and correlations with cancers and other toxic effects in offspring been used as a basis for reproductive restrictions on workers (see, for example, Hubbard and Wald (1993), who provide a substantive analysis of genetic discrimination in the workplace). While it has been women who have primarily been affected by such restrictions, growing evidence of adverse effects of such exposures on male reproductive organs could provide a basis for the extension of such restrictions to men.

11 *New Scientist* is a popular science magazine that regularly features professionally authored accounts of scientific innovations which are aimed at a cross-over professional and non-professional readership. Monk is, herself, an IVF researcher in the veterinary context.

12 Martin Barker (1981) raises a similar critique of sociobiological and ethological theories which posit racism as a natural genetic predisposition to xenophobia.

13 These views on genetic screening/counselling are forwarded, in this instance, in the context of a discussion of prenatal genetic testing.

14 The reference to social services, moreover, reveals a possible conflict of loyalties for genetic counsellors and other related practitioners – between the 'freedom of choice' of their clients and pressure from government agencies, which view disability in terms of costs, to minimise 'financial and other' burdens.

15 I found it notable (and rather surprising) how often British writers used the term 'handicap', which has, in Britain, come to be quite widely discredited for its ableist connotations and is not one which has been reclaimed by British disability rights activists.

16 See Sontag (1991), for example.

17 In this sense, the preimplantation diagnostic gaze would appear to contribute to what Illich (1985) has termed 'cultural iatrogenesis', that is, the process of the attrition, through pervasive medicalisation, of the belief that one can deal with pain and illness. Attendant on the growing currency of genetic screening is a foreclosure of a politics which addresses the oppressive social relations and discourses which dis-able.

18 As I noted earlier, in arguing that genes and women are discursively constituted as 'docile bodies' within professional discourses of IVF, I am not suggesting that they *are* docile bodies. That is to say, as bodies of knowledge are constituted through unequal power relations, they are also negotiated through hegemonic struggle. Thus 'docile bodies' are simultaneously 'bodies of resistance'.

Part III

Medico-legal genea/logics

The *Human Fertilisation and Embryology* (HFE) *Act* was passed in 1990 and represented the outcome of an eight-year authorial struggle over medical scientific practice that was, in certain key respects, unprecedented. The history of statutory regulation over medicine, for example, has rarely encroached on the actual protocols of practice; a notable exception has been in the sphere of abortion legislation.[1] Both the 1858 *Medical Registration Act*, which consolidated medicine as a licensed profession, and the statutory incorporation of the National Health Service (NHS) in 1948 represent more typical state interventions. With the NHS, the central thrust of government intervention concerned the public 'financing and allocation of health care' (Mays 1991 p. 199).[2] In both cases, legislation served primarily to validate, indeed mandate, the exclusivity of professional expertise. Even with the NHS, while a state bureaucracy was established to administrate health care resourcing, the particulars of diagnostic and treatment decision-making were left to the self-regulatory professional bodies such as the British Medical Association (BMA) and the various Royal Colleges. The HFE Act, by contrast, establishes a statutory agency to which practitioners are directly accountable for their specific IVF practices through a licensing procedure, and, in so doing, constitutes an authorial 'take-over' of one of the central aspects of professional discretion. At the same time, as the following two chapters will explore, the medical scientific agenda for IVF and related practices served as a template that substantively underpinned the terms of statutory rewriting.

Contested terrains: the 'moral' debates of IVF legislation

The HFE Act was the outcome of a many-stranded, high-profile, web of negotiations dominated by various groups, including government representatives, medical scientific professionals, religious and anti-abortion lobbies and journalists. While a number of women's groups and feminist activists attempted to intervene in the dominant debate, these efforts, as I shall discuss further below, were almost entirely eclipsed. There were a number of key moments in the consolidation of the dominant public debate on IVF that served as a key context both for the emergence of professional texts examined in the previous chapters of this book and for the shape of the HFE Act. These include: the government-commissioned Warnock Committee of Inquiry into Human Fertilisation and Embryology (1982–4), which resulted in the *Warnock Report* (1984), which outlines recommendations for legislation; the formation of the VLA (discussed in Chapter 2 of this book); the introduction of the embryo-protectionist Unborn Children (Protection) Bills (1984 and 1985) and the consolidation of the IVF 'embryo research' debate in these contexts and in the popular media.

The Warnock Inquiry

In 1982, amid growing domestic and international controversy around IVF, particularly surrounding the question of 'embryo research', the British government appointed the Warnock Committee to develop recommendations for legislation on IVF and related practices. It was the first such governmental action, and formed a prominent reference point for similar legislative proposals in a number of other countries (Spallone 1987 p. 167).[3] The membership of the Warnock Committee, chaired by philosopher Mary (now Dame Mary) Warnock, consisted of a small cross-section of representatives from élite professions including 'law, medicine, natural science, social science, theology and ethics' (p. 167). As Spallone notes, the central remit of the Warnock Committee was to define the 'fundamental questions' of infertility treatment and related scientific research as moral questions and matters of public concern' (*Warnock Report* p. 5, quoted in Spallone 1987 p. 168). Spallone identifies four central assumptions that formed the basis of the Inquiry and *Report*, including: (a) reproduction as the authorial/logical domain of medicine; (b) the special status of embryos; (c) a conventional ideology of motherhood (one that serves traditional families); and (d) the ascendant status of scientific knowledge (p. 168). To this end, the *Report* was aimed chiefly at establishing legislative guidelines that negotiated concerns to protect embryos, medical scientific progress and professional authority, the nuclear family (particularly in defining parental 'fitness') and patrilineal registration of children.[4] The *Report* was also notable for its definition of family in bio-genetic terms and for its advocacy of the development of genetic diagnostic capabilities through IVF research.[5]

The centrality of medical scientific terms and concerns to the Warnock Committee were reflected in two key ways. Firstly, the terms of reference and definitions of practice under consideration were medical scientific.[6] Secondly, the proposed resolution of the supposed conflict of interest between embryo status and IVF-based 'embryo research' was to validate a new category of embryo development – later termed the 'pre-embryo' (0–14 days gestation) within which it would be permissible to conduct research. As Crowe (1990)[7] notes, the argumentation behind the creation of the special category of embryos was heavily dependent on a medical scientific discourse asserting the development of particular embryonic tissues and structures, heretofore not regarded as significant differentiators of embryo status, as scientific 'facts'. Crowe argues that the creation of the 'pre-embryo' as a new category represented an expedient strategy by the pro-science Warnock Committee to respond to the embryo 'rights' lobby in such a way as to protect scientific 'progress'. Thirdly, as in the dominant professional texts, the *Warnock Report* utilised the medical scientific discourse of genetics to define disability only in terms of individual biological inheritance (rather than disableing social conditions), which required, therefore, medicalised prevention through screening.[8] Finally, the *Report* defined the making of judgements about parental 'fitness' on heterosexist grounds[9] as a prerogative and necessary component of medical scientific responsibility in the context of IVF and related practices.[10] Thus, the genea/logics characterising professional discourses of IVF were reproduced, in the *Warnock Report*, as proto-legislative logics.

Entrenched embryo/logics: Powell versus PROGRESS

The *Unborn Children (Protection) Bill* (1984), also known as the Powell Bill, introduced in the same year as the publication of the Warnock Report, was a particularly significant moment of contest in the chronicle of events leading to the HFE Act. The Powell Bill was the first attempt to appropriate IVF practices for state regulation. It was significant, firstly, because it was the initiative of an individual parliamentarian (i.e. a private member's Bill) that pre-empted the legislative package (beginning with the *Warnock Report*) that was being developed by the government.[11] Secondly, it sought to reverse the position taken by the Warnock Committee. Rather than supporting IVF 'embryo research' (as long as it was licensed and performed on embryos of less than 14 days' gestation), the Powell Bill proposed to ban all research on embryos on the basis that an embryo was a legal person entitled to full legal protection.

Amidst enormous media coverage, the Powell Bill quickly became a centrepiece around which a bipolar debate about embryo personhood versus scientific progress became entrenched. The consolidation of the opposition to the Powell Bill was intensified by the launch in November 1985 of the lobby group PROGRESS (an alliance of (predominantly) lay-professionals and members of the medical scientific community), which was founded specifically in order to fight the Powell Bill and regain the 'moral ground'. It was PROGRESS, for example, that coined the term 'pre-embryo' (Crowe 1990

p. 48). Consistent with the PROGRESS approach, most of the mainstream opposition to the Powell Bill mobilised a two-pronged argument in defence of IVF 'embryo research' that became the hegemonic 'pro' side of an either–or debate. This position maintained that IVF 'embryo research' promised to produce numerous 'needed' benefits (including improvement of IVF success rates, the use of IVF for the treatment of infertile men [*sic*], greater understanding of causes of miscarriage, and development of new contraceptive and genetic screening capabilities (to prevent the birth of children with 'serious genetic diseases') (PROGRESS 1985a). The second prong of the pro-'embryo research' position asserted (as had the *Warnock Report*) that, up to 14 days, embryos were not really embryos.

While the Powell Bill eventually failed to become law,[12] the Powell versus PROGRESS debate reified two competing embryo/logics. This was evident in the popular media, which consistently pitted anti-abortion constructions of embryos as 'persons' against the interests of scientific progress and the benefits of IVF (which constructed 'pre-embryos' as needed research material, while not challenging the imputation of embryo personhood after 14 days). These competing constructions of embryo special status filtered into some forms of feminist opposition to the Powell Bill, which adapted the PROGRESS logic, arguing for 'unequivoc[al] support [for] embryo research because it alleviates human suffering' (PROGRESS 1985b) to address women. For example, a leaflet distributed by the Women's Reproductive Rights Information Centre (WRRIC 1985) argued that the establishment in law of 'embryo personhood' would threaten the (already limited) legality of abortion and would also threaten 'one of the most promising forms of infertility treatment for women'. In this context, IVF was represented as a woman-centred process and pro-choice politics were elided with support for embryo research. Thus both IVF and 'embryo research' became invested with not only the power to but the intention of safeguarding women's rights, and questions of health risks and the ways in which IVF might reflect and reproduce the historical misogyny (among other oppressive social divisions) of the medical profession became marginalised.

Some feminist groups attempted to challenge the dominant embryo-centredness of debates around IVF. The Women's Reproductive Rights Campaign, York,[13] for example, argued (York WRRC 1984), even before the introduction of the Powell Bill, that 'embryo research' constituted research on *women* and that opposition to research on women was consistent with the principles underlying pro-choice politics. However, the perceived urgent necessity in most quarters of its opposition to prevent the Powell Bill from becoming law ensured that the opposition largely remained entrenched in the narrow embryo- and science-centred terms outlined above. This posed a particular irony for feminist politics, which had historically challenged the constructions of embryo interests as separate from women's in both anti-abortion and medical scientific contexts.

Pushed to the margins: feminist critiques of the Great Embryo Debate

Patricia Spallone identifies five modes through which women, feminists and woman-centred concerns were marginalised or excluded from the process leading to the HFE Act:

1. the exclusion of women's groups from submitting oral evidence to the [Warnock] committee;
2. the implication that women act 'against the best interests of children when not adhering to traditional heterosexist definitions of motherhood and sexuality';
3. the failure to acknowledge (in most quarters) the negative implications of recommendations for embryo 'special status' as 'persons' or as legitimate 'research material' for women's access to abortion or women's reproductive autonomy more generally;
4. the lack of attention to the causes (including iatrogenic and environmental) and prevention of infertility; and
5. the acceptance and fostering of the increased medicalisation of women's reproduction without considering the impact of IVF practices on women's health or recommending standards to protect it. (Spallone 1987 pp. 168–72)

Spallone also notes that, beginning with the Warnock Committee, the debate about IVF practices excluded considerations of population control, racism and the promotion of medicalised eugenics. Moreover, as I have discussed in previous chapters, the dominant representation of IVF as a response to 'desperate' infertile 'couples' eclipsed consideration of the racialised and classed character of high-technology medical science and reified the recombinant, authorial and embryo-centred genea/logics of IVF practice as popular as well as professional common sense. In this context, feminists who opposed 'embryo research' were commonly (mis)represented as sharing a platform with right-wing anti-abortionists. Within the hegemonic 'two-sides' approach, feminist critiques of the embryo-centredness of both 'sides' were largely ignored.[14]

Thus, despite the efforts of a range of feminist groups and activists to challenge the terms of the dominant debate around IVF practices, embryos emerged as the principal territory of authorial struggle. The Powell versus PROGRESS positions were not only reified in popular representations, but indeed were incorporated into the HFE Bill as a two-option clause (one allowing 'embryo research' up to 14 days, the other banning it on the grounds of embryo 'personhood') over which parliamentarians would vote.

The following chapters, then, provide a detailed examination of the HFE Act. Chapter 5 considers the constitution of authorial (jurisdictional) struggle over the principal terms and orientation of the Act. Chapter 6 investigates the implications of a number of particular provisions of the Act for women's reproductive rights. Both chapters examine the ways in which questions of embryo status constituted the pivot around which the recombinant genea/logics of IVF were mediated and on which the future of IVF was seen to be determined.

Notes

1 As Fyfe (1991) explores the history of abortion legislation, in which governmental sanctions against abortion practice and, later, limited decriminalisation can be seen as a significant territory of struggle between state

and medical scientific claims over the territories both of reproductive control and professional exclusivity.

2 Mays argues that 'the NHS represented a compromise between the principles of traditional authority and rational public administration' (Mays 1991 p. 207).

3 Subsequent Australian and West German legislative initiatives, for example, made explicit reference to the *Warnock Report* (Spallone 1987).

4 See Sections 11:16 (p. 63); 13:1 (p. 75) ; 2:5–15 (pp. 11–13); 4:26 (p. 26) in the *Warnock Report* (1984).

5 See Section 9:1–12 (pp. 48–52) in the *Warnock Report* (1984).

6 Indeed, as Spallone (1987) and Stacey and Franklin (1985) argue, the predominance of medical scientific discourse in the *Warnock Report* was acutely demonstrated in the (re)definition as medical procedures, in the same terms as IVF, of surrogacy (which does not necessarily involve any medical assistance) and donor insemination(a non-technological procedure widely used by women themselves as a non-coital method of reproduction).

7 It is important to note that Crowe's analysis here queries the scientific discourse that produced the 'pre-embryo' as a 'fact' and a 'status', and not whether or not there are material processes or sequences of development that can be experienced/observed in a woman's pregnancy.

8 See Section 9:1–12 (pp. 48–52).

9 This concern with the reproduction of heterosexuality and heterosexual family formations was not limited, of course, to medical scientific discourse, but constituted a key strand of Thatcherite and, later, Majorite politics and social policy. As many theorists have argued, legislative initiatives since 1979, more generally, have both assumed and fostered female dependency on men and the pattern of female unpaid labour traditionally associated with women's role in the family (Levitas 1986; Franklin, Lury and Stacey 1991; Pateman 1992). The privileging of the nuclear family in the *Warnock Report* reflects and elaborates this trend and has contributed to the climate in which expressly homophobic legislation about parental 'fitness' has been passed during the run-up to the HFE Act in 1990. Section 28 of the Local Government Act 1988, for example, defined lesbian and gay relationships (including lesbian and gay parents and their children) as 'pretended family relationships'. Paragraph 16 of the Children Act 1989 promotes the exclusion of lesbians and gay men from fostering children: '[their] chosen way of life … may mean that they would not be able to provide a suitable environment for the fostering of children'. The phrase 'provide a suitable environment for a child' had appeared in section 2:9 of the *Warnock Report*.

10 See Section 2:5–13 (pp. 11–15).

11 In Britain, government bills are those produced by the party in power,

announced in the Queen's speech at the opening of Parliament and usually passed into law. Private members' Bills are introduced by individuals and, unless there is overwhelming support in both houses (Commons and Lords), usually run out of time. The administrative protocols of government favour the passage of government bills and present significant barriers against the passage of private members' initiatives.

12 After the failure of the Powell Bill, it was reintroduced a year later with minor amendments as the Hargreaves Bill. This Bill also ran out of parliamentary time and failed to become law.

13 Various activists and groups, including those associated with the Feminist International Network of Resistance to Reproductive and Genetic Engineering, made similar critiques.

14 The *Warnock Report*, the DHSS [Department of Health and Social Services] Consultation Document (1986), which called for public responses to proposed terms of legislation, and the White Paper (1987) that preceded the HFE Bill 1989 acknowledged only the embryo-rights position as oppositional. The White Paper, for example, stated that 'responses to the Government's initial consultation on the *Warnock Report* revealed a diversity of strongly held views about research using human embryos' (Paragraph 3, p. 1), yet presented the characteristic two views. Both the York Women's Reproductive Rights Campaign submission (1987) in response to the DHSS consultation and that of the Feminist International Network of Resistance to Reproductive and Genetic Engineering, Britain (1987), argued that embryo research was a form of experimentation on women with IVF which endangered women's reproductive health. While challenging IVF research on women, they also opposed the restriction or banning of 'embryo research' on an embryo rights basis as a violation of women's reproductive rights. This position was not represented in the White Paper.

5

Authoria/logical contests: law, medicine and the voice of authority

The advent of IVF legislation represents the consolidation of three processes: the mediation of competing dominant interests in IVF, including medical scientific professionals (and their advocates), legislators and embryo 'rights' lobbyists (within and outside Parliament);[1] a jurisdictional claim on the terms, orientation and bodies of IVF practice; and, in the course of these processes, an interpellation of the (recombinant, authorial) bodies of IVF as bodies of law. To examine the HFE Act in this light raises two central questions for discussion. The first is the legal framework more generally, both as a mediator of competing agendas and as a form of authorial claim; and the second revolves around the specific organising principles and parameters of the HFE Act.

Adversarial bodies: law as paradigm

Elsewhere I have argued that law is a sphere that is centrally organised around the identification, construction, and mediation of adversarial interests. That is, the *jurisdiction* or territory of the law is conflict and the role and process of law — *jurisprudence* — is the mediation of conflict.[2] Thus the legal body and bodies of law are discursively constituted as adversarial bodies. This is, perhaps, most apparent in the context of criminal law, where 'crime' denotes violated boundaries (and/or bodies) and implies both transgressive (criminal) and transgressed (violated) bodies. Criminal law can follow more than one paradigm. One form, for example, may foreground the offensive 'nature' of crime and criminal (for example murder, assault) and the punitive powers of the State. The HFE Act follows what might more aptly be described as a 'protective' paradigm, foregrounding the special vulnerability of the interests to be protected and the mediatory and regulatory, rather than punitive, powers of the State. Thus, while it enumerates legal and illegal activities (offences) and provides for their punishment, this constitutes a subsidiary concern of the Law as a whole. Most of the HFE Act revolves around the delineation and arbitration of competing interests and the establishment of regulatory procedures and a regulatory agency to resolve a body of 'acceptable' compromise.

Competing authorial agency/ies

In Chapter 2, I critically assessed the agenda for the development of IVF and related practices in the medical scientific model for administering such practices. I suggested that the VLA could be understood as a model for minimally restrictive administrative policy, precisely anticipating the formation of a State Agency for that purpose. In examining the State-proposed agenda for regulating IVF and related practices, it is important to consider the kind of agency involved in State intervention into what has, so far, been a relatively 'free' (that is, professionally insulated and initiated) and ongoing medical scientific practice.

State intervention in the form of establishing legal regulatory standards and a State regulatory agency with respect to IVF practices is an *ex post facto* development. That is, it has occurred after the fact of the existence of these practices. The State did not invent IVF. Nor are legislators agents of the actual practices in question. If invention of the practices in question (and the coining of the language to describe them) could be described as the *agency of invention*, then the role of the State, in the legislative context, can be understood, in this sense, as an *'appropriative* agency', that is, a directive agency exercised by non-medical scientific professionals, after the fact

---

of the invention of practices designated for regulation. How-ever, the jurisdictional claim of the State on the authorial ter-ritories of medical scientific professionals represents not only an adversarial contest but one that involves notable interde-pendencies. Thus, on the one hand, the State, through the medium of law, can be said to be attempting to appropriate a significant dimension of the power to define and manage IVF practices. At the same time, the professional terms and defin-itions of IVF were, of necessity, a central source and reference point for the shape of legislation.[3] On the other hand, in the face of widespread public debate and controversy over IVF capabilities, and particularly over the status of embryos, pro-fessional efforts to protect the traditional exclusivity of profes-sional agency became invested with the normalising power of the State to legitimate professional authorial power and to safeguard the future of IVF. This chapter, then, will begin to consider the ways in which the HFE Act negotiates the prin-cipal terms and orientations that constitute the contested ter-rains of IVF professional practice.

Competing embryo/logics

The intent and parameters of the HFE Act are identified in its introductory summary:

> An Act to make provision in connection with Human Embryos and any subsequent development of such embryos; to prohibit certain practices in connection with embryos and gametes; to establish a Human Fertilisation and Embryology Authority; to make provision about the persons who in certain circumstances are to be treated in law as the parents of a child; and to amend the Surrogacy Arrange-ments Act 1985 (p. 1).

The order of the phrases suggest a hierarchy of importance, indicating that 'provision in connection with Human Embryos' is the priority item and central organising principle of the Act, followed by intentions to make provisions regarding medical scientific practices and definitions of legal parenthood in rela-tion to those practices. Thus, from the outset, the remit of the

Act is clearly delimited in embryo-centred terms. Embryo status is defined in relation to the authoria/logic medical scientific practices and to a legal genea/logic definition of family. The jurisdictional parameters and definitions of medical scientific practice and family revolve, in turn, around embryo status. There are three notable aspects of the embryo-protectionist orientation implicit in this summary. Firstly, and clearly responding to the embryo-'rights'-based challenges to the legitimacy of IVF practices, embryos are foregrounded as both disputed territory and endangered bodies. In this context, IVF ('certain practices') is implicitly constituted as a dangerous but desirable body of knowledge. Embryos are to be protected *from* medical science even as the imposition of statutory regulation promises to normalise IVF as a safe practice. Finally, as I have argued earlier,[4] underpinning both the construction of embryos as disembodied entities and the elaboration of principles around embryo status is an implicit construction of women as dangerous bodies. Thus, while women are absent referents of the HFE Act summary remit, a sensibility of protection *from* women resonates within the embryo-protectionist orientation through which the State is discursively constituted as both embryo protector and rational mediator.

Principal terms and jurisdictional parameters

The embryo-centredness of the HFE Act in categorising and problematising 'certain practices' is reflected in the layout of the principal terms of the Act, that is in the key definitions around which the Act is organised and in the definitions of practices in themselves.

'Embryo'

1 – (1) In this Act, except where otherwise stated –

(a) embryo means a live human embryo where fertilisation is complete, and

(b) references to an embryo include an egg in the process of fertilisation

and, for this purpose, fertilisation is not complete until the appearance of the two cell zygote.

Thus, embryos are defined without reference either to women's reproductive processes and bodies or to the sequence of events through which they come to exist. This definition presupposes, but does not refer to, the IVF procedure performed on women that makes extra-corporeal fertilisation, and identification of the 'completion' of that process, by practitioners, possible.

The second part of this definition of embryo enumerates jurisdictional parameters over embryos specifically in the context of IVF practices:

> 1 – (2) This Act, so far as it governs bringing about the creation of an embryo or the keeping or use of an embryo, applies only to bringing about the creation of an embryo outside the human [sic] body.[5]

Thus embryos are claimed only in the context of IVF and IVF is problematised and claimed for statutory authority *only* in so far as it is seen to relate to embryos. Implicitly, IVF as a treatment of women's reproductive processes and traditional professional authority in that context are normalised. Women are the absent referents on both sides.

(Un)critical distinctions: rewriting IVF authoria/logics

Rather than using the professional terms of 'clinical IVF' as distinguished from 'embryo research', the HFE Act distinguishes three separate categories of IVF practice requiring three separate licenses and three separate consent forms. Identified in the margins of the text of the Act as 'other terms', 'treatment services', 'keeping' and 'using' follow the definition of 'embryo'. The spatial arrangement of principal and 'other' terms suggests a hierarchy of jurisdictional importance; the latter are secondary to and derivative of the former. The delineation of three spheres of practice, from which, interestingly, the dangerous terms of contention – 'embryo' and 'research' – have been dropped, provides a significant illustration of the Act's recuperation of medical scientific licence (through the medium of statutory *licensing*) while appeasing embryo-'rights' challenges to it.

'Treatment services'

2 – (1) 'Treatment services' means medical, surgical or obstetric services provided to the public or a section of the public for the purpose of assisting women to carry children.

The term 'treatment services' is broader than the term 'clinical IVF' used in the VLA *Reports*. While it covers IVF, it can, in fact, encompass more than that.[6] The breadth of application of this definition is established in several significant ways. First, the phrase 'medical, surgical or obstetric services' is not specific to a particular treatment regime. This has the effect of constructing IVF as equivalent to other such services. It is important to remember that there have been no previous attempts legally to delimit or regulate any other form of medical service 'provided for the purpose of assisting women to carry children' (for example, a wide range of conventional infertility treatments). It has been, specifically, the advent of IVF that has motivated the introduction of this law. Thus IVF has not been, as this definition would imply, just another and unremarkable 'obstetric service'. The use of terminology that underplays the differences between IVF and other 'obstetric services', the ways it has obviously had different significance for legislators, normalises and banalises IVF. Similarly, the use of the terms 'services' and 'assist' eclipse conceptual association between IVF, indeed, between women (who, in one of the few moments where there is any direct reference to women, are 'assisted') and 'embryo research'. In these respects, the definition of 'treatment services' follows the logic of the VLA.[7]

A third significant phrase in this definition is 'for the purpose of'. This phrase establishes the criterion of practitioners' intent as the central index of whether or not their 'medical, surgical and obstetric' practices are 'treatment services' or not. This reinforces the authority of the medical scientific profession, the pre-eminence of its own definitions and of practitioners' judgements, and, in effect, its self-regulation. The

---

reinscription of professional authorial power is also reinforced by the rather odd notion that treatment is provided 'to the public' – a term which not only seems to distinguish patients as non-professionals but, interestingly, seems to distinguish women from 'the public'. Furthermore, in a context of the language of treatment 'services', IVF seems almost to be imbued with the character of 'public service'.

Finally, of course, comes the definition of pregnancy as 'women ... carry[ing] a child', a characteristic definition forwarded by the embryo 'rights' (anti-abortion) lobby which consistently refers to an embryo as an unborn 'child'. It also reflects the medical profession's historical view of embryos as separate entities for which women are a 'uterine environment' (Franklin 1991; Fyfe 1991). The use of this definition within and as part of the definition of 'treatment services' reinforces not only an embryo-centred understanding of IVF, but by extension, all 'other medical, surgical and obstetric' practices claimable under this section. Thus, the incorporation of IVF into the broad category of 'other ... practices' is complemented by the incorporation of 'other ... practices' into the embryo-centred agenda for the regulation of IVF. Clearly, it is an agenda that is substantively shared by both legislators and medical scientists.

'Keeping'

2 – (2) References in the Act to keeping in relation to embryos or gametes including keeping while preserved, whether preserved by cryopreservation or in any other way; and embryos or gametes so kept are referred to in this Act as 'stored' (and 'store' and 'storage' are to be interpreted accordingly) (p. 2).

Though it has not been considered as a separate category of 'IVF' practices by practitioners, the rather euphemistic term 'keeping' none the less derives and follows on from the embryo-centred logic of the clinical/research distinction. Why legislators deemed it necessary to create this third category is an interesting question.

For example, it might seem an 'obvious' and 'logical' distinction to make, since from the point of reference of embryos and gametes, creating them, storing them and researching upon them seem ostensibly separate activities. Possibly these activities occur at separate locations; different laboratories for example, or different locations within the same laboratory (the Petri dish, the storage tank, under the microscope). Yet with women as a point of reference, both 'keeping' and research on embryos ('using') are predicated on their undergoing IVF. With a similar embryo/science-centred logic as 'treatment services', the construction of 'keeping' as a separate category implies that these activities are unrelated to one another.[8]

'Using'

Interestingly, the term 'using' (as in 'using' embryos or gametes), which is the term used to mean research[9] throughout most of the Act, is not presented in the glossary of 'principal terms', though of course, effectively, it is one of them. Like the term 'keeping', 'using' would seem to have been chosen for its strategic value in linguistically eclipsing the provocative terminology of 'embryo research' and thus effectively deflating the embryo-'rights'-based rhetoric of opposition to IVF 'embryo research' practices. Certainly, with a vote pending on whether or not such IVF research would be allowed to continue, the shift of terminology that first appeared in the HFE Bill may also have been calculated to foster a pro-research outcome (thus reflecting a hegemony within Parliament of the pro-IVF embryo/logic).

Whatever the many possible reasons behind them, it remains that the construction of categorical distinctions among IVF practices, even within a narrow embryo/science-centred frame of reference, is a contradictory and arbitrary exercise. I would suggest that one of the central consequences of making these distinctions, however, is the way it makes the Law appear to be more rigorous and restrictive than it is. Indeed, having created a category that medical scientists did not use, and as I will discuss below, creating three separate licensing procedures on the basis of these distinctions, the Law appears to be doing its 'job' of 'protection' against the putative excesses of medical scientific power.

As I suggested above, a model of protective legislation constructs (or presupposes) endangering acts or practices and endangered entities and endangering agents. In this framework, legislators, through the medium of law, take the role of a protection agency. In the context of the HFE Act, and through the principal terms within it, what is problematised and what is to be protected is a key issue. In so far as the Law makes provisions in relation to embryos, it constructs, at an explicit level, 'certain' medical scientific practices, namely IVF, as potentially endangering. Thus the Law seems to offer to protect embryos against apparent danger of loose ethics among medical scientific professionals and against (some) medical scientific practices (and plans for developments in IVF technology).

However, the conceptualisation of embryos as separate entities from women participates in the anti-abortion logic that posits women as dangerous to embryo life. Thus, an implicit problematisation of women underscores the erasure of their agency and connection to embryos, an erasure that is articulated in the medical scientific agenda for IVF and reproduced in the Law. The erasure of women, on the other hand, contributes to the science-centredness of definitions of practice within the Law. Indeed, the reproduction of the medical scientific definitions of practice in the form of the Law (with only slight modifications) represents a powerful protection of the medical scientific agenda and of professional autonomy and judgements. Moreover, in utilising the medical scientific language and agenda as central reference points for the contents of the Law, stringent embryo protectionism is itself problematised. Here the Law also offers protection to IVF (embryo) researchers from the agenda of embryo 'rights' advocates.

Clearly, in terms of protection, the HFE Act is rather contradictory. The conflicts the Law constructs and arbitrates lie chiefly between the embryo 'rights' and medical scientific agendas around the 'special status' of embryos, and between the State and the medical scientific profession over which institution will have ultimate powers to define the scope of practice. What is consistent here, however, is that the Law does not provide a framework wherein the protection of women is prioritised (or perhaps possible). Indeed, that women constitute the contested bodies in authorial conflicts over embryos and IVF is effectively obscured.

Licensing the (in)distinctions

The meanings of 'licence', according to the dictionary, include: 'n. permission; leave; unrestrained liberty; legal permit to do something otherwise unlawful; v.t. to authorise by a legal permit' (Webster). To license an activity is to legitimate it, with respect to the State. Licensing, moreover, constitutes, at the same time, a jurisdictional claim by the State upon the activity (and actors) in question. Hence, in a sense, a statutorily licensed activity is transformed, by the issue of the licence, into an act of State as much as it is an act of particular (non-state) agents. The licences conferred upon medical scientists and their practices under the HFE Act promise not only to legitimate them, but also to imbue them with the 'appropriative agency' of the State.

For the most part, medical scientists and their various enterprises enjoy a *de facto* discretionary licence (which follows from their formal investiture/licence as medical practitioners). Such licence is assumed within and outside the profession, and is one which, until the introduction of the HFE Act, included IVF practices. Thus the proposal to establish a system of licensing in this sphere challenges at one and the same time the legitimacy of the practices in question, of the powers accruing to medical registration,[10] and of the traditional self-regulatory authority characterising the medical scientific profession. In the run-up to the Act, medical scientists in this field consistently argued that it was precisely their freedom of choice and practice that has made it possible to invent IVF and related procedures. State regulation was constituted, in this sense, as a harbinger of fatal impediments to the unambiguous good of medical scientific 'progress'.

At the same time, however, medical scientists have not

opposed the passage of legislation on their practices in this sphere, despite the potential such State intervention would have seriously to interfere with, or even to curtail, their practices. Indeed, they have actively advocated the introduction of a State-created licensing system. As I discussed in Chapter 2, the VLA was formed precisely anticipating legislation (and as a self-evident effort to shape, if not predetermine, its substance). The expressed support from most practitioners (who acted as spokespersons for the community) perhaps reflected a sense by the community that legislation was inevitable. Perhaps it was considered prudent by practitioners not to oppose legislative involvement in their practice, but actively to participate in its creation. Certainly it demonstrates that, however removed the community is from substantive accountability to the lay public, or even their patients/experimental subjects, they are not invulnerable to 'public opinion', or at least the opinions of powerful outsiders from powerful institutions. Moreover, if practitioners had much of their current practice at risk (i.e. 'embryo research'), they clearly had much to gain from formal State legitimation of their practices. Indeed, the licensing procedure itself, if it was organised around professionally determined standards, could bolster professional gate-keeping. Although the State proposed to appropriate some measure of the self-regulatory power of the medical science profession, at the same time it offered to protect the profession from challenges by other 'outsiders', such as embryo 'rights' activists (and feminists).

Conditions for licensing 'treatment services'

The conditions of the HFE Act for licensing 'treatment services' establish the components of 'good' IVF practice. These include: the specification of what constitutes IVF as a 'treatment service'; requirements for the selection of IVF patients; and a mandate for the provision of counselling.

Schedule 2 of the Act (entitled 'Activities for which Licences may be Granted') lists the following activities as a definition of 'treatment services':

(a) bringing about the creation of embryos *in vitro*

(b) keeping embryos

(c) using gametes

(d) practices designed to secure that embryos are in a suitable condition to be placed in a woman or to determine whether embryos are suitable for that purpose

(e) placing any embryo in a woman

(f) [interspecies fertilisation tests on sperm motility]

(g) and other practices as may be specified in or determined in accordance with regulations (Schedule 2 1(1) pp. 34–5).

Three particular points can be made about this list of activities. First is the clear embryo-centredness of the definition of 'treatment services', women being mentioned only as recipients of manipulated, extra-corporeal embryos. Second is the (indirect) inclusion of preimplantation diagnostic practices under (d). The practices of selecting embryos can include those that are intended to determine basic viability as well as those that are more explicitly genea/logic in character (i.e. genetic selection, sex pre-selection). The lack of definition for the term 'suitable' leaves the parameters of genea/logical selection open and reinscribes it as a constitutent of professional discretion. Third is the inclusion of 'keeping embryos' under the auspices of a 'treatment services' licence. If embryos may be 'kept' under a treatment licence, why is a separate 'keeping' licence necessary? The boundaries that licences are ostensibly meant to maintain are thus blurred, as the Act would seem explicitly to contradict its own categorical distinctions.

In addition to embryo selection, the Act locates screening of patients (and gamete 'donors') as a condition of licensable 'treatment services':

> A woman shall not be provided with treatment services unless account has been taken of the welfare of any child who may be born as a result of the treatment (including the need of that child for a father), and of any other child who may be affected by the birth (Section 13 (5) p. 7).

This clause, which was, as I shall discuss in the proceeding chapter, the result of much controversy over the perceived power of IVF to disrupt conventional definitions of family and

---

'proper' reproductive sexuality, constitutes, and reinscribes as a matter of law, the heterosexist genea/logics underpinning professional discourses on IVF. It provides not only a licence, but almost a mandate,[11] for eugenic selections within and through the 'treatment services' covered by the Act.[12]

Paragraph 6 of section 13, in another signficant reference to gender, provides that:

> A woman shall not be provided with any treatment services ... unless the woman being treated and, where she is being treated together with a man, the man have been given a suitable opportunity to receive proper counselling about the implications of taking the proposed steps, and have been provided with such relevant information as is proper (Section 13 (6) p. 7).

Seeming, at least superficially, to go against the grain of the embryo/science-centredness of the Act, this paragraph explicitly recognises that women (rather than the 'public') are 'provided with treatment services'. Moreover, a distinction is made between a woman receiving treatment and a woman 'being treated together with a man'. This would seem to allow for the possibility for a non-heterosexual(ly) partnered or single woman to undergo IVF, an interesting contradiction in the light of the preceding directive about children's 'need' for fathers (and the *de facto* selection practices of clinics). None the less, this provision reinforces the erasures implicit in the concept of 'IVF couple'; in the course of 'treatment together with a man', it is, of course, only the woman who receives treatment.

As a mandate for the provision of counselling as part of IVF 'treatment services', the terms 'suitable' and 'proper' are significant. While these terms imply a strong mandate for substantive counselling and information provision, what exactly constitutes 'suitable opportunity', 'proper counselling' or 'information as is proper'[13] is not spelled out, thus implicitly leaving such definition to professional discretion.[14]

The only substantive restriction attached to the licensing of 'treatment services' regards the genetic alteration of an embryo (Schedule 2 1(4) p. 35). This would legally rule out the reimplantation in women of 'transgenic embryos', and, in the light of many practitioners' investment in the future of 'gene therapy', would seem to constitute a significant restriction of practice. However, the genetic manipulation of embryos *is* legitimate under a research licence, and a practitioner may hold more than one licence at the same time. Thus, while the immediate prospect of intentional engineering of transgenic children would seem to be obviated by the conditions of 'treatment services' licensing, the process of research into transgenesis is effectively validated, if simultaneously obscured, as is the preconditional necessity of 'treatment services' for genetic research on embryos.[15]

Conditions for licences to 'keep'

Presumably, a separate licence for keeping is intended to guarantee that practitioners are specially qualified and that the equipment that they use is inspected and up to a certain standard before licences are granted. It could be argued, for example, that different skills and tools are required for IVF 'treatment services' than for cryopreservation. Yet, if this is so, why is 'keeping embryos' (and gametes) included in the treatment licence?

Perhaps the most significant provision under the conditions for licences to 'keep' embryos refers to the establishment of a statutory storage period:

> [N]o gametes or embryos shall be kept in storage for longer than the statutory storage period and, if stored at the end of the period, shall be allowed to perish (Section 14(1)(c) p. 7).

The VLA guidelines (see Chapter 2), in a similar provision, used the term 'dispose of' rather than 'perish', where 'dispose of' could be taken to mean allow to perish, but could also be taken to mean 'use'. Thus, the use of the term 'perish' here establishes a substantially more restrictive condition on practitioners' custodial 'rights' over stored embryos and gametes.[16] In particular, this provision would seem to prevent the use of gametes and embryos stored under the contingent auspices of 'treatment services' and 'keeping' licences (and consent forms) as automatic material for research at the end of the statutory storage period.[17]

However, as with other licences, licences for 'keeping' embryos require specific consent by gamete 'donors' (that is, 'donors' must give separate consent for each category of IVF practice). The Act provides that the terms of consent may be withdrawn or 'varied' throughout the storage period. There is nothing in the Act that states that 'persons' responsible for storage facilities may not contact gamete 'donors' (who did not consent in the first instance) to 'lobby' for a variation on their terms of consent; i.e. to change a consent for storage into a consent for research, before the end of the statutory storage period.

Licences for research[18]

A licence under this paragraph may authorise any of the following:
(a) bringing about the creation of embryos *in vitro*, and
(b) keeping or using embryos (Schedule 2, 3(1) p. 35).

Once more there is the characteristic blurring of ostensibly categorical distinctions among 'treatment services': 'keeping' and 'using' as licences for research would seem to obviate the need for treatment and storage licences.[19] The provision for research licences includes the following ('necessary and desirable') activities:
(a) promoting advances in the treatment of infertility
(b) increasing knowledge about the causes of congenital disease
(c) increasing knowledge about the causes of miscarriage
(d) developing more effective techniques of contraception
(e) developing methods for detecting the presence of gene or chromosome abnormalities in embryos before implantation
or for such other purposes as may be specified in regulations (Schedule 2 3(2) p. 35).

In Chapter 2, I examined a similar list proposed by the VLA, for whom 'necessary and desirable' research activities included: 'diagnosis and treatment of infertility or of genetic disorders or … the development of safe and more effective contraceptive measures (VLA 1986 p. 31). The research activities legitimated in the HFE Law include three extra categories.

In Chapter 2, I argued that the VLA-defined goals provided little substantive restriction on the study of women's reproductive processes. The expanded list of legitimate research activities provided in the HFE Act reflects a similar logic. Moreover, as with the VLA, these activities presuppose women undergoing IVF while linguistically erasing that involvement. Likewise, the Act reinscribes the professional constructions of IVF research as springboard for the creation (and application) of technological and other capabilities that are far removed from infertility treatments (the reasons most women will undergo IVF) and, indeed, from IVF practices. In turn, the genea/logics of developing contraception,[20] and genetic diagnostic capabilities colour the fundamental meaning of IVF 'treatment services'.

Prohibited activities and offences

There are two types of prohibitions outlined in the HFE Act. One set of prohibitions concerns the practice of any otherwise legitimate IVF activity without a licence, and/or exceeding the 14-day limitation on 'using'. A second set of prohibitions lists particular activities, defined as offences, that cannot be legitimated by licence. These include: interspecies embryo transfer and nuclear transfer [cloning], 'offences' that are punishable by fines and/or imprisonment.

The activities defined as offences here are significant in considering the meaning of 'protective' legislation. Firstly, they replicate the medical scientific prohibitions on IVF practice outlined in the VLA *Reports*. The difference here is that where, under the authority of the VLA, practitioners who violated these prohibitions were subject to the censure of their own community (and where the form of that censure was indeterminate), under State authority they become criminally liable and the form of punishment is specified. However, aside from practising without a licence, the other prohibited activities serve, I would suggest, as more form than substance. For example, up to the date of the passage of the HFE Act, it had not been possible to maintain a live embryo beyond 14 days gestation (indeed, even up to 14 days). Thus the prohibition on 'keeping' beyond the statutory limit is outside the range of what is, today, scientifically possible.[21]

It has proved to be the case that as scientific capabilities 'progress', laws regulating them are changed. In the case of abortion in Britain, for example, the development of neonatal technological capabilities, purportedly leading to earlier fetal viability (that is, capabilities of being born alive),[22] has been used by parliamentarians as a basis for lowering the time-limit of legal abortion (Science and Technology Subgroup 1991). Thus, it is not unlikely that, as IVF technology develops, certain prohibitions outlined in this Act will be reviewed and modified to accommodate whatever the state of the art is at the time.

Underlying the drawing up of such prohibitions is a notion of 'good' and 'bad' science. Licensed IVF activities outlined in the Act are 'good' by contrast to unlicensed activities. Moreover, cloning and human–animal hybridity have been held up as quintessential examples of 'bad' science, particularly in the media.[23] It is interesting to consider why these particular activities have become the icons of science out of control. Methodologically, for example, they are not dissimilar to IVF practices that are considered legitimate. However, the culturally inscribed 'fear' of human–animal hybridity, for example, can be linked to historical iconographies of 'mad' and physically disabled people as monstrous bodies and to deeply embedded racial hatreds underpinning the notion of miscegenation. Indeed, the 'spectre' of human–animal hybridity associated with IVF genetic capabilities can be read as a contemporary (re)inscription of miscegenation 'fears'. Human cloning is discursively constituted in similar terms, referring not only to miscegenation discourses, but also, I would suggest, to cultural disquietudes around the industrial recombinant logics of mass production. In this sense, IVF capabilities are implicitly constituted as potential 'dark satanic mills' from which a *brave new world* of animalised humans may be mass-produced (and enslaved, in turn, as workers in mass production).[24] Finally, the construction of interspecies fertilisation and nuclear transfer as unacceptable practices also draws (rather ambivalently) on cultural disquiet around human experimentation. For example, the question of IVF as a possible form of experimentation on women has not constituted a dimension of dominant 'moral' debates about reproductive technologies. Given the discursive erasures of women in professional (and legal) IVF discourse, this is not particularly surprising.

One of the effects of the constitution of interspecies fertilisation and nuclear transfer as monstrous practices is the normalisation of all other IVF practices. In this context, the methodological similarities between illegitimate and legitimate IVF practices are eclipsed, as are the questions of risks to women's (and their offspring's) health and the social implications of the embryo-centred genea/logics of IVF. Moreover, it is significant that the named banned activities are associated with 'research' rather than 'treatment services'. Here, again, the arbitrary distinction drawn between clinical/research IVF is reinforced. The location of 'bad' science only in the 'research' context implicitly reinforces the notion that IVF 'treatment services' are essentially benign. Finally, it can be argued that the fact that the prohibited activities are either not doable or not (to public knowledge) done[25] makes them strategic targets of such representations. Thus the bans on unpractised practices effectively serve further to legitimate those practices that are in use. They reinforce the notion that licensing procedures will 'protect' the public from 'bad' science while, at the same time, not presenting substantial restrictions on practice.

Upwards accountability

Taken as a whole, the HFE Act constitutes a remit for the establishment of medical scientific accountability to the State for the practices under the Law's jurisdiction. Indeed, most of the text of the Act is made up of provisions for the establishment of procedures through which that accountability will be exercised and a complex bureaucracy that administers those procedures. However, as we have seen so far, the HFE Act is organised around and substantively protects the medically and scientifically defined agenda for IVF practices. Indeed, the Law structurally provides for the continuation of the better part of professional self-regulation, co-opting as it does professional standards and aims. There are, in addition, a number of additional loopholes within the seemingly rigorous procedures established by the State to regulate IVF practices.

For example, one of the provisions of the Law requires the drawing up of a code of practice (Sections 25–6 p. 15). However, to violate the code is not a criminal offence. At worst, a violation might lead to a loss of licence to practice; but this is up to the discretion of the Authority. Thus the obligations outlined in the code of practice are not strictly binding.

Moreover, in the provisions regarding offences and punishment, there are several let-out clauses that undermine their power. Section 41 (p. 27) of the Act provides that 'it is a defence for a person ["the defendant"] charged with an offence' to prove: 'firstly, that "he" was acting under the direction of another; secondly, that "he" had reason to believe "he" was acting under a person holding a licence; and thirdly that at the time of the offence "he" was a licence holder' and 'took all such steps as were reasonable and exercised all due diligence to avoid committing the offence'. I would suggest that these provisions would/will make it difficult to convict a practitioner of an offence. Firstly, under these provisions, subordinate workers are not held responsible for their own actions.[26] Secondly, an offence is constituted not simply by undertaking prohibited activities, but doing so with express intent to break the law. In general, the difficulty of proving criminal intent, particularly in the context where crime is *defined* by intent, is exacerbated by the extent to which the defendants occupy socially privileged positions.[27] Similarly, the defence of 'diligent' avoidance would probably be argued in the technical language of medical science in front of a court composed largely of laypeople, and these circumstances would militate against the likelihood of conviction.

Under the provisions for enforcement, members and employees of the HFE Authority are given the right to enter and inspect premises, to issue warrants or confiscate material if there is suspicion of an offence, and to begin proceedings for the variation or revocation of a licence (Section 39 pp. 24–5).

However, these powers of enforcement are ambivalent in the face of the licensing procedure itself. Under the terms of the HFE Act, individuals ('persons responsible') hold licences and are responsible for the collective practices of clinics (Section 17 p. 9). The ramifications of this individualisation of responsibility are many-layered. First, it misrepresents the way IVF practices are carried out – in teams of practitioners of varying specialisations and power. The provisions, on the one hand, make one individual appear responsible for the actions of colleagues and, on the other hand, significantly erase the individual and collective agency and responsibility of most IVF practitioners.

Moreover, the term 'person' is used throughout the Act to describe anyone from the least powerful – IVF patients and their partners – to the most powerful – practitioners and members or employees of the Authority. The terminology of 'person', used indiscriminately this way, implies a manifestly false 'equality' of status and therefore a false equivalence of responsibility and agency among these 'persons'. This rhetorical erasure of power differences among 'persons', in conjunction with the individualisation of authority in the IVF context, facilitates the protection of IVF practitioners from substantive accountability to patients and to the public at large.

Aside from the very limited possibilities of prosecution for offences, the main avenue of accountability lies in record-keeping and reports, both of which are submitted to higher authorities, and both of which form central requirements in obtaining and keeping licences to practise. This, like all the measures discussed so far is a form of what might be termed 'upwards accountability'. While the Act does require the provision of information to patients, as I discussed above, what constitutes 'reasonable' information-giving is not defined. While the Authority may publish reports that are available to the public, they themselves determine their contents. The HFE Act does not offer direct or substantive protection for IVF patients nor substantive forms of accountability to the general public. Rather it protects the professional exclusivity of medical scientific agency, making profesionals accountable, but only in very limited ways, to the authority (agency) of the State, which is itself professionally exclusive.

Notes

1 The most prominent 'embryo rights' lobbyists in this context tended to be representatives of conservative organised religious groups (e.g. the Catholic Church) and powerful anti-abortion groups (e.g. the Society for the Protection of the Unborn Child (SPUC).

2 See my discussion of the legal paradigm in the context of abortion legislation in Britain in Steinberg (1991).

3 With respect to the medical scientific professions, government legislators are in the same position as most laypeople (albeit the most educationally advantaged laypeople). In order to understand what medical scientists are doing, most of us are forced to rely on those translations provided by practitioners when they are writing or speaking for those outside their own professional community. Or, if we have considerable time and resources for research (which most legislators do not have), we may be able to educate ourselves to some level of fluency in the medical scientific language. Most of us will not be able to observe actual practices, nor (unless we become medical or science students) have hands-on experience of them (although we may have experience of undergoing them as patients). Thus, our access to the profession is almost inescapably at one remove. Thus legislators, in the context of the HFE Act, have had to rely, for the most part, on medical scientific explanations of what the professionals are doing and on *ex post facto* sources, such as the mainstream media and on the assessments of powerful interest groups (such as the embryo 'rights' lobby).

4 See, for example, Raymond 1987; Baruch *et al.* 1988; Science and Technology Subgroup 1991).

5 Further refinements to its definition of the jurisdictional parameters over embryos appear as follows:
(a) references to embryos, the creation of which was brought about *in vitro* (in their application to those where fertilisation is complete) are to those where fertilisation began outside the human [*sic*] body whether or not it was completed there...
(3) This Act, so far as it governs the keeping or use of an embryo applies only to the keeping or using of an embryo outside the human body.

6 For example, clauses of the Act cover Donor Insemination (in which there are no extra-corporeal embryos 'created').

7 Maureen McNeil suggested to me that the language of 'services' is also a direct reference to consumerism. As such, she argued, 'it fits in with a more general trend to regard all aspects of health provision as consumer goods (like restaurant service, etc.).' It also, arguably, locates the 'con-

sumption' of IVF 'services' with what is generally considered to be 'women's work' of consumption (e.g. shopping) in our culture – an occupation that is more often seen as leisure than as labour (Winship 1987). IVF, in this light, can appear to be, if not precisely a leisure activity, then at least an activity that is not associated with work (or hardship).

8 It is also possible that one of the rationales for defining 'keeping' as a separate sphere of IVF practice has to do with concerns about potential custody disputes that could arise over 'kept' embryos (for example, in cases where a sperm 'donor' has died, or where the 'IVF couple' have divorced). However, as the issue of custodial power over the future of embryos is outlined in the regulations on 'donor' consent (see Chapter 5), where the future 'use' of embryos depends upon consent of both 'donors', it is not clear how having a separate 'keeping' category clarifies the issue (or indeed would prevent custody suits regardless of (and challenging) the tenets of the law).

9 Although 'using' is not definitively limited to research.

10 The HFE Act establishes the need for a second licence to practise IVF, thus introducing a significant limitation on professional definitions of medical hierarchy, discretion and entitlements to practise.

11 The phrase 'unless account has been taken' does not constitute a direct injunction against treatment of unmarried, non-heterosexual women with IVF and related practices. Like the ambiguous prohibition against the 'promotion of homosexuality' in Section 28 of the Local Government Act 1988, 'account taken' establishes a punitive and restrictive climate without clarifying the terms of the burdens of proof one way or the other.

12 As I discuss in Chapter 6, this clause was initiated by a furore over the provision of Donor Insemination to unmarried women, and both DI and IVF are covered by the terms of the HFE Act.

13 Indeed, the phrase 'such relevant information as is proper' could be taken to imply that there is relevant information that it is not proper to provide (I am grateful to David Phelps for this insight.)

14 This provision also does not rule out the possibility of counselling's being offered by a member of the IVF team (or a genetic counsellor).

15 The phrase 'genetic alteration of embryos' poses ambiguities in itself. Presumably, it refers to the intentional alteration of embryos by practitioners (i.e. genetic research under a research licence). However, 'genetic alteration' may occur as a 'side-effect' of IVF treatment. Indeed the entire IVF 'treatment service' process, which includes hormonal induction to women, extraction and manipulation of their eggs in a chemical culture medium, 'keeping' and preimplantation diagnosis (which may include the excision of one or more embryonic cells for genetic analysis [embryo biopsy]), all 'necessary and desirable' practices licensed as 'treatment', could have mutagenic effects on embryos. The indices of practice distinctions seem to rely, then, on statements of practitioner intent in the face of what are, at an

empirical level, clearly shaky boundaries.

16 One possible motive for the change in wording that is observable between the VLA Guidelines and the HFE Act may have been the desire to obviate potential adverse publicity from the 'embryo rights' lobby that might otherwise have been excited by the strong linguistic associations between the verb 'dispose of' that appears in the earlier wording and its most characteristic objects, viz 'rubbish' or 'garbage': it could be argued that it might not have appeared very politic or 'caring' to speak in such terms. (I am grateful to David Phelps for this insight).

17 The tensions underpinning the compromise of conflicting embryo/logic interests encapsulated in this change of terminology were dramatically brought to the fore in July 1996 when news broke that some 3000 to 4000 (of an estimated 10 million) stored embryos in IVF clinics around Britain were due to be destroyed on August 1 1996 (the end of the statutory storage period) due to the inability of clinics to trace parents to renew their consent for storage. The media moral panic which ensured was infused with anti-abortionist rhetoric. A consensus appeared to emerge that this disposition of frozen embryos represented the destruction of potential children; neither journalists nor IVF practitioners/researchers mentioned the interests of research in their opposition to what one newscaster termed a 'prenatal massacre'. Indeed, the newsprint debate focused almost entirely on the need to find parents to *renew* consent for storage; the possibility that they might wish to *vary* (or be asked to consider varying) their consent to allow for research (a possibility expressly allowed by the HFE Act) was never mentioned. The implicit disavowal of research in this context would seem to accrue directly from the tensions encoded into the distinction so strenuously pursued both by practitioners and by legislators between 'treatment embryos' (as potential children) and 'research embryos', a distinction which obscures the fact that both sets of embryos are produced in the 'treatment' context. Ironically, the concession by IVF researchers to embryo-protectionist interests in supporting this distinction in order to *protect* research interests would seem, at the very least, to be a fragile contract. Whether this event and the panic in its wake will herald a shift in the regulations for storage (or in *de facto* practices with respect to the securing of consent and keeping of contact with parents) and in which direction remains to be seen. What is clear is that competing embryo/logic interests create profound contradictions in the negotiation and regulation of what is perceived to be legitimate IVF practice. (See, for example, Mihill, 23.7.96; Dudley-Edwards, 24.7.96.)

18 Interestingly, the term 'research' is used in this section of the Act as opposed to the more inclusive (and less direct) term 'using', which appears throughout most of the Act.

19 This provision seems to allow for the possibility that women might go through IVF practices only to provide embryos for research.

20 At a conference on women's health that I attended in Bangladesh in 1989

a number of speakers raised the issue of the possible development of genetically engineered contraceptive vaccines in the context of IVF research – a 'product' which, it was argued, would be targeted for distribution in countries (typically non-Western) where long-term (experimental) hormone contraceptives were currently being used in population control programmes.

21 Moreover, if there have been interspecies transfer or cloning experiments involving human embryos or gametes, these have not been allowed to reach public attention. I would suggest that either they have not been seriously attempted or, where they are, it is beyond the boundaries of lay scrutiny (and probably beyond the scrutiny of any statutory Authority).

22 The capability of being born alive does not necessarily mean the capability of staying alive. It has been the case, for example, that where neonatal technologies have prolonged the lives of extremely premature infants, devastating damage to the bones, organs and brains of these infants has often resulted and rates of infant/child mortality remain extremely high.

23 This 'fear' has, it seems, been mostly limited to the notion of fusing human/animal interspecies gametes and birthing human/animal hybrids. At a molecular level, the incorporation of human genes in animals (e.g. the 'super mouse') has not been interpellated into the horror genre of journalism. Nor have interspecies animal hybrids (e.g. the 'geep', which fuses sheep and goat gametes) generated a comparable degree of popular alarm to that generated by the possibility of human/animal hybridity. (A wide selection of media representations (from Britain and a range of other countries) around this issue can be found at the GEN/ARCHIV, Essen, Germany).

24 This was precisely the theme of Aldous Huxley's *Brave New World* (1977 [1932]) and is, indeed, a common dystopian vision of reproductive technologies in science fiction.

25 These practices are currently carried out in the context of IVF veterinary research. However, veterinary research, while the basis and origin for most medical scientific practices used on humans, has been subject to far less professional (and legal) limitation on possible practices – for which it has been the target of considerable social protest but little social restriction.

26 Indeed, the terminology of 'following orders' is rather disturbing, given its recent historical prominence in the context of the Nuremberg trials of National Socialist 'war criminals' (Arendt 1963/4).

27 White, middle-class 'respectable' male professionals are not, typically, arrested or convicted of crimes. (And when they are, they tend to serve comparatively lighter sentences.)

6

Rewriting recombinant bodies

The implications of reproductive law for women's reproductive and social status have been a central concern within feminist politics. As Lupton (1994) notes, the contemporary women's health movement has been grounded both in a critique of the erosion of women's reproductive health, rights and social status through professional and state claims on (and about) women's reproductive bodies and in a politic of *reclaiming* and redefining women's bodily self-determination as a right (pp. 125–9). In this context, feminist struggles for reproductive autonomy have involved contradictory investments *in* and rejections *of* law and medical science as sites through which women may empower themselves and find remedy for the oppressions accruing from medico/legal struggles over women's wombs. The extent to which these discourses may be *rewritten* in feminist terms has been a point of considerable dispute and is a key question underpinning my examination of the medico/legal discourses of IVF.

In the first part of this book, I examined the ways in which women are discursively constituted as recombinant bodies within professional languages and practices of IVF. In the last chapter, I argued that in so far as the HFE Act constitutes a reconstitution of professional agendas for IVF futures, so too are the bodies of professional knowledges *rewritten* as bodies of law. The embryo/logic contests that have shaped IVF legislation, both in Britain and elsewhere, reflect historical preoccupations with and a history of competing claims over the *captured wombs*[1] of women. The HFE Act, in this context, follows a trajectory of medico/legal inscriptions of women's reproductive bodies and agency in which notions of endangerment (of embryos and/or of the social order) are seen to inhere. Yet within the embryo and science-centred agendas mediated by the HFE Act, women are constituted as dangerous (docile and divided) bodies and presupposed as the bodily vessels and yet beneficiaries of scientific progress.

These contradictory currents within the Act's *rewriting* of IVF futures and their implications for women's civil status are the concerns of this chapter. Here, a number of the Act's provisions will be assessed not only in terms of their implications for women undergoing IVF and related practices, but also in terms of the ways in which the legal principles elaborated in the Act may interpellate all women, in variable ways, whether or not they will ever be IVF patients.

Exclusionary bodies and legal languages

The endorsement of the medical scientific terminology and framework in the HFE Act reflects and extends the discursive erasures of women as principles of law. Where women are and are not referred to, in a legislative framework that is organised around treatments only women will undergo, constitute significant markers of a legislative agenda for a reconstitution of women's reproductive and civil status. I have noted in the preceding chapter that women do not feature largely in the linguistic matrix of the Act and in its substantive re-presentation of professional definitions of IVF practice and policy. In this context, the linguistic conventions of legal discourse would seem to reify the constitution of women as the absent/present bodies of professional inquiry. At the same time, however, there are significant tensions in the terms through which the Act mediates the reproductive and civil agency of women.

'Person'

The term 'person', for example, is used throughout the Act but has different meanings depending upon (but not necessarily made clear by) the particular context in which it appears. At different times throughout the text of the Act, 'person' refers variously to: members of the Licensing Authority, committee members, licence holders, practitioners and other persons to whom licences apply, women receiving IVF, their presumptively male partners and other providers of gametes. Deciphering which 'person' is being referred to in any particular clause is made more difficult when more than one referent is involved (not an infrequent occurrence).

The indiscriminate use of 'person' seems clearly to be a product of the linguistic conventions of legal discourse. However, to dismiss it for this reason would be to fail to appreciate the way such a convention reflects, (re)organises and at the same time denies unequal power relations among the 'persons' lumped together under the same linguistic category. For example, as I discussed in the last chapter, the terminology of 'persons' individualises the deployment of State and medical scientific institutional power, and thus obscures both the institutional character of power relations in the IVF context and the ways in which these relations are gendered. Conversely, intrinsic to the appellation of 'person' is an attribution of legal *personhood*. The designation of women as 'persons' would seem, therefore, to constitute a straightforward recognition (indeed, protection) of women as reproductive and civil agents, as subjects rather than objects of professional practice. As we shall see, however, in the light of the Act's preoccupation with definitions of embryo 'personhood' and 'fit' parenting, the personhood of women necessarily constitutes a question rather than a given.

'He'

In addition to, and qualifying, the standard use of 'person' is a similar use of the pronoun 'he'. The standardised use of 'he', also characteristic of legal discourse, both interpellates and

---

erases women not only as bodies of male knowledge but even, rather bizarrely, as male bodies. For example:

3 – (1) Before a person gives consent under this Schedule –
(a) *he* must be given a suitable opportunity to receive proper counselling about the implications of taking the proposed steps, and
(b) *he* must be provided with such relevant information as is proper (Schedule 3, 3(1), p. 37, my emphasis).

The 'provisions under this Schedule' are those which outline the conditions of consent for IVF (treatment, storage or research). 'Person' and 'he' in this clause refer to those providing the gametes for IVF procedures. 'He', then, means women (as well as men).

While both men and women 'provide' gametes for it, only women will undergo IVF procedures; and while the hierarchy of the profession is dominated by male practitioners, patients are exclusively women. Both constitute gendered divisions of labour that are entirely obscured by the terminology of 'he'. The use of male generics has long been problematised by feminists both for the ways they obscure (and in so doing reinforce) power differences between men and women and for the way, when referring to those holding power, they actually refer primarily to men. To use 'he' in this context is a particularly acute illustration of the exclusionary sexism of legal conventions, and the contradictions that arise when the law deals with (women's) reproduction.

'Donors'

Besides male-centred terminology, the Act also uses gender-'neutral' formulations such as 'persons whose gametes are kept and used' and 'gamete donors'. The gender-'neutrality' of both formulations reconstitutes a false equivalence of position between men and women with respect to IVF procedures. As a legal inscription of the notion of 'IVF couples', 'gamete donors' (along with the notion of a woman treated 'together with a man') construct the civil personhood of women as relational rather than autonomous.[2] Moreover, when 'donor' refers

to women undergoing IVF 'treatment services', it also dis-
claims precisely the position of women *as* patients.[3] Indeed
'donor' perhaps most pointedly encapsulates the discursive
recombinant logic of IVF, which, in making material the conceptual separation not only of women from embryos, but of
women from the corporeal processes of reproduction, would
seem to make women's reproductive experiences much more
like men's.

Embryo/logic precedents 1: rewriting the parameters of pregnancy

The first explicit reference to women occurs in the definition
of 'treatment services', which, as we will recall, refers to 'medical, surgical or obstetric services provided for the purpose of
assisting women to carry children' (Section 2(1) p. 1). Indeed,
throughout the Act, 'treatment services' is the only context in
which women are referred to as women rather than through
the euphemistic media of gender-'neutral' or male generics
and, as such, eclipses the preconditional involvement of women
in all other practices covered by the Act. Moreover, as I noted
in the last chapter, underpinning this definition of 'treatment
services' is a definition of pregnancy that not only posits a clear
division between women and embryos, but indeed incorporates an unprecedented legal construction of an embryo as a
'child'.

The embryo-centred definition of pregnancy is further consolidated as one of the Act's principal terms:

> For the purposes of this Act, a woman is not to be treated as car-
> rying a child until the embryo is implanted (Section 2(3) p. 2).

Within both modern medical and popular common sense, conception has been considered the moment where a woman has
become pregnant. One remarkable aspect of this definition is
the unprecedented way that pregnancy is redefined in terms of
implantation. It is a particularly important definition for the
way that it both utilises and at the same time contradicts the
arguments of would-be 'embryo protectors' and for the way it

has clearly emerged from and serves a professional authorial agenda.

Firstly, to use implantation as a marker of pregnancy is consistent with the embryo-centred logic of the IVF treatment/research distinction. It is significant, for example, at what point in this definition women are constructed as entering a relationship to embryos. If they are 'not to be treated as carrying a child' until implantation, embryos are then implicitly defined as not in relation to women until that point. This not only obscures the (IVF) process by which embryos can be removed from relationship to women in the first place, but conceptually locates IVF embryos in the first instance within medical scientific and statutory arenas and only secondarily (*ex post facto*) in women.

Moreover, if a pregnancy does not exist until implantation, neither then does a 'child'. Embryos *in vitro*, with this definition, cannot then be considered 'persons'. This implicitly protects IVF (embryo) research from the embryo 'rights' argument that embryos are 'persons' from conception. At the same time however, this definition, reinforced by the phrase 'carrying a child', suggests that embryonic 'personhood' can be interpreted to be established at the point of implantation. Thus the concept and imperative of embryo 'protection' is reinforced, exempting only early (before implantation) embryos.

I would suggest that one of the reasons it was possible to formulate this novel definition of pregnancy is the very technological process that made it possible to remove early embryos from women's bodies and make them available to medical scientific 'use'. It would seem difficult to define pregnancy as beginning at conception when conception takes place in a Petri dish. However, the removal of embryos from women's bodies, in itself, does not obviate a definition of an embryo as a 'person' from conception or the possibility of banning IVF embryo research on this basis. It is the linking of an implied embryo 'personhood' expressly to *pregnancy-as-implantation* that offers a compromise to the conflicting agendas of medical scientists and would-be embryo 'protectors'.

Thus the reference to women here seems to serve both embryo- and science-centred interests.

Defining pregnancy in terms of implantation has jurisdictional implications that will affect women both in and outside the IVF context. The prepositional phrase 'for the purposes of this Act' has at least two possible jurisdictional meanings. First, with respect to IVF, the jurisdiction of the legislation over embryos extends to the point where a woman can 'be treated as carrying a child', that is, over the period of time after embryos are transferred into her and until implantation is diagnosed by practitioners. Implantation thus delimits the power of the Act. This means in effect, that practitioners, through their state-empowered jurisdiction over the non-implanted embryos within them, have jurisdiction over women. The direct State claim on women's bodies during the period of time between embryo transfer and implantation is (implicitly) effected through continued medical scientific surveillance (presupposed for the diagnosis of implantation). Likewise the dual jurisdictional claims on women's bodies during this period are organised around (and constructed as) an embryo-centred imperative accruing specifically from the recombinant logic of the IVF process and the role of the State as embryo 'protector'. Thus the subordination of women to State and medical scientific interests in their embryos is presupposed as a matter of both technical logic and legal principle.

Secondly, 'for the purposes of this Act' suggests that this definition of pregnancy only applies with reference to the practices covered by this legislation. Yet while the Act might not, in itself, establish embryo 'personhood' (after implantation) outside the IVF context, I would suggest that it serves as a powerful basis for extending the embryo 'protectionist' principle that characterises it (either through case law or subsequent legislation). The definition of pregnancy, beginning at implantation and conceptualised as 'carrying a child', as law represents perhaps the most succesful attempt, to date, to establish that women and the 'children' they 'carry' are entirely separate beings, with separate (and adversarial) interests. Until the passage of this Act, a fetus has been given no personhood status within the law. However, the language used here, I would suggest, creates a legal (precedential) basis for arguing that embryos in or outside the IVF context are legal persons (after implantation), thus narrowing the parameters of the (limited) legality of abortion (which is based on the non-personhood status of embryos). However, as I shall consider below, the implicit attribution of personhood to (post-implantation) embryos in this definition constitutes only one facet of the contradictory mediation of embryo status and women's civil personhood that threads through the Act as a whole. Competing constructions of the indices of embryo 'personhood' infuse contestations over the parameters of legitimate IVF research as well as over the limits of legal abortion – both of which are redefined under the auspices of the Act.

Embryo/logic precedents 2: primitive streaks and the research embryo

The term 'pre-embryo' is not used in the Act; however, the 14-day period it demarcates is. The Act invalidates the 'use' of *in vitro* embryos beyond the formation of the 'primitive streak' (presumed to occur at roughly 14 days). Thus, in keeping with the distinction made between 'treatment services' and research, the ascribed marker of embryo 'personhood' *in vitro* is distinct from that *in vivo*. The appearance of this distinction in the Act heralds a transformation of what seemed chiefly to be a medical scientific public relations category into a legal one. In so doing, what was formerly a strategy to side-step adverse public perceptions of IVF research on embryos and to undermine anti-embryo research initiatives, is legislatively reinscribed as a second embryo/logic precedent that threatens the already tenuous autonomy of women, both within and outside the IVF context, over their bodies and reproductive decision-making.

Balloting research futures

Contestations around embryo 'personhood' were manifested with particular acuity in relation to questions around IVF as

---

research. Indeed, the relative status of embryos and of IVF research were constructed both as the central terrain of contestation and as contingent questions that were resolvable only by means of a general parliamentary vote. As foregrounded in the White Paper (1987):

> Since the publication of the Warnock Report, embryo research has been the subject of considerable public debate. Those who favour the continuation of embryo research argue that it offers very important benefits − for example in the improvement of infertility treatment itself and in detecting genetic disorders − which cannot be obtained in other ways. Opponents of research argue that, from the point of conception, embryos have the same status as a child or an adult, and it is improper to conduct research, whatever the benefits for others, that would lead to their eventual destruction ...
>
> The key distinction in the debate surrounding embryo research appears to be between the use of an embryo with the intention of achieving (with that embryo) a successful pregnancy leading to a healthy baby, and its use for other reasons (e.g. the improvement of knowledge about disease) ... The Government therefore proposes that the alternative draft clauses ... made available to Parliament should be along [these] lines (p. 6).

Thus the embryo 'rights' opposition is understood within the White Paper as sharing many of the fundamental assumptions that characterise the pro-embryo research position: that is, that IVF is a source of 'benefits'; that IVF on women is neither a research practice nor a site of contestation regarding embryo status and the ethics of human research. Similarly, both positions posit a marker of embryo 'personhood'. The point of contestation and the terms of the vote effectively revolved around which moment was to be invested with that significance.

As we saw with its redefinition of pregnancy, the Act has adverse jurisdictional implications for women's control over their own bodies, both in the context of IVF (where State/medical jurisdiction over women is established through their jurisdiction over embryos until implantation is diagnosed) and outside it (where the definition of an implanted embryo as a 'child' provides a basis for the erosion of access to abortion). While it held substantive implications for validating

---

or limiting the scope of professional discretion in IVF practice, the vote on embryo research presented adverse implications for women, whichever 'side' won. Both options forged an implicit jurisdictional claim on women's bodies and reproductive decision-making through an explicit claim on their embryos.

Ultimately, a majority of parliamentarians voted in favour of the 14-day pro-research alternative. This victory for IVF researchers was not surprising. I would suggest that, despite the impression to the contrary one might have got from the vehement lobbying efforts by IVF practitioners at the time, the outcome of the vote was almost a foregone conclusion. From the *Warnock Report* on, the legislative run-up to the Act was clearly slanted in favour of the 14-day limit on research, presented as a rational and balanced compromise between maverick scientists (who would want no limit) and embryo 'rights' lobbyists (who would ban progress). The outcome of the vote (and the ways in which this outcome was foregrounded in the legislative process) reflect the extraordinary currency of the notion of scientific progress, particularly in the face of the powerful iconographies of endangered embryos[4] and recent legislative and jurisprudential trends in many countries, towards the strengthening of embryo 'rights'.[5]

Embryo/logic precedents 3: embryo status and the abortion amendment

Section 37 of the HFE Act constitutes an amendment to the 1967 *Abortion Act*. The 1967 Act had permitted the legal termination of pregnancy under certain conditions until 28 weeks' gestation.[6] The amendment provides substantive changes to both the parameters of and grounds for legal abortion. Firstly, it reduces the upper time-limit of abortion to 24 weeks (with similar grounds and under the same conditions as those provided in the 1967 Act). Secondly, it stipulates several conditions under which the limit may be held not to apply because the continuance of the pregnancy would involve: risk of permanent[7] mental or physical injury or death to the woman, or 'substantial risk that if the child were born it would suffer from such physical or mental abnormalities as to be seriously handicapped [*sic*]' (Section 37 p. 23). The abortion amendment thus effectively establishes two further, and substantively divergent, markers of putative fetal (embryo) 'personhood' under the auspices of the HFE Act. As such, it constitutes a further arena of compromise through which conflicting technical, embryo-centred and genea/logic interests are negotiated.

The move to attach an abortion law amendment to the HFE Act followed on the heels of the unsuccessful attempt in 1987–9 by MP David Alton to legislate a reduction of the upper time-limit for legal abortion to 18 weeks. A central argument posited during the Alton (Abortion Amendment) Bill debate to justify such a reduction in the time-limit for legal abortion was that a fetus, after 18 weeks' development, should be regarded as a legal person (because advances in neonatal technology had lowered the age of fetal viability, and, within existing law, fetal viability is taken as a marker of personhood).[8] The dominant argument of the parliamentary opposition to the Bill posited that parents [*sic*] should have the right to terminate a pregnancy if the fetus is diagnosed as 'abnormal', and that, given the limitations of pre-natal diagnostic technology, it would be necessary to have 'late' abortions in many cases. This oppositional argument did not challenge the embryo-protectionist logic of the Alton position, but rather justified existing time-limits on abortion in exemptionist eugenic (ableist) terms (rather than, for example, in terms of women's rights to bodily self-determination). Both sides used the state of the art of medical scientific technology as a reference point for their arguments. Ultimately, the Alton Bill ran out of time in Committee and so failed to become law. However, it was successful in setting the agenda for future legislative attempts to 'reform' abortion law – as evidenced by the inclusion of the abortion amendment in the HFE Act. Indeed, this amendment incorporates both sides of the Alton debate: it lowers the time-limit for legal abortion *except* in cases of diagnoses of fetal 'abnormality' – where the time-limit has been removed.[9]

However, in addition to its mediation of embryo-'rights'

and eugenic sensibilities characterising both the Alton and HFE Act debates, the amendment also establishes two further contradictory standards regarding embryo/fetal status. While the amendment stipulates a reduction in the legal time-limit for abortion to 24 weeks, it none the less (re)confirms the legality of abortion up until that time. Under the terms of this amendment, then, an embryo/fetus is not presumed to be a 'person' until 24 weeks. Thus, the principle regarding fetal status under this amendment contradicts the implicit embryo 'protection' logic and implications of both the 14-day rule and the implantation definition of pregnancy. With these latter provisions, it is illegitimate after 14 days (with the appearance of the primitive streak) to do research on embryos, and, after implantation, an embryo becomes a 'child' carried by a woman. Yet under the abortion provision, it is permissible to terminate a pregnancy from conception to 24 weeks (and beyond in cases of fetal 'abnormality'). Moreover, with the inclusion of an exemption to the 24-week limit in cases of 'serious handicap [sic]', there is, effectively, no marker of personhood.[10]

Given the ways in which it rather dramatically confuses the embryo/logic remit of the HFE Act, it is interesting to speculate on the reasons for the inclusion of this amendment. Firstly, it is not unusual in Government-initiated legislation for parliamentarians to add provisions that can ride on the coat-tails of a Bill that is almost certainly destined to become law (as most Government-introduced Bills, unlike private members' Bills, are destined). While the Alton Bill had failed to become legislation, the overriding sentiment within Parliament was that the time-limit for abortion should be lowered (although 18 weeks was considered by most to be too low) (Science and Technology Subgroup 1991). The HFE Act provided an opportunity for a relatively untroubled passage of this position into law. Moreover, despite contradictions regarding the markers of embryo/fetal personhood, both the amendment and the main body of the Act share a similar embryo 'rights/protection' logic. At this level, the provisions are not fundamentally incompatible.

Conversely, as I noted earlier, one important theme in the

defence of IVF research was the argument that a ban on embryo research would threaten women's access to abortion. To include an amendment that appears to guarantee this access (under limited conditions and albeit at a lower time-limit) reinforces the rejection of the notion that embryos are persons from conception and thus appears to protect women's interests. Moreover, it can be seen to undermine the potential (anti-abortion) embryo 'rights' implications of the 14-day rule and definition of pregnancy in the main body of the Act, and thus to protect the professional investments in IVF research.[11] Finally, the suspension of the 24-week limit in cases of 'serious handicap' mediates (ableist) genea/logic preoccupations prominent in both abortion and IVF debates.

Commercial logics: endorsing 'organic economies'

As Brown *et al.* (1990) point out, IVF is a 'money-spinner' (p. 95). It constitutes a range of products and services, the development of which has enormous commercial potential in an international market. This includes profits to be made from selling patented procedures and products (including drugs and laboratory/surgical equipment). IVF is also the basis for a wide range of research projects, genetic and hormonal, that contribute to the (already established and growing) multinational drug and genetics industries (pp. 96–9). Moreover, in Britain, as in other countries offering IVF, 'treatment services' are largely offered by private clinics or hospitals, which are institutions run for profit.

Many commentators have argued that the increasingly commercial character of IVF (Brown *et al.* 1990; Burfoot 1990; Koval 1990) has become a central factor guiding priorities in IVF policy and development. Koval, examining the company 'IVF-Australia' as a case study of the formation of an IVF business enterprise, argues that the commercialisation of IVF research has led to increased secrecy about research on the one hand, and the prioritisation of commercially exploitable directions in research on the other (Koval 1990 pp. 113–15).[12]

Koval identifies a number of additional consequences arising from the market orientation of IVF: (1) that babies are increasingly conceptualised as products (p. 117); (2) that 'success rates' are characteristically inflated to make IVF more marketable pp. 126–7);[13] and (3) that the indications for use of IVF treatment are expanding, with the consequence of drawing increasing numbers of women into 'treatment' programmes (p. 127). I would add also that through the institutionalisation of IVF in market terms, women's reproductive material (eggs, and other tissue) becomes increasingly viewed (and treated) as commodities in the research marketplace. In this context, regardless of their reasons for undergoing IVF 'treatment services', women (their bodies and labour) are interpellated into the commercial logics of IVF enterprise, which presuppose (and are predicated upon) the participation of women in IVF programmes (and through that participation, in research that may have little or nothing to do with women's reasons for seeking IVF treatment).[14]

Characteristically, women's position within the commercial enterprise of IVF was not problematised within dominant debates about IVF and IVF legislation. While some disquiet was expressed over the exploitation of human embryos for commercialised research ends, none was raised in relation to the treatment of women for this purpose. Indeed, the commercial character of IVF research *per se* was obscured in the rhetoric of human benefit, increase of knowledge and new medical cures.

Regulating traffic in embryos and gametes

The inclusion of regulations in the HFE Act for the legitimate conduct of trade in reproductive tissues presupposes an already established practice. As with other IVF practices, the transfer of reproductive tissues from one party or institution to another was already well established before the HFE Bill was drawn up. Some of these practices received uneasy media attention, for example the transfer of sperm, eggs and particularly embryos from a 'donor' to recipients who did not 'fit' the conventional profile of the socially acceptable parent. The *Warnock Report* and subsequent Government documents also problematised these practices for creating confusion over legal parentage, and, as I discuss further below, recommended that the legislation regulate these transfers in that light. However, the economics of trade in embryos and gametes among clinics was not an issue in the run-up to legislation. Several questions must be asked, then, in the light of the sections of the HFE Act that are specifically concerned with this aspect of IVF practice. (1) What is entailed in the transfer of reproductive material both from the woman or man from whom the material is taken and among various IVF clinics or practitioners? (2) How does the Act propose to regulate such transfers?

Organic commodities

The transfer of reproductive materials is, at several levels, a market transaction. Firstly, reproductive tissues (along with other types of human tissue or organs) can be given a direct commodity value; 'donors' [*sic*] of the material can be paid. A significant example is the long-established practice of paying sperm 'donors' a small fee (Scott 1981 p. 211).[15] Although a thorough discussion of it is beyond the scope of this project, it is none the less important to note that the issue of direct payment to organ/tissue 'donors' has not gone without public controversy. In 1989, for example, there was a great deal of critical media attention in Britain given to the issue of payment to a kidney 'donor' (Evans 1989; Ballantyne 1989). Although it is difficult to say how much the mainstream media reflect larger public opinion more broadly, one can say that the opinions of journalists writing at the time were consistently disquieted at the very idea of the commodification of body parts (and the exploitation of people living in poverty in this way) that direct payment for organs/tissues seems to imply. In any case, it seems that it is only the payment of 'donors' that raises the spectre of unethical commercial exploitation of human bodies.[16]

As I noted above, the medical scientific professions (whether or not they are private, profit-making institutions[17]) and the professionals within them are entities and actors within a commercial market that spans many sectors of production, including biomedical engineering firms, multinational pharmaceutical companies, research institutes and hospitals. While I do not suggest that the priorities of individual practitioners are necessarily defined by profit motives, it is none the less the case that the professional structures in which they work operate within a commercial market. This inescapably includes the raw materials or resources on which, for example, research work is practised. Among the reasons that the economic base (and breadth) of organ/tissue traffic is rarely raised as a public issue, I would suggest, are both the use of the term 'donor' to describe the persons from whom the tissues/organs are obtained[18] and the general cultural perception/construction of medicine as the 'healing profession'. The altruistic connotations of transplant terminology and the predominant image of benign medicine can obscure the question of the commodification of human tissues and organs.

IVF also constitutes an organic economy, both as a form of 'transplant' technology and as an enterprise within the broader commercial marketplace of medical science. Indeed, IVF is a gateway practice through which traffic in body parts (between persons and between medical scientific institutions) can now include eggs and embryos. As is noted by researchers themselves, the futures (including economic) of genetic and other forms of bio/chemical research are predicated on the movement of eggs and embryos from women through IVF 'treatment services'.

Trafficking restrictions for relatively unrestricted traffic

Throughout his study of the trade in human body parts, Russell Scott documents the fact that the historical trend in (or standard model for) legal intervention in the 'organic economy' has been regulatory. A regulatory framework assumes (and (re)confers) the basic legitimacy of the practice in question. As we have seen so far, most of the provisions dealing with IVF practices in the HFE Act follow the regulatory model, and this includes provisions regarding the movements of gametes and embryos between 'persons' and between institutions.

Paragraph (e) of Section 12 (conditions for treatment licences), explicitly considers the economics of gamete and embryo movements:

> no money or other benefit shall be given or received in respect of any supply of gametes or embryos unless authorised by directions (p. 6).

There are two significant features of this provision. Firstly, though it may seem otherwise from the 'no' in 'no money or other benefit', the paragraph authorises direct payment for gametes as long as it is under the auspices of directions from the Licensing Authority. The absence of both subject and object in this sentence (to or from whom 'money' and 'other benefit' is given or received) can also be interpreted to refer to monetary transactions between institutions – a possible inference that is strengthened by the market-orientated resonances of the term 'supply'. Thus the section implicitly legitimates the assignment of commodity value to gametes through direct payment to 'donors' and through the trafficking economy of gamete/embryo supply and demand. The use of the term 'gametes', moreover, suggests that the long-established practice of paying sperm 'donors' could legitimately be extended to include egg 'donors'.[19] This is particularly interesting in the light of the Surrogacy Arrangements Act 1985 (which is amended in Section 36 of the HFE Act),[20] which prohibits commercial surrogacy arrangements (that is, the direct payment of 'surrogate mothers') and constitutes the only restriction placed on IVF commerce.[21]

The remaining sections authorise, under the auspices of a licence (and subject to particular Directions from the HFE Authority), the movements of gametes and embryos between persons and institutions within the UK and internationally (Section 24 (3) and (4) p. 13), with the only proviso being that all information about such movements must be recorded and submitted to the Authority (Section 24 (2) p. 13).[22]

However, while the Act effectively sanctions the commercial trafficking of gametes and embryos, this is obscured by the use of euphemistic language regarding 'the course of their carriage' (Section 24 (3) p. 13) and the language of negation used in the validation of payment to gamete and embryo providers. Similarly, the interpellation of women in the commercial logic of gamete and embryo transactions between 'persons' and institutions is obscured by the elision of male and female gamete providers, the altruistic language of 'donation' (including where 'donors' are actually women undergoing IVF as patients), and the characteristic discussion of gametes and embryos as 'supplies' without reference to their sources.

Heritage and heterosexism: genea/logic regulations

Several dimensions of the HFE Act are aimed at, and have the effect of, reinforcing conventional genea/logic notions of the nuclear family. The provisions regarding the keeping of genealogical records (which include genetic genealogies), the definitions of legal mother- and fatherhood, and the explicit provision promoting heterosexual family units, as well as the pervasive language of IVF 'couples', together constitute a framework that regulates reproductive 'fitness' through the regulation of IVF and related practices.

Heterosexual heritage and biological relatedness

Erica Haimes argues that, in conventional terms, the 'structural requirements of normal families [are] the wish to have a family and the assumption that an ordinary family includes children' (Haimes 1990 p. 167). The policies (and legislative initiatives) around IVF and donor insemination have been centrally informed by associations between family and nature: natural urges and natural (i.e. genetic) inheritance. Indeed, they have been developed to mediate the threat posed by IVF and donor insemination to precisely these assumed 'natural' components of the 'ordinary' family.

The provisions that mandate record-keeping in terms of the origin and movement of gametes constitute a framework for the monitoring of genetic relatedness. As Erica Haimes argues in an article (1990) exploring IVF and donor insemination policies, 'natural', i.e. biological, relatedness has been held as a primary definitional parameter of kinship throughout the process leading to the introduction of the HFE Act. Haimes notes that the Warnock Committee, for example, 'suggested that a child should be informed of her/his method of conception and that, at the age of eighteen, she/he should be able to obtain further "basic information" (non-identifying) on the ethnic origins and genetic health' where anonymous sperm donation has been used (Haimes 1990 p. 157). This recommendation appears in the Act as Section 35 (p. 22). As Haimes argues, the considerable concern generated around the question of sperm donor anonymity revolved centrally around the desire to contain the disruptive potential of IVF and donor insemination for conventional notions of reproductive sexuality and relatedness within the ideology of the natural, nuclear family. The issue of contention is the way IVF and DI procedures separate penetrative sexual intercourse from childbearing. Haimes argues that the registration of husbands as legal fathers in the context of the use of donor sperm; the 'mixing of the husband's sperm with donor sperm [which leaves] some ambiguity about who might be the genetic father'; and 'where egg donation occurs, permitting the receiving woman to become pregnant and to give birth' and other such practices seek to 'minimise the role of the donor' in order to harness IVF and donor insemination within the parameters of heterosexual familial 'normality' (1990 p. 156). Underlying these provisions and policies, then, are several interlinked notions of what constitutes a 'normal' family, namely: marriage; genetic relatedness; and 'legitimate' patrilineal heritage. Not only are these the central indices of IVF and donor insemination record-keeping, but as such, they are clearly established to contain the confusion these procedures cause to conventional notions of legitimate familial relationships.

Legitimacy: definitions of legal parentage

Section 27, a very brief section, defines a legal mother, in the context of the practices covered by the Bill, as the woman 'carrying the child', that is, the woman who bears the pregnancy (and gives birth) (p. 15). This definition seems to resolve a potential 'crisis' of definition emerging from the way IVF procedures can separate genetic relationships from pregnancy.[23] This definition of 'mother' seems aimed at preventing custody disputes in 'egg donation' cases, and as such, offers to stabilise the disruptive potential of such practices for family relationships.

Section 28, which numbers 9 separate clauses, offers an elaborate definition of legal 'fatherhood' and the 'legitimacy' of offspring in patrilineal terms (pp. 15–17). The 9 clauses appear to cover every possible permutation of male position in relation to women undergoing IVF or donor insemination. Such detail in itself reinforces the perceived disruptive potential of these practices in relation to paternity, legitimacy and custody rights. Legal paternity is chiefly defined by reason of marriage to a woman undergoing IVF or donor insemination (whether or not the husband provided the sperm).

Clearly then, IVF and donor insemination create a conflict between the assumptions around marital and genetic relatedness that inform conventional notions of the family. The perceived need to elaborate on this question legislatively reflects how profoundly entrenched and yet, paradoxically, how fragile 'the family' is.[24]

Reproducing heterosexuality: and the 'need' for fathers

As I have noted earlier, the reproduction of heterosexual domestic arrangements, with particular emphasis on the primary importance of there being male and female (married) parents, has informed a number of legislative moves in recent years, as well as having been a significant area of debate in the run-up to the HFE Act. This was consolidated during the Committee Stage of the Bill, where in the House of Lords Lady Saltoun 'moved an amendment [number 21] which would prohibit the "placing of an embryo in an unmarried woman"' (WRRIC 1989). It is worth quoting Lady Saltoun's argument in full:

The object of the amendment is to prohibit the provision of AID to unmarried women, lesbian couples or unmarried couples. It is true that many single women have succeeded in giving their child a good home and upbringing and that their children are wanted and very much loved. No one would deny that fact: but their children must, in the nature of things, suffer some disadvantage from the lack of a father, if only that they have just one parent who loves them and belongs to them instead of two. It does not end there. Children learn primarily from example, by copying what they see ... It is for ... role model reasons ... that the Committee may consider that lesbian couples should not be legible [*sic*] to receive AID or *in vitro* fertilisation service ... There is also the question of whether *in vitro* techniques should be made available to couples who are not legally married. Many people believe that it is all right to make such services available to unmarried couples only in what is called 'a stable relationship', but if the relationship is that stable, why will they not marry? ... All of the arguments I have heard against my amendments put the interests of the woman concerned before those of the child [*sic*] ... I am not really interested in morality, in the rights of women to have children, or in prevalent sexual mores. I am concerned with ... a compromise between private interests and society's interests, which in this case I think means the children's interests. I entirely agree ... that we should support the family as it is, but I do not think that we should necessarily always assist it to become as it is (Lords 1990).

The language of 'nature' again predominates in this call for the restriction of IVF and donor insemination practices to heterosexual couples. Not only does this statement reinforce heterosexist notions about legitimate familial relationships, but it clearly establishes the reproduction of heterosexuality/ism as a primary responsibility of the medical profession, indeed, a central component of the profession's accountability to the State. The meaning of 'nature' in this context was also shaped by the controversy caused by a 'leak' to the media, precisely during the period of discussion of Lady Saltoun's proposed amendment, that unmarried women were seeking and obtaining Donor Insemination services at BPAS clinics. Interestingly, the 'Virgin Birth' controversy revolved expressly around the case of a single heterosexual woman who none the less eschewed sex and men in favour of 'science' in order to become pregnant. What was stigmatised in this context was not only the prospect of lesbian motherhood, but of single motherhood as a deviant heterosexuality. IVF and DI were constituted as dangerous gateways to the expression of both. As in the context of IVF clinic patient-screening practices, the concern in the legislature (and popular media) with the reproduction of *acceptable* heterosexualities presupposes a range of social divisions that have historically constituted the meaning of 'fit' parenting.

Although the amendment was narrowly defeated (61 against, 60 in favour), Lady Saltoun's arguments influenced the injunction that 'treatment services' cannot be provided without consideration of the 'need' of children for fathers that was eventually incorporated as Section 13(5) of the Act.

Genea/logical contracts: the establishment of male reproductive rights

6 – (2) An embryo, the creation of which is brought about *in vitro* must not be received by any person unless there is an effective consent by *each person* whose gametes were used to bring about the creation of the embryo ... (Schedule 3 6(2) p. 37, emphasis mine).

The provisions of Schedule 3 establish that, for the creation, transfer, 'keeping' and 'use' of IVF embryos, consent is required from both the man and the woman who 'provide' the gametes for them. The terminology of 'each person', as I have argued above, posits a false equivalence between the procedures whereby men and women 'provide' gametes in the IVF context. It also constructs an ostensible 'equality' between male and female consent, and thus an 'equal' status with respect to IVF treatment. Underlying this language is an implicit attribution of 'ownership' of one's gametes for both men and women. It is, in effect, an articulation of reproductive 'rights' for men and women over the disposition of their gametes and the decision-making process associated with that use.

However, this implied 'equality' in status between female and male 'gamete providers' is misleading. Consider, for example, a case where a woman might wish to have a stored embryo

---

reimplanted in her body. This use, as with all other uses, of an embryo requires the consent of both herself and the man who provided the sperm. If he declines to consent, she cannot 'receive' this embryo. In effect, his consent is necessary for her attempt to become pregnant with these embryos. Considering that only she has gone through IVF treatment, the requirement of his consent gives him significant power over her reproductive decision-making; although she bears the treatment burden, she is not allowed commensurate power over decisions taken in this context.

Perhaps more worrying are the broader implications of the attribution of male reproductive rights over sperm in the context of women's reproduction (and reproductive decision-making). These provisions in the HFE Act establish a precedent for the argument that if men have rights over their sperm in the IVF context, then they should in any other context – a logic that would make a woman's 'right' either to terminate or to continue her pregnancy contingent on male consent. The argument that men have rights over the embryos in women's bodies was, in fact, one of the bases (along with the argument that embryos have 'personhood') of the much publicised and unsuccessful attempt by an Oxford student, before the passage of the HFE Act, to prevent his girlfriend from obtaining an abortion (Science and Technology Subgroup 1991).[25]

The 'equal rights' of men and women over embryos laid down in the HFE Act extend both the embryo 'protection' and heterosexist genea/logics articulated throughout the Act. Here, linked to the putatively endangered embryo 'interests' are those of the men who provide the sperm. Thus even as 'equal rights' between embryos and women effectively means the subordination of women to embryo 'protectors',[26] so too are women potentially subordinated to individual men through men's 'equal rights' over embryos. Male reproductive rights over sperm, once sperm is incorporated in an embryo and part of (and/or inside) women's bodies, are male reproductive rights over women.[27]

Conclusion

As we have seen, then, the HFE Act elaborates a regulatory framework for IVF (and related) practices that heralds a number of potentially devastating consequences for women's reproductive health and 'rights' both within and outside the context of IVF. Firstly, it reproduces the general linguistic erasure of women and validates and reproduces the recombinant, embryo-centred genea/logics underpinning professional IVF discourses. Secondly, it implicitly validates the interpellation of women into the commercial (and commodifying) logics of the IVF enterprise and explicitly validates their interpellation into the recombinant genea/logics of professional IVF discourse. Finally, through its definition of contradictory indices of embryo personhood it establishes unprecedented (though conflicting) standards for the protection of embryos. This, in addition to the establishment of male reproductive 'rights' over gametes and embryos, *rewrites* the bodies of women as jurisdictional territories of the State, medical scientific professionals and men.

Notes

1 See Oakley (1984), who coined this phrase in her examination of the ways in which women's bodies have been interpellated in medico/legal struggles to control reproduction.

2 The construction of women's civil status in relational or derivative terms is characteristic of the history of legal discourse. As Pateman (1992) notes, women have historically been constituted as definitional outsiders to the public world of citizenship and the state.

3 The terminology of 'donor' has, in this respect, certain similarities to the legal construction of women who have been raped, as 'witnesses'.

4 See, for example, Petchesky (1987) and Franklin (1991).

5 See, for example, Baruch *et al.* (1988), Cohen and Taub (1989), and Feinman (1992), who examine the distinctive rise of embryo-rights-based legislation in contemporary politics.

6 The 1967 Abortion Act decriminalised abortion under the conditions that it is performed by a licensed doctor; permission is granted by two doctors, one of whom is a consultant; and it is performed only in cases where there is risk to the life of the mother or to her physical or psychological well being, or in cases where fetal 'abnormality' is diagnosed.

7 It is the risk of 'permanent' injury that is the criterion for the suspension of the 24-week limit. In cases of risk of injuries which are not deemed to be permanent, 24 weeks is the upper limit.

8 Those parliamentarians making this argument made it clear that they regarded embryos from conception as entitled to the status of legal 'person' and that this was a strategy to erode the legality of abortion incrementally, beginning with 'late' abortions (a term invented by Alton and his supporters).

9 For detailed discussion of the parliamentary debate on the Alton Bill, see Steinberg (1991).

10 The suspension of concerns with fetal personhood in cases of risk of permanent injury or death to the woman can be read in two ways. It might suggest that while fetal personhood may be assumed at 24 weeks, in the face of grave risks the woman's life and personhood take precedence. On the other hand, the exemption can also be read as suggesting that fetal personhood cannot be taken to be established in cases of serious risk to the mother's life.

11 In this context, though it did not figure in the HFE debates, it is also possible that the inclusion of the abortion amendment reflected medical scientific interests in fetal tissue research. As Scott (1981) notes, fetal research is prominent in a wide variety of medical scientific projects and the source for fetal material is mainly from abortions (pp. 36–7). Scott also notes that governmental support for fetal research was also formalised (though not legislated) in the *Peel Report* 1972:

> During our discussions we have been constantly aware of the public concern and of the ethical problems surrounding the use of fetuses, fetal tissues and fetal material for research …In general we feel that the contribution to the health and welfare of the entire population is of such importance that the development of research of this kind should continue subject to adequate and clearly defined safeguards (*Peel Report* 1972 as quoted in Scott 1981 p. 38).

It can be argued that the medical research-orientated philosophy of the *Peel Report*, as with the practice of fetal research, has significantly foregrounded the terms of the HFE Act, including its relegitimation of abortion. It is also important to note that whether or not medical scientists interested in doing 'fetal research' contributed (directly or indirectly) to the inclusion of the abortion amendment in the HFE Act, the amendment none the less effectively provides for its continuation.

12 Koval argues that there is increased secrecy (including in publically funded labs) over research 'claimed to be commercially sensitive but [which] may, in fact, be ethically sensitive' as well as the 'distinct and alarming danger that technical advances in Universities will be directed towards those with commercially exploitable outcomes' (Koval 1990 pp. 113–15).

13 See also Corea and Ince (1987).

14 It can be argued that in this respect, participation as patients of IVF treatment becomes a form of exploited female labour (not only unpaid, but indeed paid for by women) in a profit-making industry.

15 Scott writes:

> In Britain, the RCOG [Royal College of Obstetricians and Gynaecologists] inquiry of 1977 into the practices of AI clinics discovered that nearly 80 percent of clinics paid their donors, the price varying between £2 and £15 per sample, with a most common fee of £5. Euphemisms such as "reimbursement of expenses" are common ... AI clinics commonly say that they would be unable to obtain semen if they did not pay for it. It is interesting that the Council of Europe draft rules do not equivocate about payment: "No payment shall be made for donation of semen. However the loss of earnings as well as traveling and other expenses directly caused by the donation may be refunded to the donor. A person or a private entity which offers semen for the purpose of artificial insemination shall not do it for profit' (Scott 1981, p. 211).

16 On 22 November 1989, BBC2's *Antenna* series screened a programme entitled 'Spare Parts', which examined kidney transplantation as a trade. The programme revealed that in New York City, for example, some victims of violent crime were used as kidney 'donors', and patients who were legally brain-dead were maintained on life-support machines to keep organs alive until consent from the family could be obtained for 'donation'. The programme also tracked the movements of traffic in kidneys, focusing in particular on the USA United Network of Organ Sharing (UNOS), an organ-trafficking control centre. The programme also identified Euro-Transplant as a European equivalent. The cost of shipping a kidney overseas for transplant, at that time, was £5,000, which included medical salaries and shipping costs. Kidney 'brokers', those who mediate transactions in kidney traffic, were paid, according to the programme, somewhere in the region of £40,000. Moreover, the programme documented the fact that poor countries, such as the Philippines, were used as cheap sources of kidneys that were routinely taken from (male) prisoners in the penitentiaries.

17 Public services such as the British National Health Service (NHS) and publically funded research in, for example, non-private Universities, do not operate outside commercial interests (and often have direct commercial interests themselves). As Mays (1991) notes, Conservative government reforms of the 1980s and 1990s have been guided by a commercial ethos (in which the NHS, along with other public services, has been reformed, residualised or privatised under the auspices of a market-led logic – for example patients have increasingly been reconceptualised as customers and Public Services as 'bad' businesses).

18 The term 'donor' includes, for example, those who are paid for their organs or tissues, dead bodies, and – in the IVF context – persons who are undergoing treatment (i.e. women IVF patients are referred to as egg 'donors' for their own treatment).

19 It is interesting to consider the earlier wording of this provision as it appeared in the HFE Bill (1989):

> No person providing gametes for the purpose of treatment services shall be given any money or money's worth for doing so other than such sums (if any) as directions may authorise (13(7) p. 7).

What 'money's worth' means in relation to the very different processes of acquiring sperm from men and eggs from women is not specified. However, given the consistent elision of the two processes throughout the legislative process, it would not be unlikely that 'sums' would be similar for each. This is not to suggest that paying women more would compensate for the disproportionate burden of risks borne by women in this context or for the many ways in which women's civil and reproductive rights may be undermined in the IVF context and through the provisions of HFE.

20 The amendment provides that, in addition to the invalidation of commercial surrogacy established in the original Act (1985), surrogacy contracts (arrangements) are not enforceable. It also clarifies the definition of 'legal mother' in the light of specific IVF practices.

21 Strongly underpinning opposition to commercial surrogacy in Britain was an opposition (both in the context of IVF and non-technologically assisted surrogacy) to the commodification of children as products and of reproduction as a form of prostitution, which were seen as implicit in the conduct of surrogacy for payment.

22 The obligation to keep records is part of the general conditions that apply to all licences.

23 For example, a woman may become pregnant with 'donated' eggs and sperm.

24 Patrilineal registration (and establishment of paternity) are the defining indices, along with marriage, of 'legitimate' children and 'legitimate' parentage outside the context of IVF.

25 The Court ultimately held that the woman could not be prevented from exercising her right to legal abortion. However, while the case was being decided, a temporary injunction was issued preventing her from exercising her rights under the 1967 Abortion Act. By the time the decision was handed down, her pregnancy had developed to a stage that approached the upper time-limit of legal abortion. It was said that this plus the harrowing publicity the case had received led her to feel unable to go through with the abortion. She subsequently gave birth to a daughter, who was then given into the custody of the student who had brought the case.

26 As a case in point, in Ireland in 1992 a 14-year-old girl who had become pregnant after being raped by her friend's father was prevented from travelling to England (in order to stop her from obtaining an abortion). According to the Irish Constitution, women and embryos have 'equal' civil

status. Effectively this translated into the young woman's being denied her civil right to travel because of the State interest in 'protecting' the 'equal rights' of her embryo. Ultimately, and in the wake of international controversy, the Irish court set aside the injunction. The case clearly demonstrated that 'equality' between embryo and woman is a contradiction in terms.

27 This is not to suggest that any definition of male reproductive rights is at the expense of women's rights. For example, it can be argued that men have the reproductive 'rights' over their own bodies – including over their sperm, until that sperm is incorporated in a woman's body (or embryo).

Conclusion

I began this book by suggesting that discursive possibilities and closures are inherent in and negotiated through the authorial standpoint. I have argued that parameters of imagination and distinctive trajectories of theory and practice accrue through the premises, analytical indices, logics and historical context that shape both subjects and objects of knowledge. In this context, my examination of the dominant authorial cultures of IVF foregrounds the terms of both hegemonic and oppositional authorship, of processes of meaning and interrogative possibilities and foreclosures as contested currents of perspective and practice that are embedded in relations of power. Thus the terms through which I construct myself as critical author have implications for the questions that come to the fore in relation to the dominant authorial sphere of IVF practice specifically and of medicine, science and the State more generally. Similarly, the terms of my analysis of dominant IVF discourses contribute to and raise questions about the premises and logics of feminist politics in this context.

Anti-oppressive indices and the decoding of dominant discourses

Through my evaluation of dominant IVF politics, I have attempted to elaborate an anti-oppressive feminist standpoint analysis of science, medicine and technology. Thus I began with the premiss that complex power relations not only under-pin the social conditions of the use of technology, but are embedded both in the conditions of its invention and, as it were, in the character of the 'machine'. I posited that an analy-sis of the ways in which dominant authorial discourses medi-ate social inequalities constitutes a concomitant mediation of the relative agency of professionals and women (both as patients and more broadly). In prioritising social relations of inequality as key indices of analysis, it has been my intention to challenge the identification of women undergoing IVF as representative of all women's (potential) experiences and to reject the elision of the question of professional IVF agendas from that of women's investments in (or opposition to) IVF practices. Thus, in *reading reproductive technologies*, I have been concerned to do two things: firstly, to evaluate profes-sional authorship as a context in which women's agency, repro-ductive possibilities and positionalities are discursively delimited; and secondly, to shift the interrogative trajectories through which IVF has been evaluated in professional and pop-ular debates and within the context of much feminist theory.

A *reading* of dominant IVF discourses through the medium of anti-oppressive analytical indices clearly relocates a number of issues to the foreground that have otherwise been eclipsed by the terms of popular and professional debate. The critical standpoint of this book has prioritised the consideration of the racist, classist, (hetero)sexist and ableist dynamics that consti-tute the discursive field of IVF. Within this interrogative framework, questions of authorial ethos and the ways in which power relations of expertise are embedded in technological languages and practice, in the agency of invention and in the institutional processes of provision and administration become central. Also brought to the fore are the recombinant, genea/logic and embryo-centred sensibilities inscribed in authorial visions of IVF futures and praxis. Such considerations highlight the broader historical matrices of oppression that have underpinned professional and State claims on women's bodies as territory through which reproductive 'fitness' and futures are to be determined.

The analysis elaborated in this book has implications for the constitution of feminist reproductive politics around reproductive technologies. Important in this context are questions about the extent to which these technologies can be *rewritten* in feminist terms and how, in the light of such an analysis, we understand women's investments in IVF and related practices.

Recuperating recombinant bodies?

As Theresia Degener (1990) has noted, feminist debates about reproductive technologies and the meaning of 'women's reproductive rights' have been underscored by tensions around the perceived liberatory or oppressive potentials within dominant medico/legal institutions, languages and practices. Investments, for example, in the use of IVF to *help* women or in the vision of appropriating control of the technology *by* women clearly constitute investments in the belief that these professional bodies of knowledge can be recuperated for a feminist (woman-centred) agenda. Indeed, the desire to capture the authorial voice in this context can be read as a desire to dramatically shift existing power relations around women's reproduction, processes of social control and medical scientific monopolies of expertise. I would suggest, however, that investments in using or appropriating IVF for women are often grounded in a number of problematic presuppositions.

For instance, while it cannot be denied that IVF has helped some women, the question of which women, under what conditions, and of the terms and character of that 'help', are often eclipsed. The significance of professional and State agendas and the power relations of professional agency are similarly dismissed in rhetorical claims for women to control the technology. I am not suggesting that the subversion of dominant discourses is impossible or that dominant social institutions are impervious to anti-oppressive feminist redefinition. However, it is clearly not enough simply to assert an agenda of appropriation and leave the questions of how and the terms through which this is to be accomplished unasked. Given the extent to which eugenic, embryo/logic and recombinant sensibilities are embedded in the dominant discursive field of IVF, such considerations would seem to be in need of considerable elaboration.

Take, for example, the issue of reproductive choice and the patient-screening practices through which IVF is organised. It would seem imperative, in the light of the arguments advanced in this book, to raise two related questions: firstly, whether a democratisation of access to IVF-related treatments is possible; and secondly, whether this would more fundamentally subvert the selective/eugenic rationality of IVF-related practices.

It is certainly possible to imagine regulations against direct screening on some of the grounds discussed (for example banning the selection of patients on heterosexist grounds and providing IVF services on the NHS). Clearly, such a move would seem to subvert important barriers against access to treatment for groups that are clearly marginalised by current screening priorities and the high costs of treatment. There are, however, a number of problems with such an argument. Firstly, as I noted in my discussion of patient selection, the mechanisms of screening in this context are not always overt or direct. How would it be possible, in this context, to develop effective anti-discriminatory regulations against the considerable discretionary power of medical professionals in defining and applying diagnostic criteria for treatment? Moreover, unless one assumes that public medicine has or will have unlimited resources, the idea of unlimited access to high-investment, high-technology treatments such as IVF is, at best, utopian.[1] The limitations on the possibility of democratisation, in other words, are extensive and complex. Moreover, the questions of feasibility and the political economy of public health provision cannot be divorced from other considerations – the historical power of reproductive medicine and its centrality in the formation of dominant discourses of family and miscegenation, as well as racialised, classed and ableist languages of risk (all of which are mediated through the patient- and embryo-screening practices and ethos constituting IVF). Democratising access to IVF treatment would not only not substantively subvert these relations but, indeed, would seem to extend their currency. Nor would it address the social relations, causes and context of infertility, or the social relations, formal properties and risks of treatment itself.

To ask whether it is possible to democratise access to IVF-related treatments is, in essence, to entertain the possibility of divorcing this sphere of reproductive medicine from conventional discourses of family and from the historical role of medicine as an agency of sexual and reproductive regulation and control. It also divorces women's investments in choosing IVF or genetic screening from social context and the social relations through which only some women's infertility is constituted as a medical/social problem and disability is socially constituted as a 'natural' disaster. I would suggest that widening access to IVF treatments is not only not enough, but indeed, as a proposition, side-steps the more fundamental questions about the power of medical discourse and professionals, the character and political economy of medicine generally and reproductive medicine specifically, and the wider social climate around notions of 'fit' parenting and 'monstrous' bodies (in which the former have been centrally implicated). Similarly, to define reproductive choice/rights in terms of democratisation of access to treatment would seem to assume that women's reproductive agency is both without and transcendent of context.

Indeed, there is a danger in framing the central questions of IVF around how IVF can be used for or claimed by women. Implicit in both formulations is a presumption that women's desires for children are intransigent rather than contingent and that their investments in IVF are similarly predetermined. There is also a positivistic construction, here, of the inevitability of IVF that divorces the shape and character of the technology from the conditions of its making. An assertive faith that professional definitions of IVF practice can be captured and rewritten for women ignores the social conditions that have made IVF and genetic screening thinkable to their inventors and desirable for some women but not others and obscures the discursive closures embedded in the logics of IVF languages and practice.

Redefining reproductive rights

One of the core arguments of this book is that women IVF patients, whatever their personal motives for undergoing IVF, are interpellated into the dominant discursive logics of the process. This analysis has significant implications both for questions around (some) women's investments in IVF technologies and the liberatory possibilities they may perceive in them and for definitions of a feminist politics of reproductive rights in this context. There is a danger here that the terms of such a critique may be constituted or taken as reproducing the construction of women as the culpable yet 'docile' bodies inscribed in dominant IVF discourses. Such a construction would seem inevitable if we ignore the material conditions and social relations that foster investments in IVF and genetic screening as options. A romanticised notion of (feminist) resistance as if it were always progressive ignores the ways in which choosing IVF or screening reflect acute perceptions of the social consequences of childlessness and the profound oppressions surrounding disability, and as such do constitute forms of resistance. As I posited at the start of this book, a feminist politics that views women IVF patients as suffering from false consciousness and that argues for women to refuse IVF implicitly burdens women with the obligation of resistance while ignoring the consequences of that resistance. It would seem clear that the material implications of having a disabled child in an ableist society, of being childless when occupying social positions in which one is expected to have children, or of desiring a biologically related child in a context in which only 'natural' kinship is privileged as 'real', make sense of women's choices to resist *through* these technologies. Indeed, practitioners' motives for helping women may be underpinned precisely by an awareness of these adverse social conditions even as they discursively reinscribe them.

However, if it is a problem to elide women's agency and investments in IVF with that of professionals and of personal motives with institutionalised agendas, it is also a problem to claim that women are not implicated in the dominant ethos underpinning choices they make, even where they are explicitly opposed to that ethos but feel they have no other option. This formulation also participates in the victimological construction of women as docile bodies. Moreover, as a feminist politic, it both invests notions of 'reproductive rights' in processes and political/ethical economies of medicalisation and technology and ignores the historical investments of feminist reproductive politics in eugenic and racial hygiene theories.[2] Davis (1990), for example, has argued that the failure to consider the history of racist, classist and, as Degener (1990) further notes, ableist definitions of women's reproductive 'freedom' has constituted a refusal to construct a feminist reproductive rights movement in anti-oppressive terms.[3] To divorce women's need's and choices from the dominant logics of IVF and to claim IVF, on this basis, as a 'right' without considering questions of positionality or the character of that which is claimed, constitutes both a denial and a reinscription of this historical trajectory.

To constrain the scope of our questions to whether women should use or refuse IVF and genetic screening technologies reproduces the unbearable contradictions inherent in the dominant logics of these processes. Clearly, feminist politics around reproductive choice must be more than simply a call for access to choices not of our own making or an injunction against the use of technologies in a context where there appears to be no better options. It seems to me that the question is not why do women do IVF or genetic screening and what do we do about those women, but what are the social conditions which make IVF thinkable and desirable and how does IVF reinscribe those social conditions? And, perhaps more importantly, if eugenic conceptions are integral to the technology, how can women be enabled not to want it?

Notes

1 While I was completing this book, I was told anecdotally by a GP friend that in one region, a decision has been made by the health authority that instead of limiting services (a necessity in economic terms) by screening

patients on the grounds discussed in this book, one cycle of IVF/GIFT treatment would be made available to any patient for whom it would be deemed physiologically appropriate. While this move obviates overt practices of selection, to offer one cycle is almost no better than offering none – as the likelihood of live birth from one cycle of treatment is virtually nil.

2 See, for example, Davis (1990), Degener (1990) and Lupton (1994).

3 Degener (1990) has argued that:

> [i]n demanding rights that only [address] the problems of a certain section of women, the old and new women's liberation movement has often unwittingly renounced the principle of equality. Our approach to the question of abortion and contraception is a clear example of this. In the western part of the world we fight for contraception and abortion because we see them as ... essential instruments of female self-determination. Yet we overlook the fact that for many women in Third World countries, and for many disabled women in our own countries, this right only exists in the form of a ban on having children in the interests of population control (p. 97).

In this context, Davis (1990) has argued that what has been demanded as a 'right' for the privileged has been constituted as a duty for the poor.

Bibliography

(For government publications, see after alphabetical entries.)

Abbott, Pamela and Claire Wallace, 1989. 'The Family', in Brown, Philip, and Richard Sparks (eds), *Beyond Thatcherism: Social Policy, Politics and Society*. Milton Keynes, Open University Press.

Aitken, R. J. and D. W. Lincoln, 1986. 'Human Embryo Research: the Case for Contraception', in CIBA Foundation, *Human Embryo Research: Yes or No?*, pp. 122–36. London, Tavistock.

Akhter, Farida, 1987. 'Wheat for Statistics: A Case Study of Relief Wheat for Attaining Sterilization Target in Bangladesh', in Spallone, Patricia and Deborah Lynn Steinberg (eds), *Made to Order: The Myth of Reproductive and Genetic Progress*, pp. 154–60. Oxford, Pergamon.

Amos, Valerie and Pratibha Parmar, 1984. 'Challenging Imperial Feminism'. *Feminist Review*, 17, Autumn, 3–20.

Anderson, Mary, 1987. *Infertility: A Guide for the Anxious Couple*. London, Faber and Faber.

Annual Editions, 1978. *Focus Biology: The New Evolution – Genes: Handle with Care*, 3rd edn. Guilford, CT, C. N. Dushkin Publishing Group.

Antenna, 1989. 'Spare Parts'. (Screened 22 November, 8pm, Channel 4.)

Anthias, Floya and Nira Yuval Davis, 1993. *Racialised Boundaries: Race, Nation, Gender, Colour and Class and the Anti-Racist Struggle*. London, Routledge.

Arditti, Rita, Renate Duelli Klein and Shelley Minden, 1984. *Test-Tube Women: What Future for Motherhood?* London, Pandora.

Arendt, Hannah, 1963/4. *Eichmann in Jerusalem: A Report on the Banality of Evil*. New York, Penguin.

Austin, C. R., 1989. *Human Embryos: The Debate on Assisted Reproduction*. New York, Oxford University Press.

Ballantyne, Aileen, 1988. 'Go to Work on an Egg', *Guardian*, 14 December 1988.

Ballantyne, Aileen, 1989. 'Kidney Sale Clinic Bans Two Doctors', *Guardian*, 8 February 1989.

Barker, Graham H., 1981. *Your Search for Fertility: A Sympathetic Guide to Achieving Pregnancy for Childless Couples*. New York, William Morrow.

Barker, Martin, 1981. *The New Racism: Conservatives and the Ideology of the Tribe*. London, Junction Books.

Barrett, Michele, 1991. *The Politics of Truth: From Marx to Foucault*. London, Polity.

Baruch, Elaine Hoffman, Amadeo F. D'Adamo Jr., and Joni Seager (eds), 1988. *Embryos, Ethics and Women's Rights: Exploring the New Reproductive Technologies*. New York, Huntington Press.

Benston, Margaret Lowe, 1992. 'Women's Voices/Men's Voices: Technology as a Language', in Kirkup, Gill and Laurie Smith Keller (eds), *Inventing Women: Science, Technology and Gender*. London, Polity.

Blane, David, 1991. 'Health Professions', in Scambler, Graham (ed.), *Sociology as Applied to Medicine*, pp. 221–35. London, Baillière Tindall.

Blane, David, 1991. 'Inequality and Social Class', in Scambler, Graham (ed.), *Sociology as Applied to Medicine*, pp. 109–28. London, Baillière Tindall.

Blatt, Robin J. R., 1988. *Pre-Natal Tests: What They Are, Their Benefits and Risks and How to Decide Whether to Have Them or Not*. New York, Vintage.

BMA (British Medical Association), 1988. *Philosophy and Practice of Medical Ethics*. London, BMA/Unwin.

Bocock, Robert and Kenneth Thompson (eds), 1992. *Social and Cultural Forms of Modernity*. Cambridge, Polity and Open University Press.

Bowles, Gloria and Renate Duelli Klein (eds), 1983. *Theories of Women's Studies*. London, Routledge.

Bradish, Paula *et al.*, 1989. *Frauen Gegen Gen und Reproduktionstechnologien: Beitrage vom 2. Bundesweiten Kongress Frankfurt, 28–30.10.1988*. Frankfurt, Frauenoffensive.

Bradley, Harriet, 1992. 'Changing Social Divisions: Class, Gender and Race', in Bocock, Robert and Kenneth Thompson (eds), *Social and Cultural Forms of Modernity*. Cambridge, Polity and Open University Press.

Braham, Peter, Ali Rattansi and Richard Skellington (eds), 1992.

Racism and Anti-Racism: Inequalities, Opportunities and Policies. London, Sage.

British Broadcasting Corporation, 1992. *Doctors to Be.* Series screened on BBC2, November–December 1992.

Brock, D. J. H., 1982. *Early Diagnosis of Fetal Defects.* New York, Churchill Livingstone.

Brown, Phillip and Richard Sparks (eds), 1990. *Beyond Thatcherism: Politics and Society.* Milton Keynes, Open University Press.

Brown, Marion, Kay Fielden and Jocelynne A. Scutt, 1990. 'New Frontiers or Old Recycled? New Reproductive Technologies as Primary Industry', in Scutt, Jocelynne A. (ed.) *The Baby Machine: Reproductive Technologies and the Commercialisation of Motherhood,* pp. 77–107. London, Green Print.

Bruel and Kjaer (UK) Ltd, 1986. *A Bridge to New Life* (publicity brochure published in the UK).

Bryan, Beverley, Stella Dadzie and Suzanne Scafe, 1985. *Heart of the Race: Black Women's Lives in Britain.* London, Virago.

Bryman, Alan and Duncan Cramer, 1990. *Quantitative Data Analysis for Social Scientists.* London, Routledge.

Bullard, Linda, 1987. 'Killing Us Softly: Towards a Feminist Analysis of Genetic Engineering', in Spallone, Patricia and Deborah Lynn Steinberg, *Made to Order: The Myth of Reproductive and Genetic Progress.* Oxford, Pergamon.

Burfoot, Annette, 1990. 'The Normalisation of a New Reproductive Technology', in McNeil, Maureen, Ian Varcoe and Steven Yearley (eds), *The New Reproductive Technologies,* pp. 58–73. London, Macmillan.

Butler, Judith, 1990. *Gender Trouble: Feminism and the Subversion of Identity.* London, Routledge.

Canaan, Joyce, 1991. 'Is "Doing Nothing" Just Boys' Play?: Integrating Feminist and Cultural Studies Perspectives on Working Class Young Men's Masculinity' in Franklin, Sarah, Celia Lury and Jackie Stacey (eds), *Off-Centre: Feminism and Cultural Studies.* London, Harper Collins.

Carby, Hazel, 1981. 'White Women Listen: Black Feminism and the Boundaries of Sisterhood', in CCCS, *The Empire Strikes Back: Race and Racism in 70s Britain,* pp. 212–35. London, Hutchinson.

Carter, Cedric O., 1962. *Human Heredity.* Harmondsworth, Penguin.

Carter, Cedric O. (ed.), 1983. *Developments in Human Reproduction and Their Eugenic, Ethical Implications: Proceedings of the Nineteenth Annual Symposium of the Eugenics Society.* London, Academic Press.

CCETSW (Central Council for the Education and Training of Social

Workers), 1991. 'DipSW Requirements and Regulations for the Diploma in Social Work: Paper 30'. The Council, London.

Childright, 1991. 'Fostering Advice is Homophobic', *Childright: A Bulletin of Law and Policy Affecting Young People in England and Wales*, 74 (March 1991), 2.

Childright, 1991. 'Government Issues First Volumes of Final Children's Act', *Childright: A Bulletin of Law and Policy Affecting Young People in England and Wales*, 77 (June 1991), 7–10.

CIBA Foundation, 1986. *Human Embryo Research: Yes or No?* London, Tavistock.

Cixous, Hélène, 1992. *Talking Liberties.* (Series, Channel 4, Britain.)

Clarke, Cyril, 1987. *Human Genetics and Medicine*, 3rd edn. London, Edward Arnold.

Clarke, Maxine, 1985. 'Chances of Legislation Fade', *Nature*, 318, 197.

Cohen, J., 1989. *The Privileged Ape: Cultural Capital in the Making of Man.* Lancaster, Parthenon.

Cohen, Sherrill and Nadine Taub (eds), 1989. *Reproductive Laws for the 1990s*, Clifton, NJ, Humana Press.

Coleman, Vernon, 1975. *The Medicine Men: A Shattering Analysis of the Drugs Industry.* London, Arrow.

Collins, Patricia Hill, 1990. *Black Feminist Thought: Knowledge, Consciousness and the Politics of Empowerment.* London, Harper Collins.

Collins, Patricia Hill, 1991. 'The Outsider Within', in Fonow, J. and M. M. Cook (eds), *Beyond Methodology*. Indianapolis, Indiana University Press.

Connell, R.W., 1995. *Masculinities.* Cambridge, Polity.

Corea, Gena, 1979. *The Hidden Malpractice: How American Medicine Mistreats Women.* New York, Harper and Row.

Corea, Gena, 1985. *The Mother Machine: Reproductive Technologies from Artificial Insemination to Artificial Wombs.* New York, Harper and Row.

Corea, Gena and Susan Ince, 1987. 'Report of a Survey of IVF Clinics in the USA', in Spallone, Patricia and Deborah Lynn Steinberg (eds), *Made to Order: The Myth of Reproductive and Genetic Progress*, pp. 133–45. Oxford. Pergamon.

Corea, Gena *et al.* 1985. *Man-Made Women: How New Reproductive Technologies Affect Women.* London, Hutchinson.

Crook, Nikita A., 1986. DES Action/Toronto: Fact Sheet. DES Action/ Toronto, 60 Grosvenor St., #442, Toronto, Ontario, Canada M5S 1B6.

Crowe, Christine, 1987. '"Women Want It": In Vitro Fertilization and Women's Motivations for Participation', in Spallone, Patricia and

Deborah Lynn Steinberg (eds), *Made to Order: The Myth of Reproductive and Genetic Progress*, pp. 84–93. Oxford, Pergamon.

Crowe, Christine, 1990. 'Whose Mind over Whose Matter? Women, In Vitro Fertilisation and the Development of Scientific Knowledge', in McNeil, Maureen, Ian Varcoe and Steven Yearley (eds), *The New Reproductive Technologies*, pp. 27–57. London, Macmillan.

Cunha, G. R. *et al.*, 1987. 'Teratogenic Effects of Clomiphene, Tamoxifen and Diethylstilbestrol on the Developing Human Female Genital Tract', *Human Pathology*, pp. 1–12.

Daly, Mary, 1978. *Gyn/Ecology: The Metaethics of Radical Feminism*. Boston, MA, Beacon Books.

Daniels, Cynthia R., 1993. *At Women's Expense: State Power and the Politics of Fetal Rights*. Cambridge, MA, Harvard University Press.

David, Miriam, 1986. 'Moral and Maternal: The Family in the Right', in Levitas, Ruth (ed.), pp. 136–66. *The Ideology of the New Right*. Cambridge, Polity.

Davis, Angela, 1991[1982]. *Women, Race and Class*. London, The Women's Press.

Davis, Angela, 1984. *Women, Culture and Politics*. London, The Women's Press.

Davis, Angela, 1990. 'Racism, Birth Control and Reproductive Rights', in Fried, Marlene Gerber (ed.), *From Abortion to Reproductive Freedom: Transforming a Movement*, pp. 15–26. Boston, MA, South End Press.

De Beauvoir, Simone, 1974[1952]. *The Second Sex*. New York, Vintage.

Degener, Theresia, 1990. 'Female Self-Determination Between Feminist Claims and "Voluntary" Eugenics, Between "Rights" and Ethics.' *Issues in Reproductive and Genetic Engineering: Journal of International Feminist Analysis*, 3 (2), 87–100.

Di Stefano, Christine, 1990. 'Dilemmas of Difference: Feminism Modernity and Postmodernism', in Nicholson, Linda J. (ed.), *Feminism/Postmodernism*, pp. 63–82. London, Routledge.

Direcks, Anita, 1987. 'Has the Lesson Been Learned?: The DES Story and IVF', in Spallone, Patricia and Deborah Lynn Steinberg (eds), *Made to Order: The Myth of Reproductive and Genetic Progress*, pp. 161–5. Oxford, Pergamon.

Doerr, Edd and James W. Prescott (eds), 1989. *Abortion Rights and Fetal Personhood*. Long Beach, CA, Center Line Press.

Dominelli, Lena, 1992. 'An Uncaring Profession? An Examination of Racism and Social Work', in Braham, Peter, Ali Rattansi and Richard Skellington (eds), *Racism and Anti-Racism: Inequalities, Opportunities and Policies*, pp. 164–78. London, Sage.

Douglas, Mary, 1966. *Purity and Danger: An Analysis of the Concepts of Polution and Taboo*. London, Routledge and Kegan Paul.

Doyal, Lesley, 1987. 'Infertility – A Life Sentence? Women and the National Health Service', in Stanworth, Michelle (ed.), *Reproductive Technologies: Gender, Motherhood and Medicine*, pp. 174–90. Cambridge, Polity.

Dreifus, Claudia, 1977. *Seizing Our Bodies: The Politics of Women's Health*. New York, Vintage.

Dudley-Edwards, Ruth, 'Today 3,000 Embryonic Human Beings will be Sentenced to Death. What a Sad Victory for the Witch Doctors of the 20th Century', *The Daily Mail*, 24 July 1996.

Dworkin, Andrea, 1974. *Woman Hating*. New York, E. P. Dutton.

Edwards, R. G. *et al.*, 1984. 'Factors Influencing the Success of In Vitro Fertilization for Alleviating Human Infertility', *Journal of In Vitro Fertilization and Embryo Transfer*. New York, Plenum Publishing Corporation.

Ehrenreich, Barbara and Deirdre English, 1979. *For Her Own Good: 150 Years of Experts' Advice to Women*. London, Pluto.

Elkington, John, 1985a. *The Poisoned Womb: Human Reproduction in a Polluted World*. London, Viking.

Elkington, John, 1985b. *The Gene Factory: Inside the Biotechnology Business*. London, Century.

Epstein, Debbie, 1991. Changing Classroom Cultures: An Examination of Anti-Racist Pedagogy, INSET and School Change in the Context of Local and National Politics. Unpublished Ph.D. Thesis, University of Birmingham.

Epstein, Debbie, 1993. *Changing Classroom Cultures: Anti-Racism, Politics and Schools*. Stoke-on-Trent, Trentham Books.

Epstein, Debbie, 1993. 'Defining Accountability in Education', *British Educational Research Journal: Special Issue: Equal Opportunities and Educational Reform*, 19 (3), 243–57.

Esbjornson, Robert (ed.), 1984. *The Manipulation of Life*. (SF.) London, Harper and Row.

ESHRE (European Society of Human Reproduction and Embryology), 1986. Brussels Conference Abstracts, June. *Human Reproduction*, Vol. 1.

Evans, Martyn, 1989. 'Donors and Do Nots', *The Guardian*, 1 February 1989.

Evening Mail, 1992. 'Rape Girl Abortion Ban to go on Appeal', 18 February 1992.

Faulder, Caroline, 1985. *Whose Body Is It? The Troubling Issue of Informed Consent*. London, Virago.

Feinman, Calrice (ed.), 1992. *The Criminalization of a Woman's Body*. New York, Harrington Park Press.

Feminist International Network on the New Reproductive Technologies (FINNRET), 1984. *Reproductive Wrongs: Male Power and the New Reproductive Technologies*. Manchester, Amazon Press.

Feminist International Network of Resistance to Reproductive and Genetic Engineering (FINRRAGE Britain), 1987. 'Statement in Response to the DHSS Consultation Paper Regarding Legislation on Human Infertility Services and Embryo Research' (submitted to DHSS 30 June 1987; unpublished).

Ferguson-Smith, M. A. and M. E. Ferguson-Smith, 1983. *Problems of Prenatal Diagnosis*. Duncan Guthrie Institute of Medical Genetics, Yorkhill, Glasgow.

Finch, Janet, 1984. 'It's Great to Have Someone to Talk To', in Bell, Colin and Helen Roberts (eds), *Social Researching, Politics, Problems and Practice*. London, Routledge and Kegan Paul.

Foucault, Michel, 1975. *The Birth of the Clinic*. New York, Vintage.

Foucault, Michel, 1977. *Discipline and Punish: The Birth of the Prison*. London, Penguin.

Fox Keller, Evelyn, 1992. 'How Gender Matters, or Why it is so Hard for Us to Count Past Two', in Kirkup, Gill and Laurie Smith Keller (eds), *Inventing Women: Science, Technology and Gender*, pp. 42–56. Cambridge, Polity.

Franklin, Sarah, 1990. 'Deconstructing "Desperateness": The Social Construction of Infertility in Popular Representions of New Reproductive Technologies', in McNeil, Maureen, Ian Varcoe and Steven Yearley (eds), *The New Reproductive Technologies*, pp. 200–29. London, Macmillan.

Franklin, Sarah, 1991. 'Fetal Fascinations: New Dimensions to the Medical–Scientific Construction of Fetal Personhood', in Franklin, Sarah, Celia Lury and Jackie Stacey (eds), *Off-Centre: Feminism and Cultural Studies*, pp. 190–205. London, Harper Collins.

Franklin, Sarah, Celia Lury and Jackie Stacey (eds), 1991. *Off-Centre: Feminism and Cultural Studies*. London, Harper Collins.

French, Marilyn, 1985. *Beyond Power: Women, Men and Morals*. London, Jonathon Cape.

Fried, Marlene Gerber (ed.), 1990. *From Abortion to Reproductive Freedom: Transforming a Movement*. Boston, MA, South End Press.

Friedson, Eliot, 1970. *Profession of Medicine: a Study of the Sociology of Applied Knowledge*. New York, Dodd, Mead.

Fromer, Margot Joan, 1983. *Ethical Issues in Sexuality and Reproduction*. St Louis, MO, Mosby.

Frye, Marilyn, 1983. *The Politics of Reality: Essays in Feminist Theory*. Trumansburg, NY, Crossing Press.

Fyfe, Wendy, 1991. 'Abortion Acts: 1803 to 1967', in Franklin, Sarah,

Celia Lury and Jackie Stacey (eds), *Off-Centre: Feminism and Cultural Studies*, pp. 160–74. London, Harper Collins.

Gallagher, Janet, 1987. 'Eggs, Embryos and Fetuses: Anxiety and the Law', in Stanworth, Michelle (ed.), *Reproductive Technologies: Gender, Motherhood and Medicine*, pp. 139–50. Cambridge, Polity.

Giddens, Anthony, 1989. *Sociology*. Cambridge, Polity.

Glover, Jonathon, 1984. *What Sort of People Should there Be? Genetic Engineering, Brain Control and their Impact on our Future*. Harmondsworth, Pelican.

Gordon, Linda, 1983 [1974]. *Birth Control in America: Woman's Body, Woman's Right*. Harmondsworth, Penguin.

Greer, Germaine, 1984. *Sex and Destiny: The Politics of Human Fertility*. London, Picador.

Guardian, 1987a. 'Prenatal Test Could Eliminate Hare Lip', 27 August 1987.

Guardian, 1987b. 'Tests Beginning Soon on Vaccine to End Tooth Decay', 27 August 1987.

Haimes, Erica, 1990. 'Recreating the Family? Policy Considerations Relating to the "New" Reproductive Technologies', in McNeil, Maureen, Ian Varcoe and Steven Yearley (eds), *The New Reproductive Technologies*, pp. 154–72. London, Macmillan.

Hall, Stephen S., 1987. *Invisible Frontiers: The Race to Synthesize a Human Gene*. New York, Atlantic Monthly Press.

Hall, Stuart, 1977. 'The Political and the Economic in Marx's Theory of Classes', in Hunt, Alan (ed.), *Class and Class Structure*, pp. 15–60. London, Lawrence and Wishart.

Hall, Stuart, 1992. Raymond Williams Memorial Lecture, Midlands Arts Centre, Birmingham. (Forthcoming in *Cultural Studies in Birmingham*, 1993.).

Hammersley, Martyn, 1992. 'On Feminist Methodology'. *Sociology*, 26(2) 187–206.

Hanmer, Jalna and Sheila Saunders, 1984. *Well Founded Fear: A Community Study of Violence Toward Women*. London, Hutchinson.

Haraway, Donna, 1989. *Primate Visions: Gender, Race and Nature in the World of Modern Science*. New York, Routledge.

Harding, Sandra, 1986. *The Science Question in Feminism*. Milton Keynes, Open University Press.

Harding, Sandra, 1990. 'Feminism and Anti-Enlightenment Critiques', in Nicholson, Linda J. (ed.), pp. 83–106. *Feminism/Postmodernism*. London, Routledge.

Harding, Sandra, 1991. *Whose Science? Whose Knowledge? Thinking From Women's Lives*. Milton Keynes, Open University Press.

Harding, Sandra, 1992. 'How the Women's Movement Benefits Science', in Kirkup, Gill and Laurie Smith Keller, *Inventing Women: Science, Technology and Gender*, pp. 57–72. London, Polity.

Harding, Sandra (ed.), 1987. *Feminism and Methodology*. Milton Keynes, Open University Press.

Harding, Sandra and Jean F. O'Barr (eds), 1987. *Sex and Scientific Inquiry*. Chicago, University of Chicago Press.

Hartl, Daniel L., 1978. 'Genes: Handle with Care', in *Focus: Biology* 3rd edn, pp. 96–101. Guilford, CT, Dushkin Publishing Group.

Hartmann, Betsy, 1987. *Reproductive Rights and Wrongs: The Global Politics of Population Control and Contraceptive Choice*. New York, Harper and Row.

Henriques, Julian *et al.*, 1984. *Changing the Subject: Psychology, Social Regulation and Subjectivity*. London, Methuen.

HFEA (Human Fertilisation and Embryology Authority), 1992. 'Annual Report.'

HFEA (Human Fertilisation and Embryology Authority), 1992. 'Code of Practice.'

HFEA (Human Fertilisation and Embryology Authority), 1992. 'List of Licensed Centres' (1 July 1992).

HFEA (Human Fertilisation and Embryology Authority), 1992. 'Statistical Analysis of the United Kingdom: IVF and GIFT Data 1985–1990'.

Hillier, Sheila, 1991. 'The Health and Health Care of Ethnic Minority Groups', in Scambler, Graham (ed.), *Sociology as Applied to Medicine*, pp. 146–59. London, Baillière Tindall.

Hirst, Paul, 1977. 'Economic Classes and Politics', in Hunt, Alan (ed.), *Class and Class Structure*, pp. 125–54. London, Lawrence and Wishart.

hooks, bell, 1982. *Ain't I a Woman: Black Women and Feminism*. London, Pluto Press.

hooks, bell, 1989. *Talking Back: Thinking Feminist – Thinking Black*. London, Sheba.

hooks, bell, 1991. *Yearning: Race, Gender and Cultural Politics*. London, Turnaround Press.

Hubbard, Ruth, 1990. *The Politics of Women's Biology*. New Brunswick, Rutgers University Press.

Hubbard, Ruth and Elijah Wald, 1993. *Exploding the Gene Myth: How Genetic Information is Produced and Manipulated by Scientists, Physicians, Employers, Insurance Companies, Educators and Law Enforcers*. Boston, MA, Beacon.

Hubbard, Ruth, Mary Sue Henifin and Barbara Fried (eds), 1982. *Biological Woman: The Convenient Myth*. Cambridge, MA, Schenkman Publishing.

Hunt, Alan (ed.), 1977. *Class and Class Structure*. London, Lawrence and Wishart.

Huxley, Aldous. 1977[1932]. *Brave New World*. London, Grafton.

Illich, Ivan, 1985[1976]. *Limits to Medicine: Medical Nemesis: The Expropriation of Health*. Harmondsworth, Pelican.

Illman, John, 1989. 'Cell Test has Key to Future', *Guardian*, 1 March 1989.

Issues in Reproductive and Genetic Engineering: Journal of International Feminist Analysis. Vols 1–5, 1988–92. New York, Pergamon.

Jackel, E., 1981. *Hitler's World View: A Blueprint for Power*. Cambridge, MA, Harvard University Press.

Jayaratne, Toby Epstein, 1983. 'The Value of Quantitative Methodology for Feminist Research', in Bowles, Gloria and Renate Duelli Klein (eds), *Theories of Women's Studies*, pp. 140–61. London, Routledge Kegan and Paul.

Jones, D. Gareth, 1985. *Brave New People: Ethical Issues at the Commencement of Life*. Grand Rapids, MI, Eerdmans.

Jordan, June, 1989. *Moving Towards Home*. London, Virago.

Jordanova, Ludmilla (ed.), 1986. *Languages of Nature: Critical Essays on Science and Literature*. London, Free Association Books.

Kamal, Sultana, 1987. 'Seizure of Reproductive Rights? A Discussion on Population Control in the Third World and the Emergence of the New Reproductive Technologies in the West', in Spallone, Patricia and Deborah Lynn Steinberg (eds), *Made to Order: The Myth of Reproductive and Genetic Progress*, pp. 146–53. Oxford, Pergamon.

Kelly, Liz, Linda Regan and Sheila Burton, 1992. 'Defending the Indefensible? Quantitative Methods and Feminist Research', in Hinds, Hilary *et al.* (eds), *Working Out: New Directions for Women's Studies*, pp. 149–60. London, Falmer.

Kennedy, Ian, 1983. *The Unmasking of Medicine: A Searching Look at Health Care Today*. London, Paladin.

Kenner, Charmian, 1985. *No Time for Women: Exploring Women's Health in the 1930s and Today*. London, Pandora.

Kevles, Daniel J., 1985. *In the Name of Eugenics: Genetics and the Uses of Human Heredity*. Harmondsworth, Penguin.

Kirkup, Gill and Laurie Smith Keller (eds), 1992. *Inventing Women: Science, Technology and Gender*. London, Polity.

Klein, Renate Duelli, 1983. 'How To Do What We Want To Do: Thoughts on Feminist Methodology', in Bowles, Gloria and Renate Duelli Klein (eds), *Theories of Women's Studies*, pp. 88–104. London, Routledge and Kegan Paul.

Klein, Renate, 1989a. 'The Exploitation of Our Desire: Women's Experiences with In Vitro Fertilisation.' Women's Studies Summer Institute, Deakin University, Victoria, Australia.

Klein, Renate D. (ed.), 1989b. *Infertility: Women Speak Out about Their Experiences of Reproductive Medicine.* London, Pandora.

Klein, Renate and Robyn Rowland, 1988a. 'Hormonal Cocktails: Women as Test-Sites for Fertility Drugs: Summary.' Deakin University, Victoria, Australia.

Klein, Renate and Robyn Rowland, 1988b. 'Women as Test-Sites for Fertility Drugs: Clomiphene Citrate and Hormonal Cocktails', in *Reproductive and Genetic Engineering: Journal of International Feminist Analysis*, 1(3), pp. 251–74. New York, Pergamon.

Koonz, Claudia, 1987. *Mothers in the Fatherland: Women, the Family and Nazi Politics.* New York, St Martin's Press.

Koval, Ramona, 1990. 'The Commercialisation of Reproductive Technology', in Scutt, Jocelynne A. (ed.), *The Baby Machine: Reproductive Technologies and the Commercialisation of Motherhood*, pp. 108–34. London, Green Print.

Laborie, Françoise, 1987. 'Looking for Mothers, You Only Find Fetuses', in Spallone, Patricia and Deborah Lynn Steinberg (eds), *Made to Order: The Myth of Reproductive and Genetic Progress*, pp. 48–57. Oxford, Pergamon.

Laing, R. D., 1960. *The Divided Self.* London, Penguin.

Lancaster, Paul A. L., 1987. 12 December 1987. 'Congenital Malformations After In-Vitro Fertilization.' *The Lancet.*

Langan, Mary, 1992a. 'Who Cares? Women in the Mixed Economy of Care', in Langan, Mary and Lesley Day (eds), *Women, Oppression and Social Work: Issues in Anti-Discriminatory Practice.* London, Routledge.

Langan, Mary, 1992b. 'Introduction: Women and Social Work in the 1990s', in Langan, Mary and Lesley Day, *Women, Oppression and Social Work: Issues in Anti-Discriminatory Practice.* London, Routledge.

Langan, Mary and Leslie Day (eds), 1992. *Women, Oppression and Social Work: Issues in Anti-Discriminatory Practice.* London, Routledge.

Larrain, Jorge, 1979. *Concepts of Ideology.* London, Hutchinson.

Larrain, Jorge, 1983. *Marxism and Ideology.* London, Macmillan.

Latour, Bruno and Stephen Woolgar, 1979. *Laboratory Life: The Social Construction of Scientific Facts.* London, Sage.

Laws, Sophie, 1990. *Issues of Blood: The Politics of Menstruation.* London, Macmillan.

Leach, Penelope, 1979. *Who Cares: A New Deal for Mothers and Their Small Children.* Harmondsworth, Penguin.

Leeson, Joyce and Judith Gray, 1978. *Women and Medicine.* London,

Tavistock.

Levitas, Ruth (ed.), 1986. *The Ideology of the New Right*. London, Polity.

Lifton, Robert Jay, 1986. *The Nazi Doctors: A Study of the Psychology of Evil*. London, Macmillan.

Locker, David, 1991. 'Social Causes of Disease', in Scambler, Graham (ed.), *Sociology as Applied to Medicine*, pp. 18–32. London, Baillière Tindall.

Loney, Martin, 1986. *The Politics of Greed: The New Right and the Welfare State*. London, Pluto Press.

Lorde, Audre, 1984. *Sister Outsider*. Trumansburg, NY, The Crossing Press.

Lupton, Deborah, 1994. *Medicine as Culture: Illness, Disease and the Body in Western Societies*. London, Sage.

McDonnall, Kathleen (ed.), 1986. *Adverse Effects: Women and the Pharmaceutical Industry*. Toronto, Women's Press.

McKie, Robin, 1987. 'Birth Defect Discovery Hailed by Doctors', *The Observer*, 15 March 1987.

McKie, Robin, 1988. 'Doctors Plan to Weed out Sick Embryos', *The Observer*, 24 January 1988.

MacKinnon, Catharine, 1987. *Feminism Unmodified: Discourses on Life and Law*. Cambridge, MA, Harvard University Press.

Mclaren, Ann, 1986. 'Prelude to Embryogenesis', in CIBA Foundation, *Human Embryo Research: Yes or No?* London, Tavistock.

McNeil, Maureen (ed.), 1987. *Gender and Expertise*. London, Free Association Press.

McNeil, Maureen, 1990. 'Reproductive Technologies: A New Terrain for the Sociology of Technology', in McNeil, Maureen, Ian Varcoe and Steven Yearley (eds), *The New Reproductive Technologies*, pp. 1–26. London, Macmillan.

McNeil, Maureen, 1991. 'Putting the Alton Bill in Context', in Franklin, Sarah, Celia Lury and Jackie Stacey (eds), *Off-Centre: Feminism and Cultural Studies*, pp. 149–59. London, Harper Collins.

McNeil, Maureen, Ian Varcoe and Steven Yearley (eds), 1990. *The New Reproductive Technologies*. London, Macmillan.

Mama, Amina, 1989. 'Violence Against Black Women: Gender, Race and State Violence.' *Feminist Review*, 32, 30–48.

Mama, Amina, 1992. 'Black Women in the British State: Race, Class and Gender Analysis for the 1990s', in Braham, Peter, Ali Rattansi and Richard Skellington (eds), *Racism and Anti-Racism: Inequalities, Opportunities and Policies*. London, Sage.

Marsh, David and Joanna Chambers, 1981. *Abortion Politics*. London, Junction Books.

Martin, Emily, 1987. *The Woman in the Body: A Cultural Analysis of Reproduction*. Boston, MA, Beacon Press.

Mays, Nicholas, 1991. 'Origins and Development of the National Health Service', in Scambler, Graham (ed.), *Sociology as Applied to Medicine*, pp. 199–220. London, Baillière Tindall.

Medical Research Council (MRC), 1984/5. 'Annual Report: Cell Biology and Disorders Board'. The Council, London.

Meek, Sue, 1986. 'Reproductive Technology: Present Practices and Future Implications', in *Commission for the Future: Biotechnology Revolution: Future Challenges for Australia (Selected Papers (1986))*.

Melrose, Diana, 1983. *Bitter Pills: Medicines and the Third World Poor*. Oxford, Oxfam.

Merchant, Caroline, 1980. *The Death of Nature: Women, Ecology and the Scientific Revolution*. (SF.) London, Harper and Row.

Merkin, Donald H., 1976. *Pregnancy as a Disease: The Pill in Society*. Washington, Kennkat Press.

Mies, Maria, 1983. 'Towards a Methodology for Feminist Research' in Bowles, Gloria and Renate Duelli Klein (eds), *Theories of Women's Studies*, pp. 117–39. London, Routledge and Kegan Paul.

Mihill, Chris, 'Frozen Human Embryos to be Destroyed', *The Guardian*, 23 July 1996.

Milunsky, Aubrey, 1977. *Know Your Genes*. Harmondsworth, Penguin.

Mitchell, Juliet, 1990[1974]. *Psychoanalysis and Feminism: A Radical Reassessment of Freudian Psychoanalysis*. London, Penguin.

Modleski, Tanya, 1991. *Feminism Without Women: Culture and Criticism in a 'Post-Feminist' Age*. London, Routledge.

Moi, Toril, 1985. *Sexual/Textual Politics: Feminist Literary Theory*. London, Methuen.

Monk, Marilyn, 1990. 'Embryo Research and Genetic Disease', *New Scientist*, 6 January 1990, pp. 56–9.

Morgan, Derek and Robert G. Lee, 1991. *Blackstone's Guide to the Human Fertilisation and Embryology Act 1990: Abortion and Embryo Research, the New Law*. London, Blackstone Press.

Morris, Jenny, 1991. *Pride Against Prejudice: Transforming Attitudes to Disability*. London, The Women's Press.

Morris, Jenny, 1995. 'Disabled by Society.' *Community Care*, 20–26 July 1995.

Mort, Frank, 1987. *Dangerous Sexualities: Medico-Moral Politics in England since 1830*. London, Routledge and Kegan Paul.

Moser, C. A., 1958. *Survey and Social Investigation*. London, Heinemann.

Moyser, George and Margaret Wagstaffe (eds), 1987. *Research Methods for Elite Studies.* London, Unwin Hyman.

Newell, John, 1988. 'On the Muscular Tracks', *The Guardian*, 29 March 1988.

Newill, Robert, 1974. *Infertile Marriage.* London, Penguin.

Nichols, Eve K., 1988. *Human Gene Therapy.* Cambridge, MA, Harvard University Press.

Nicholson, Linda J. (ed.), 1990. *Feminism/Postmodernism.* London, Routledge.

Nicholson, Linda J. and Nancy Fraser, 1990. 'Social Criticism Without Philosophy: An Encounter Between Feminism and Postmodernism', in Nicholson, Linda J. (ed.), *Feminism/Postmodernism*, pp. 19–38. London, Routledge.

O'Brian, Mary, 1981. *The Politics of Reproduction.* Boston, MA, Routledge and Kegan Paul.

O'Donovan, Oliver, 1984. *Begotten or Made.* Oxford, Oxford University Press.

Oakley, Ann, 1976. 'Wisewoman and Medicine Man: Changes in the Management of Childbirth', in Oakley, A. and J. Mitchell (eds), *The Rights and Wrongs of Women*, pp. 17–45. Harmondsworth, Penguin.

Oakley, Ann, 1980. *Women Confined: Towards a Sociology of Childbirth.* Oxford, Martin Robertson.

Oakley, Ann, 1981. 'Interviewing Women: A Contradiction in Terms', in Roberts, Helen (ed.), *Doing Feminist Research.* London, Routledge and Kegan Paul.

Oakley, Ann, 1981. *Subject Women.* London, Fontana.

Oakley, Ann, 1984. *The Captured Womb: A History of Medical Care of Pregnant Women.* Oxford, Basil Blackwell.

Oakley, Ann, 1987. 'From Walking Wombs to Test-Tube Babies', in Stanworth, Michelle (ed.), *Reproductive Technologies: Gender, Motherhood and Medicine*, pp. 36–56. Cambridge, Polity.

OUT, 1992. 'Gay Sera Sera', Channel 4, Britain, 29 July 1992.

Overall, Christine, 1987. *Ethics and Human Reproduction: A Feminist Analysis*, Boston, MA, Allen and Unwin.

Panorama, 1988. 'The Agony and the Ecstasy.' (Screened on BBC 1, Great Britain.)

Pateman, Carol, 1992. 'The Patriarchal Welfare State', in McDowell, Linda and Rosemary Pringle (eds), *Defining Women: Social Institutions and Gender Divisions*, pp. 223–45. London, Polity.

Petchesky, Rosalind Pollack, 1987. 'Foetal Images: The Power of Visual Culture in the Politics of Reproduction', in Stanworth, Michelle (ed.), *Reproductive Technologies: Gender, Motherhood and Medicine*, pp. 57–80. Cambridge, Polity.

Pfeffer, Naomi, 1987. 'Artificial Insemination, In-vitro Fertilization and the Stigma of Infertility', in Stanworth, Michelle (ed.), *Reproductive Technologies: Gender, Motherhood and Medicine*, pp. 81–97. Cambridge, Polity.

Phillips, Anne, 1987. *Divided Loyalties: Dilemmas of Sex and Class.* London, Virago.

Pipes, Mary, 1986. *Understanding Abortion.* London, Women's Press.

Price, Frances V., 1990. 'The Management of Uncertainty in Obstetric Practice: Ultrasonography, In Vitro Fertilisation and Embryo Transfer', in McNeil, Maureen, Ian Varcoe and Steven Yearley (eds), *The New Reproductive Technologies*, pp. 123–53. London, Macmillan.

Proctor, Robert N., 1988. *Racial Hygiene: Medicine Under the Nazis.* Cambridge, MA, Harvard University Press.

PROGRESS (no date). PROGRESS: Campaign for Research into Human Reproduction. 'PROGRESS Information Pamphlet on Reproductive and Genetic Technologies.' (PROGRESS Information Pack.)

PROGRESS, 1985a. PROGRESS: Campaign for Research into Human Reproduction. (PROGRESS Information Pack.)

PROGRESS, 1985b. PROGRESS: Campaign for Research into Human Reproduction. 'Aims of PROGRESS.' (PROGRESS Information Pack.)

PROGRESS, 1985–6. PROGRESS: Campaign for Research into Human Reproduction. 'PROGRESS Report' November 1985–June 1986. (PROGRESS Information Pack.)

PROGRESS, 1986. PROGRESS: Campaign for Research into Human Reproduction. 'PROGRESS Constitution' June 1986. (PROGRESS Information Pack.)

Ramazanoglu, Caroline, 1992. 'On Feminist Methodology: Male Reason versus Female Empowerment.' *Sociology*, 26(2) (May), 207–12.

Randles, Tess, 1991. 'The Alton Bill and the Media's "Consensual" Position', in Franklin, Sarah, Celia Lury and Jackie Stacey, *Off-Centre: Feminism and Cultural Studies*, pp. 206–13. London, Harper Collins.

Raymond, Janice, 1987. 'Fetalists and Feminists: They Are Not the Same', in Spallone, Patricia and Deborah Lynn Steinberg (eds), *Made to Order: The Myth of Reproductive and Genetic Progress.* Oxford, Pergamon.

Registrar General's Office, 1991. *Census of the Population of Britain.* London, HMSO.

Reinharz, Shulamit, 1983. 'Experiential Analysis: A Contribution to Feminist Research' in Bowles, Gloria and Renate Duelli Klein (eds), *Theories of Women's Studies*, pp. 162–91. London, Routledge and Kegan Paul.

Reissman, Catherine Kohler, 1992. 'Women and Medicalisation: A New Perspective', in Kirkup, Gill and Laurie Smith Keller (eds), *Inventing Women: Science, Technology and Gender*, pp. 123–44. Cambridge, Polity.

Rich, Adrienne, 1978. 'Compulsory Heterosexuality and Lesbian Existence', *Signs* 5 (4), 631–60.

Rifkin, Jeremy, 1984. *Algeny: A New Word, a New World.* Harmondsworth, Penguin.

Rights of Women (ROW) Lesbian Custody Group, 1986. *Lesbian Mothers' Legal Handbook.* London, Women's Press.

Roberts, Helen, 1981. 'Women and their Doctors: Power and Powerlessness in the Research Process', in Roberts, Helen (ed.), *Doing Feminist Research.* London, Routledge and Kegan Paul.

Roberts, Helen, 1981. *Doing Feminist Research.* London, Routledge.

Roberts, Helen, 1985. *The Patient Patients: Women and their Doctors.* London, Pandora.

Roberts, Helen (ed.), 1981. *Doing Feminist Research.* London, Routledge and Kegan Paul.

Romalis, Shelly, 1981. *Childbirth: Alternatives to Medical Control.* Texas, University of Texas Press.

Rorvik, David M. and Landrum B. Shettles, 1980. *Your Baby's Sex: Now You Can Choose.* New York, Bantam.

Rose, Gerry, 1982. *Deciphering Sociological Research.* London, Routledge.

Rose, Hilary, 1987. 'Victorian Values in the Test-Tube: The Politics of Reproductive Science and Technology', in Stanworth, Michelle (ed.), *Reproductive Technologies: Gender, Motherhood and Medicine*, pp. 151–73. Cambridge, Polity.

Rose, Steven (ed.), 1982. *Against Biological Determinism: The Dialectics of Biology Group.* New York, Alison and Busby.

Rosser, Sue V. (ed.), 1988. *Feminism Within the Science and Health Care Professions: Overcoming Resistance.* Oxford, Pergamon.

Rothman, Barbara Katz, 1982. *In Labour: Women and Power in the Birth-Place.* London, Junction Books.

Rothman, Barbara Katz, 1986. *The Tentative Pregnancy: Prenatal Diagnosis and the Future of Motherhood.* New York, Penguin.

Rothschild, Joan (ed.), 1983. *Machina ex Dea: Feminist Perspectives on Technology.* Oxford, Pergamon.

Ryan, Joanna and Frank Thomas, 1987. *The Politics of Mental Handicap.* London, Free Association Books.

Savage, Wendy, 1986. *A Savage Inquiry: Who Controls Childbirth?*

London, Virago.

Sayers, Janet, 1982. *Biological Politics: Feminist and Anti-Feminist Perspectives*. London, Tavistock.

Scambler, Graham (ed.), 1991. *Sociology as Applied to Medicine*. London, Baillière Tindall.

Science and Technology Subgroup, 1991. 'In the Wake of the Alton Bill: Science, Technology and Reproductive Politics', in Franklin, Sarah, Celia Lury and Jackie Stacey (eds), *Off-Centre: Feminism and Cultural Studies*, pp. 147–220. London, Harper Collins.

Scott, Russell, 1981. *The Body as Property*. London, Penguin.

Scutt, Jocelynne A., 1990. *The Baby Machine: Reproductive Technologies and the Commercialisation of Motherhood*. London, Green Print.

Serono Laboratories, (no date). 'If Nature Can't Deliver.' Hertfordshire, Serono Laboratories (UK) Ltd.

Shettles, L. B. and David Rorvik, 1985. *How to Choose the Sex of Your Baby: A Complete Update on the Method Best Supported by the Scientific Evidence*. North Ryde, NSW, Australia, Angus and Robertson.

Shiva, Vandana, 1988. *Staying Alive: Women, Ecology and Survival in India*. London, Zed Books.

Smart, Carol, 1987a. 'Securing the Family? Rhetoric and Policy in the Field of Social Security', in Loney, Martin *et al.* (eds), *The State or the Market: Politics and Welfare in Contemporary Britain*. Milton Keynes, Open University Press.

Smart, Carol, 1987b. '"There is of Course a Distinction by Nature": Law and the Problem of Paternity', in Stanworth, Michelle (ed.), *Reproductive Technologies: Gender, Motherhood and Medicine*, pp. 98–117. Cambridge, Polity.

Smith Keller, Laurie, 1992. 'Discovering and Doing: Science and Technology, an Introduction", in Kirkup, Gill and Laurie Smith Keller (eds), *Inventing Women: Science, Technology and Gender*, pp. 5–11. London, Polity.

Sontag, Susan, 1991. *Illness as Metaphor // AIDS and its Metaphors*. London, Penguin.

Spallone, Patricia, 1987. 'Reproductive Technology and the State: The Warnock Report and its Clones', in Spallone, Patricia and Deborah Lynn Steinberg (eds), *Made to Order: The Myth of Reproductive and Genetic Progress*, pp. 166–83. Oxford, Pergamon.

Spallone, Patricia, 1989. *Beyond Conception: The New Politics of Reproduction*. London, Macmillan.

Spallone, Patricia, 1992. *Generation Games: Genetic Engineering and the Future for our Lives*. London, The Women's Press.

Spallone, Patricia and Deborah Lynn Steinberg (eds), 1987. *Made to Order: The Myth of Reproductive and Genetic Progress*. Oxford, Pergamon.

Spelman, Elizabeth V., 1978. 'On Treating Persons As Persons'. *Ethics*, 88(2), 150–61.

Stacey, Jackie, 1991. 'Promoting Normality: Section 28 and the Regulation of Sexuality', in Franklin, Sarah *et al.* (eds), *Off-Centre: Feminism and Cultural Studies*, pp. 284–304. London, Harper Collins.

Stacey, Jackie and Sarah B. Franklin, 1985. 'The Warnock Report: Some Thoughts on the New Reproductive Technologies and the Links Between Oppressions.' (Unpublished essay, Kent University, Women's Studies MA.)

Stanley, Liz (ed.), 1990. *Feminist Praxis*. London, Routledge.

Stanley, Liz and Sue Wise, 1990. 'Method, Methodology and Epistemology in Feminist Research Processes', in Stanley, Liz (ed.), *Feminist Praxis*, pp. 20–62. London, Routledge.

Stanworth, Michelle (ed.), 1987. *Reproductive Technologies: Gender, Motherhood and Medicine*. Cambridge, Polity.

Steel Bank Film Co-operative. 1988. 'Soft Cell: A Feminist Analysis of Genetic Engineering.' (Screened Channel 4, 11 January 1988.)

Steinberg, Deborah Lynn, 1986. 'On the Question of Being Heard: Legal Protection and Legal Remedies for Women.' (Unpublished Master's Thesis, The University of Kent, Canterbury, England.)

Steinberg, Deborah Lynn, 1987. 'Selective Breeding and Social Engineering: Discriminatory Policies of Access to Artificial Insemination by Donor in Great Britain', in Spallone, Patricia and Deborah Lynn Steinberg, *Made to Order: the Myth of Reproductive and Genetic Progress*, pp. 184–9. Oxford, Pergamon.

Steinberg, Deborah Lynn, 1989. 'Die Politik der Ausgrenzung', in Bradish, Paula *et al.*, *Frauen Gegen Gen- und Reproduktionstechnologien: Beitrage vom 2. Bundesweiten Kongress, Frankfurt 28–30.10.1988*, pp. 136–42. Frankfurt, Frauenoffensive.

Steinberg, Deborah Lynn, 1990, 'The Depersonalisation of Women Through the Administration of "In Vitro Fertilisation"', in McNeil, Maureen, Ian Varcoe and Steven Yearley (eds), *The New Reproductive Technologies*, pp. 74–122. London, Macmillan.

Steinberg, Deborah Lynn, 1991. 'Adversarial Politics: The Legal Construction of Abortion', in Franklin, Sarah, Celia Lury and Jackie Stacey (eds), *Off-Centre: Feminism and Cultural Studies*, pp. 175–89. London, Harper Collins.

Steinberg, Deborah Lynn, 1992. 'Genes and Racial Hygiene: Studies of Science under National Socialism' in *Science as Culture*, 3(14), 116–29.

Steinberg, Deborah Lynn, 1993. '"Pure Culture": A Feminist Analysis of IVF Ethos and Innovation', Ph.D. thesis, Department of Cultural Studies, University of Birmingham, Birmingham, England.

Thurnham, Peter and Sarah Thurnham, 1986. 'When Nature Fails – Why Handicap? The Case for Legalising Pre-Embryo Research into Congenital Handicap'. London, Conservative Political Centre (CPC).

Times Higher Education Supplement, 1988. 'Wellcome Maternal Health', *THES*, 23 December 1988.

Tormey, Judith Farr, 1976. 'Exploitation, Oppression and Self-Sacrifice', in Gould and Wartofsky (eds), *Women and Philosophy: Toward a Theory of Liberation*. New York, G. P. Putnam's Sons.

UBINIG (Policy Research Development Alternative, Bangladesh), 1991. *Declaration of Comilla: Proceedings of FINRRAGE–UBINIG International Conference 1989*. Dhaka, Bangladesh, UBINIG.

Usher, Jane, 1991. *A Women's Madness: Misogyny or Mental Illness?* Hemel Hempstead, Harvester Wheatsheaf.

Veitch, Andrew, 1985. 'Embryo Tests Await Go-Ahead', *The Guardian*, 19 November 1985.

Veitch, Andrew, 1987a. 'Couples Will be Able to Check "Healthy" Embryos', *The Guardian*, 11 June 1987.

Veitch, Andrew, 1987b. 'Scientists Claim Breakthrough on Genetic Probe for Sperm', *The Guardian*, 30 June 1987.

Verp, Marion S., 1985. 'Genetic Counselling', in Gleicher, N. (ed.), *Principles of Medical Therapy in Pregnancy*, pp. 1217–22. New York, Plenum.

Vines, Gail, 1987. 'Test-Tube Embryos.' *New Scientist*, 19 November 1987, 1–4

Vines, Gail, 1989. 'Why Experiment on Human Embryos?' *New Scientist*, 4 November 1989, 48–50.

VLA (Voluntary Licensing Authority), 1986. 'First Report of the Voluntary Licensing Authority.' VLA, London.

VLA (Voluntary Licensing Authority), 1987. 'Second Report of the Voluntary Licensing Authority.' VLA, London.

VLA (Voluntary Licensing Authority), 1988. 'Third Report of the Voluntary Licensing Authority.' VLA, London.

VLA (Voluntary Licensing Authority), 1989. 'Fourth Report of the Voluntary Licensing Authority.' VLA, London.

VLA (Voluntary Licensing Authority), 1990. 'Fifth Report of the Voluntary Licensing Authority.' VLA, London.

VLA (Voluntary Licensing Authority), 1991. 'Sixth Report of the Voluntary Licensing Authority.' VLA, London.

Walkowitz, Judith R., 1980. *Prostitution and Victorian Society: Women,*

Class and the State. Cambridge, Cambridge University Press.

Walters, William and Peter Singer (eds), 1984[1982]. *Test-Tube Babies: A Guide to Moral Questions, Present Techniques and Future Possibilities*. Melbourne, Oxford University Press.

Warnock, Mary, 1984. *A Question of Life: The Warnock Report on Human Fertilisation and Embryology*. Oxford, Blackwell.

Warren, Mary Ann, 1985. *Gendercide: The Implications of Sex Selection*. Totowa, NJ, Rowman and Allan Held.

Watson, James D., John Tooze and David T. Kurtz, 1983. *Recombinant DNA: A Short Course*. New York, Scientific American Books.

Weatherall, D. J., *et al.* 1986. 'Analysis of Foetal DNA for the Diagnosis and Management of Genetic Disease', in Ciba Foundation, *Human Embryo Research: Yes or No?* pp. 83–99. London, Tavistock.

Weeks, Jeffrey, 1991. *Against Nature: Essays on History, Sexuality and Identity*. London, Rivers Oram Press.

Weindling, Paul, 1989. *Health, Race and German Politics between National Unification and Nazism: 1870–1945*. Cambridge, Cambridge University Press.

Weiss, Sheila Faith, 1987. *Race Hygiene and National Efficiency: The Eugenics of Wilhelm Schallmayer*. Berkeley, University of California Press.

Wheale, Peter and Ruth McNally, 1988. *Genetic Engineering: Catastrophe or Utopia?* New York, Harvester Wheatsheaf.

White, Evelyn C. (ed.), 1990. *The Black Women's Health Book: Speaking for Ourselves*. Washington, The Seal Press.

WHO (World Health Organisation), 1990. *Injectible Contraceptives: Their Role in Family Planning Care*. Geneva, WHO.

Williamson, R., 1986. 'Research Needs and the Reduction of Severe Congenital Disease', in Ciba Foundation, *Human Embryo Research: Yes or No?*, pp. 105–14. London, Tavistock.

Willis, Paul, 1980. 'Notes on Method', in Hall, Stuart *et al.* (eds), *Culture, Media, Language*, pp. 88–95. London, Hutchinson.

Wilson, Sarah, 1989. 'The Other Egg Crisis', *New Statesman and Society*, 24 February 1989, 31.

Winship, Janice, 1987. *Inside Women's Magazines*. London, Pandora.

Winston, Robert, 1987. *Infertility: A Sympathetic Approach*. London, Optima.

Witz, Anne, 1992. *Professions and Patriarchy*. London, Routledge.

Wood, Carl and Ann Westmore, 1984. *Test-Tube Conception*. London, Allen and Unwin.

WRRIC (Women's Reproductive Rights Information Centre), 1985. 'Information Sheet: Legislation and Embryo Legislation'. London,

The Centre.

WRRIC (Women's Reproductive Rights Information Centre), 1989. 'Information Sheet: The Embryo Bill'. London, The Centre.

Yanchinski, Stephanie, 1985. *Setting Genes to Work: The Industrial Era of Biotechnology*. Harmondsworth, Penguin.

York WRRC (York Women's Reproductive Rights Campaign), 1987. 'DHSS Legislation on Human Infertility Services and Embryo Research Consultation Paper.' (Submitted to DHSS 30 June 1987; unpublished.)

Yoxen, Edward, 1983. *The Gene Business: Who Should Control Biotechnology?* London, Free Association Press.

Zimmerman, Jan, 1986. *Once Upon the Future: A Woman's Guide to Tomorrow's Technology*. London, Pandora.

Government publications (London, HMSO)

Statutes

Surrogacy Arrangements Act, 1985. UK.
Local Government Act, 1988. UK.
Children Act, The, 1989. UK.
Human Fertilisation and Embryology Act, The, 1990. UK.

Bills

Unborn Children (Protection) Bill, 1984. UK.
Unborn Children (Protection) No. 2 Bill, 1985. UK.
Human Fertilisation and Embryology Bill, 1989. UK.

Other government publications

Department of Health and Social Security, 1986. 'DHSS Legislation on Human Infertility Services and Embryo Research: Consultation Paper.' London, DHSS.

Department of Health and Social Security, 1987. 'Human Fertilisation and Embryology: A Framework for Legislation.' London, HMSO.

Department of Social Security, 1991. 'Working Together Under the Children Act 1989: A Guide to Arrangements for Inter-Agency Co-operation for the Protection of Children from Abuse.' London, HMSO.

Home Office, 1992. 'Race and the Criminal Justice System.' London, HMSO.

Index

---

religious 92–5
'stability' 86–8
selective breeding 1
selective rationalities 31–2, 78–100, 104, 193
self-determination 27, 162
self-regulation, professional 55–72, 129, 143, 148, 156 *see also* Voluntary Licensing Authority
sex preselection 149
sexual morality 4
sexuality, regulation of 77–8
single women 82–100, 150, 182
social control, medicine as 76–8
social engineering 75–8
social work 17
social workers 87
Society for the Protection of Unborn Children (SPUC) 93
Stanworth, (Michelle) 6–8, 10, 15
state agendas 138–58, 165–85, 192
statutory storage period 151–2
success rates 38–9, 50, 133
superovulation 34–5, 38
'surplus embryos' 64

technological determinist 3 *see also* preimplantation diagnosis
teratogens 118
terminology
    Human Fertilisation and Embryology Act (1990) 140–2, 145, 146
    IVF 32–41
    preimplantation diagnosis 105–6
text
    bodies as 28–9
    IVF as 31–51
    technology as 28–9
thalidomide 34

traffic in eggs and embryos 4, 175–9
transgenic embryos 150–1

Unborn Children (Protection) Bills 130

Virgin Birth controversy 1, 83, 182–3
Voluntary Licensing Authority (VLA) 3, 55–72, 115–16, 130, 139, 151, 152–3
    clinical/research distinction 57–72
    consent 65–70, 71–2
    custody of embryos 67–70
    First Report 58–72
    membership 57–8
    professionalism 60–1
    Reports 55, 58–72, 60, 80
    safety of IVF 59, 61, 63
    scientificity 61–3
    Third Report 60

Warnock Committee 56, 130–2, 135
    membership 130–1
    Report (1984) 82, 130–2, 170, 171, 175
Winston, Robert 105
Women's Reproductive Rights Campaign, York 134
Women's Reproductive Rights Information Centre (WRRIC) 133
women's reproductive rights 2, 4, 19, 20, 57–8, 135, 185, 192–6
women
    as dangerous 26–9, 105, 141, 146, 163 *see also* 'risk'; maternal
    single 82–100, 150, 182